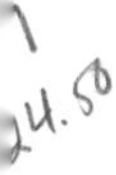

BookClub
ROTARY CLUB OF EVANSTON LIGHTHOUSE

Presented in Honor of

Dr. Robert Buchanan
Trustee
Aga Khan University

Rotary Club of Evanston Lighthouse

PAKISTAN

IAN TALBOT

Pakistan

A New History

Columbia University Press
New York

Columbia University Press
Publishers Since 1893
New York
cup.columbia.edu

Library of Congress Cataloging-in-Publication Data

Talbot, Ian.
Pakistan : a new history / Ian Talbot.
p. cm.
Includes bibliographical references and index.
ISBN 978-0-231-70318-5 (alk. paper)
1. Pakistan—History. I. Title.

DS382.T354 2012
954.9105—dc23

2012022119

∞

Columbia University Press books are printed on permanent and durable acid-free paper. This book is printed on paper with recycled content.
Printed in India

c 10 9 8 7 6 5 4 3 2 1

For
Lois and Martin

CONTENTS

CONTENTS

PREFACE AND ACKNOWLEDGEMENTS

It is now thirteen years since I completed my first text on the history of Pakistan. The original version published by Hurst (*Pakistan: A Modern History*) has since been revised and appeared in a second edition. It concluded that 'further polarisation and instability' could only be avoided by 'the genuine political participation of previously marginalised groups such as women, the minorities and the rural and urban poor. This would not only redeem the "failed promise" of 1947, but also provide hope that Pakistan can effectively tackle the immense economic, social and environmental challenges of the next century'. Now well over a decade into that century, while some of the dramatis personae have changed, most tragically through the passing of Benazir Bhutto, the structural problems of governance and the economy that I highlighted in my narrative not only remain unaddressed but persist in a more critical form.

The current volume is reflective of Pakistan's mounting problems. My regard for the country and my friendships with many Pakistanis have made it sometimes painful to lay these bare. They cannot however be denied, if all that is good in the country, the generosity and hospitality of its people, the dynamism of the young, are to survive an uncertain future. This book seeks to look beyond the headlines and to uncover the continuities and contingencies that have shaped Pakistan's historical travails. It is intended as a work of interpretation and reflection which builds on the earlier narrative account I laid down. It is this as much as its updating that constitutes its newness. The aim is to highlight major turning points and trends during the past six decades. In particular there is emphasis on the increasing entrenchment of the army in Pakistan's politics and economy; the issues surrounding the role of Islam in public life; the tensions between centralising tendencies and local identities and democratic urges; and the impact of geo-political influences on internal development. While this is a study in failure—failure of governance, political and economic development, and most of all of the hopes vested in the project of a separate Muslim homeland—the text attempts to reveal that this was not pre-ordained. Such a fatalistic interpretation does not do justice to the complexities of historical developments, individual actors and the state's own possibilities. This understanding offers the comfort that, while acknowledging that Pakistan's gravest crises may lie ahead, there still remain opportunities for a reappraisal of priorities and a reform of institutions which could yet enable the state not just to muddle through, but to achieve political and economic sustainability.

The work reflects my own understanding of Pakistan's history, which has developed over many years of scholarly engagement. It has been influenced not only by the extensive sources cited in this volume, but as a result of numerous formal and informal academic exchanges. Not all of the following will agree with my line of reasoning in its entirety, but I nevertheless wish publicly to acknowledge their contributions to my assessment: Professor Iftikhar Malik, Professor Yunas Samad, Professor Mohammad Waseem, Professor Imran Ali, Professor Gurharpal Singh, Professor Francis Robinson, Dr Farzana Shaikh.

Finally, I am grateful to Michael Dwyer for encouraging me to write this volume, amidst the responsibilities of running a major History Department. Any errors of fact or omission are my responsibility alone.

IAN TALBOT

Southampton, July 2011

GLOSSARY

abadkar	settler
abaya	traditional over-garment worn by women in parts of the Islamic world
alim	a religious scholar (pl. *ulema*)
amir	commander, chief
biraderi	kinship group
dacoit	bandit
dawa	call (to Islam)
diya	compensation for murder or injury paid by the guilty party
fatwa	ruling of religious law
fiqh	Islamic jurisprudence
hadith	recorded saying or story of the Prophet
hartal	strike
hawala	informal money transfer based on trust
hudood	Islamic penal code
ijtehad	independent judgement, reasoning
ijma	consensus
izzat	honour
jihad	struggle for the sake of Islam ('lesser *jihad*' alone traditionally refers to armed struggle)
jirga	tribal council
kafir	unbeliever, non-Muslim
lascar	sailor
lashkar	army
lathi	wooden club

madrasa	Islamic school (pl. *madaris*)
maulana	Muslim scholar learned in the Quran
Majlis-i-Shura	consultative council
mohajir	person who migrates for the sake of Islam; in Pakistan refers to Partition-migrant
mujahid	Islamic warrior
mullah	preacher
murid	disciple of a *pir*
Nizam-e-Adl	system of justice based on *shari'ah*
nazim	elected mayor
panchayat	village council
pardah	seclusion of women
pir	Muslim Sufi saint, spiritual guide
qazi	Islamic judge
razakars	armed volunteers
riwaj	custom
sajjada nashin	custodian of a Sufi shrine
salafi	resoration of 'pious', strict Islam
sardar	tribal head
shari'ah	Islamic law
sulah	truce Sufi Muslim mystic
umma	global Islamic community
urs	death anniversary of a Sufi saint
ushr	Islamic tax on agriculture
wadero	large landowner in Sindh
zakat	Islamic alms tax
zamindar	landholder responsible for paying land revenue to the government

ABBREVIATIONS

AIML	All-India Muslim League
ANP	Awami National Party
APMSO	All-Pakistan Mohajir Students' Organization
BLA	Balochistan Liberation Army
CCI	Council of Common Interests
CDNS	Council of Defence and National Security
CIA	Central Intelligence Agency
CII	Council of Islamic Ideology
COP	Combined Opposition Parties
CSP	Civil Service of Pakistan
DIM	*Dawat ul-Irshad* (Centre for Preaching and Guidance)
EBDO	Elective Bodies (Disqualification) Order
ESAF	Enhanced Structural Adjustment Facility
FATA	Federally Administered Tribal Areas
FSF	Federal Security Force
HUA	*Harkat-ul-Ansar* (Movement of the Helpers)
HUJI	*Harkat-ul Jihad al-Islami* (Movement for Islamic Jihad)
HUM	*Harkat-ul-Mujahadin* (Movement of the Mujahadin)
IJI	*Islami Jumhoori Ittehad* (Islamic Democratic Alliance)
IJT	*Islami Jamiat-i-Tulaba* (Islamic Students' Movement)
ISI	Inter-Services Intelligence
JCSC	Joint Chief of Staff's Committee
JeM	*Jaish-e-Muhammad* (Army of Muhammad)
JI	*Jamaat-i-Islami* (Islamic Society)
JKLF	Jammu and Kashmir Liberation Front
JuD	*Jamaat-ud-Dawa* (Organization for Preaching)

JUI	*Jamiat-ul-Ulama-e-Islam* (Association of the Ulama of Islam)
JUI(F)	JUI Fazlur Rahman faction
JUP	*Jamiat-ul-Ulama-e-Pakistan* (Association of the Ulama of Pakistan)
JWP	Jamhoori Watan Party
KPP	Krishak Praja Party
KSP	Krishak Sramik Party
LFO	Legal Framework Order
LeJ	*Lashkar-e-Jhangvi* (Army of Jhangvi)
LeT	*Lashkar-e-Taiba* (Army of the Pure)
LTTE	Liberation Tigers of Tamil Eelam
MMA	*Muttahida Majlis-i-Amal* (United Council of Action)
MQM	*Muttahida Qaumi Mahaz* (United National Movement)
MRD	Movement for the Restoration of Democracy
NAP	National Awami Party
NiM	*Nizam-i-Mustafa* (Introduction of a Prophetic Order)
NWFP	North West Frontier Province
OIC	Organisation of the Islamic Conference
PATA	Provincially Administered Tribal Areas
PDA	Pakistan Democratic Alliance
PML	Pakistan Muslim League
PML (J)	PML Junejo faction
PML(N)	PML Nawaz faction
PML(Q)	PML (Quaid)
PNA	Pakistan National Alliance
PODO	Public Offices (Disqualification) Order
PONM	Pakistan Oppressed Nationalities Movement
PPP	Pakistan People's Party
PRODA	Public and Representative Offices (Disqualification) Act
PSF	People's Student Federation
PTI	*Pakistan Tehreek-e-Insaf* (Pakistan Movement for Justice)
RAW	Research and Analysis Wing (Indian Intelligence Agency)
SAARC	South Asian Association for Regional Cooperation
SEATO	South-East Asia Treaty Organisation
SMP	*Sipah-i-Muhammad Pakistan* (Soldiers of Muhammad)
SSP	*Sipah-i-Sahaba Pakistan* (Army of the Companions of the Prophet in Pakistan)

TJ	*Tablighi Jamaat* (Society for Spreading Faith)
TKN	*Tehreek Khatm-e-Nabawat* (Movement for the Finality of the Prophethood)
TNFJ	*Tehreek-i-Nifaz-i-Fiqh Jafariya* (Movement for the Implementation of Shia Law)
TNSM	*Tehreek-e-Nifaz-e-Shariat-e-Muhammadi* (Movement for the Enforcement of Islamic Law)
TTP	*Tehreek-e-Taliban Pakistan* (Pakistan Taliban Movement)
UP	United Provinces
WAF	Women's Action Forum
WAPDA	Water and Power Development Authority

INTRODUCTION

Osama bin Laden's death on 2 May 2011 reverberated around the world. The undetected US covert operation took place at a compound which was within walking distance of Pakistan's elite military academy near Abbottabad. Pakistan had repeatedly claimed that the Al-Qaeda leader was holed up in Afghanistan. His long-term presence in Abbottabad provoked outrage at Pakistan's 'complicity' with international terrorism. Washington's growing awareness, however, that neither the Pakistan Army Chief nor the head of its Inter-Services Intelligence agency (ISI) had known of Osama's presence was cold comfort. If Pakistan was not a 'rogue state', then it was fast moving towards a 'failed state'.

Five years before the Abbottabad affair, Ralph Peters, a retired army officer, had speculated that Balochistan and the NWFP, long the scene of ethno-nationalist movements, would break away, prompting conspiracy theory claims in Pakistan that this was the US intention.[1] The veteran Pakistan expert Stephen Cohen, in his study *The Idea of Pakistan* published in 2004, had warned that major transformation was necessary to prevent the troubled state from sliding into crisis.[2] There followed a seemingly endless round of pessimistic predictions on Pakistan's future. The Delhi-based Institute for Defence Studies and Analyses produced, for example, the *Whither Pakistan* report and held out the possibility of implosion and 'Lebanonization' alongside a scenario of stability.[3] Pakistan's future was also assessed by Bruce Riedel, a US former analyst, and John R. Schmidt, a former American diplomat based in Islamabad.[4] Riedel openly speculated about the carving out of an Islamic Emirate from part of Pakistan's territory. The most impressive and scholarly analysis was produced shortly before the Osama bin Laden debacle by the Brooking Institute, in the form of Stephen Cohen's essay on *The Future of Pakistan* and the conference collection of papers compiled by him, *Pakistan's Future: The Bellagio Papers*.[5]

Despite their different methodologies, the studies commonly echoed the idea that Pakistan was on the brink of a major crisis and that its possession of nuclear weapons and strategic role in the 'War on Terror' gave it the status of 'pivotal state'.[6] State failure would adversely affect regional and global stability. The creation of the Friends of Democratic Pakistan aid consortium and the US Congressional Kerry-Lugar Act, with its support for non-military expenditure, were policy responses to the realization that Pakistan was too important to fail. The growing importance of FATA, comprising the seven tribal agencies of Bajaur, Mohmand, Khyber, Kurram, Orakzai, North Waziristan and South Waziristan, to Western security interests, also drew a crop of policy briefs[7] and initiatives such as the FATA Sustainable Development Plan 2007–2015.[8]

Policy-orientated works address the 'problem' of Pakistan, rather than seeking to understand the country and its people in their terms.[9] Much of this literature has been designed to uncover the roots of instability and the state's linkages with militant groups.[10] Robert Looney, for example, has posited a link between what he terms as 'Pakistan's failed economic take-off' and the spread of terrorism within Pakistan.[11] He cites institutional rigidities and poor governance as stifling economic growth. This has created an environment in which 'large segments of the population have become weary and frustrated' and Pakistan has emerged as a classic example of a 'terrorist breeding ground'.[12] Niazi, on the other hand, has argued that it has not so much been the failure to achieve economic development as its uneven distribution that has fuelled militancy. Uneven development has reinforced conservatism in the minority provinces. At the same time the state has deployed Islam as a political resource to undercut Pakhtun and Baloch nationalism, which is in part rooted in the social and economic disparities present in the Punjab-dominated Pakistan state.[13] Yusuf similarly links socio-economic polarization with instability. He especially draws attention to this with respect to education: with the elite abandoning the collapsed public schooling system, whose poor standards and anti-Western attitudes are increasing the prospects for a Talibanized Pakistan.[14]

It is, however, Christine Fair who has most extensively interrogated the role of education and militancy.[15] She has questioned the post 9/11 Western assumption of the general threat posed by *madaris'* (religious schools') encouragement of the perpetration of violence, while acknowledging that a handful of well-known *madaris* do have *jihadist* links.[16]Drawing on surveys conducted by Tariq Rahman,[17] she has highlighted that militant attitudes are also espoused by public-school as well as *madari* students.[18] Moreover, she cites the 2005 work of Tahir Andrabi et al. to maintain that the reach of the *madaris* has been grossly exaggerated.[19] She also questions the link between poverty and education in the *madaris*, which was a commonplace of much literature.[20] In an assessment of militant recruitment, she argues that for some groups the *madari* cadres are unsuitable for the complex operations for which they are tasked. Militant organizations with a regional operational capability, such as *Lashkar-e-Taiba* (LeT), are more likely to recruit highly-educated and well-off operatives. Sectarian organizations, such as *Sipah-i-Sahaba Pakistan* (SSP), on the other hand, which have a more limited operational reach, are likely to favour *madari* products who in any case are likely to be highly motivated against sectarian rivals.[21]

Sir Hilary Synnott, the former British High Commissioner in Islamabad, has produced one of the more historically aware policy reports.[22] He acknowledges that 'chronic domestic problems...date from the country's earliest years'. He also, in contrast for example with the *Whither Pakistan* report, admits that 'Pakistan has paid a heavy price for other countries' behaviour towards it'.[23] Synnott is cautiously optimistic that the 'country (can) urgently put its own house in order' with 'prolonged, intensive and well-directed effort' assisted by 'external counsel, financial help and the input of a broad range of concerned outsiders'.[24]

A much weaker historical understanding is displayed in Zahid Hussain's *Frontline Pakistan: The Struggle with Militant Islam*.[25] There is limited discussion of the longer-term factors behind the contemporary militant threat to Pakistan. The focus begins with the most recent period of military rule, that of Pervez Musharraf (1999–2008), and highlights his regime's ambiguous response to the threat of Islamic extremism. This understanding, with its concomitant call for a return to democracy, fails to appreciate the long-term ties between the state and militancy and the fact that democratic regimes as well as the army had cultivated *jihadists* in the pursuit of strategic aims. Hassan Abbas[26] and Husain Haqqani share Hussain's view that democracy is the key to ending the state's involvement with extremists. Both writers extend the analysis to the military regimes of Ayub Khan (1958–69) and Zia-ul-Haq (1977–88). Haqqani coined the term the 'mullah-military' nexus to explain Pakistan's emerging political model in the Zia era.[27]

Policy analysts also began to focus on a new 'problem' posed by the emergence of the so-called Punjab Taliban, following a rise in attacks on government installations and 'soft targets' in the Punjab heartland of Pakistan in 2008–9. Recent work has been produced by Riikonen, Abbas and Upadhyay.[28] This has analysed the Punjab Taliban as a loose network of pre-existing radical Sunni groups which had previously been engaged in sectarian activities and the Kashmir *jihad*.[29] While recruitment was identified as coming from South Punjab, there was disagreement over why it should have emerged as a hub of extremism, despite the existence of 'poverty clusters' in the rural areas of the Bahawalpur, Rahimyar Khan, Muzaffargarh and Dera Ghazi Khan districts;[30] for the Pakistan National Human Development Report of 2003 had revealed that no district from Punjab was ranked in the last one third of Pakistan's 91 districts.[31]

Whilst the best policy-oriented writing as produced by Christine Fair and Hilary Synnott is nuanced, it can easily fall into stereotypical portrayals of Pakistan and its people. This overlooks the diversity and dynamism of a country which is too easily pigeon-holed in monochromic Islamist terms. The recent collection *Pakistan: Beyond the 'Crisis State'*, edited by Maleeha Lodhi, successfully addresses these issues by bringing together pieces both on Pakistan's historical development and its contemporary problems of security, governance and economic challenges.[32] It thus avoids the tendency in some US-based studies of adopting a teleological approach which sees Pakistan consigned from the outset to a career as an increasingly 'failed' state. In contrast, Maleeha Lodhi and her contributors regard Pakistan's problems as 'surmountable', although they will require a gradual but far-reaching process of reform, involving governance, education, the economy and restructuring of civil-military relations. The volume sees a new social activism, epitomized by the lawyers' movement, the rise of the middle class and a new media, as 'transformational trends'. *Pakistan: Beyond the 'Crisis State'* also points to Pakistan's rich and varied cultural heritage, which in the words of another optimistic assessment 'may yet salvage a pluralist alternative consistent with democratic citizenship'.[33]

Lodhi's collection is expansive in its scope. Many analysts will not commit themselves to looking beyond the next three to five years when predicting Pakistan's future. Jonathan Paris's work is typical of this approach. He sees Pakistan as 'muddling through' the next few years, unable to bring about major reforms, but coping with fissiparous ethnic threats and that of a Taliban takeover.[34] Paris is a somewhat easy target for criticism, as like a latter-day James Mill he had not set foot on the subcontinent before venturing his expert analysis of its failures.[35] Many of the other recent experts on Pakistan can draw on extensive professional careers with resultant engagements and exposures to its culture. Few, however, of the think-tank experts possess a historical training or approach Pakistan's contemporary crisis through this perspective. Policy-orientated works, as we have noted, address the 'problem' of Pakistan, rather than seeking to understand the country and its people in their terms.[36] I have previously argued that such awareness is crucial; this is especially the case as Pakistan currently faces complex and multi-dimensional problems.[37]

Historical study of Pakistan reveals that, despite a seemingly chaotic rush of events and enduring crises, much has remained unchanged since 1947. Many of the same political families who were prominent in the colonial era continue to win political office. This political class continues to operate in terms of narrow personal interests rather than national ones. Personalities and patronage, rather than programmes and policies, continue to dominate politics. Moreover, problems which preoccupy contemporary analysts, such as the distribution of power between the executive and the legislature or the state's use of Islamic militants as 'strategic assets', are present from the state's very formation. Within months of Pakistan's emergence, for example, popularly elected governments in Sindh and the North West Frontier Province had been dismissed by the nation's founding father and first Governor General, Mohammad Ali Jinnah; whilst *jihadist* tribesmen had been used by the army in an attempt to wrest Jammu and Kashmir from Indian control.[38] What changed with respect to the latter policy down the years were its scale and the ability of *jihadist* groups to secure their own sources of funding.

Before turning to some of the historical themes which will run through this work, it is necessary to introduce the cautionary note that preoccupations with Pakistan's viability are not solely the prerogative of the post 9/11 scenario. British officials and Congress politicians alike were sceptical about the survival of Pakistan on the eve of its creation. This was rooted in concerns about the Muslim state's economic viability. An important recent understanding of the reasons for Congress's late conversion to the acceptance of India's partition is that figures such as Sardar Patel thought that Pakistan would collapse at birth, forcing a chastened Muslim League elite to accept a 'reunification' on Congress's terms of centralization. Patel was mistaken, but certainly his membership of the Partition Council, established after the acceptance of the 3 June Plan, would have alerted him to Pakistan's unfavourable economic prospects.[39]

The growing regional and class tensions in Pakistan, resulting from the skewed development of the 1960s, led the young firebrand Tariq Ali to argue in 1970 that only a people's revolution could save Pakistan from disintegration.[40] He was as scathing of the inability of the establishment elite to bring about structural reform as are some contemporary analysts, who fear that internal pressures resulting from entrenched inequalities will explode in an Islamist revolution rather than a socialist one. Disillusionment with the limited reforms of the Zulfiqar Ali Bhutto era, followed by the right-wing ascendancy of the army and its religious allies, provoked Tariq Ali into a further questioning of Pakistan's survival in 1983.[41] Nearly three troubled decades later, Pakistan continues to 'muddle through'. For the historian this raises the need to uncover the roots of the state's sustainability, alongside the more obvious quest to explain why it has been crisis-ridden throughout most of its existence.

The contemporary analysis of Pakistan variously as a 'failed state', a 'failing state', a 'troubled state', a 'fragile state', thus needs to be accompanied by a historical analysis of its post-independence development which sheds light both on the causes of its continuous crises and on its resilience. This analysis needs to be sufficiently sophisticated to track historical trajectories, to identify continuities and change-the 'game changing' events of political science conceptualization. Is Pakistan's contemporary crisis rooted in recent and largely unforeseen developments, whether deliberate disasters such as 9/11 and the apparent harbouring of Osama bin Laden, or natural calamities such as the 2005 earthquake and the 2010 floods? Conversely is it the result of the burden of history with respect not only to domestic dimensions, but in its external dimensions? Can the crisis be seen as a cumulative failure to introduce structural economic reform and achieve democratic consolidation? Equally important, however, are questions concerning Pakistan's resilience. Has the recent expansion of the middle class and civil society strengthened the underpinnings for democracy? Can patron-client relations in the countryside be seen as simultaneously perpetuating instability through entrenching inequalities while at the same time inhibiting mass movements directed against prevailing asymmetries of power? Similarly, can ethnic divisions and sectarianism both inhibit social cohesion and encourage violence, whilst acting as a barrier to Islamist revolution? Finally, will ongoing population increase and accompanying urbanization, with their attendant educational, employment and environmental pressures, ultimately put pay to Pakistan's ability to 'muddle through'?

These questions will be addressed within an overarching historical analysis which focuses on five key areas of Pakistan's development: namely, its historical inheritances; the civil-military relationship; the external dimension; centre-province relations; and the role of Islam in Pakistan's public life. The first concerns the legacies of the colonial era and the immediate post-independence experience of massive social dislocation arising from Partition and its impact on statecraft and nation-building. These are the long-term causes of domestic problems alluded to in the quotation from Synott's work, *Transforming Pakistan*. Following on from my earlier studies, I will argue that although at first blush India and Pakistan had similar inheritances of governance from the British Raj, in reality these were different because the bulk of what became West Pakistan formed a British 'security state' in North West India. The compromises the Muslim League had to make with entrenched landed and tribal elites in this region and the dislocations of 1947–8 further reinforced a tradition of governance which privileged administrative efficiency and 'security' over political representation and democratic development.

This historical inheritance has played a part in the second major theme of Pakistan's development, the skewing of civil-military relations in favour of the latter. It is now well-established that even during the periods of civilian rule the army has wielded immense influence behind the scenes with respect to key aspects of foreign and security policy. The surrender of civilian initiative in these areas may be voluntary, as appears to be the case in the Zardari-Kayani current phase, or it may be a cause of major friction as it was in the 1990s. Ideally, the military is prepared to cede day-to-day matters of governance to elected politicians, while it retains a veto over strategic issues and its institutional interests. In the immediate wake of the Abbottabad affair, there was unprecedented criticism of the military in parliament and the media. The PPP-led government did not, however, make any moves to push back military influence. Moreover, while public opinion in terms of support for army action against militants dropped, the military's long-term portrayal of itself as the guardian of Pakistan ensured that 79 per cent of the respondents in the Pew Survey still said that it had a good influence on the country.[42] In reality the military has been more effective as a state usurper than a state saviour. It has increasingly expanded its tentacles into civilian institutions and business activity. It has, however, always struggled to achieve political legitimacy and to introduce structural reforms. Rather than being a modernizing force, the military has sustained traditional hierarchies. A number of important consequences have stemmed from this pattern of authority.

Firstly, the military has recognized the need for a strategic withdrawal to barracks if unpopularity or corruption were tarnishing its standing. This explains the periodic 'civilianization' of martial law and return to a fragile democracy. Secondly, even at the outset of martial law, the need has been recognized for technocratic expertise and for a degree of legitimization flowing both from civilian political support and legal cover. The former has been provided largely by religious parties and conservative landholders, the latter by sections of the judiciary. Its existence helps explain the relatively benign authoritarianism of military rule, in comparison with some Latin American and African countries. Thirdly, the military's inability to provide markedly superior administration or economic management to that of civilians has contributed to Pakistan's downward spiral in governance. Despite this fact, not only the army but also sections of Pakistan's society continue to view it as the most efficient state institution and the guarantor of stability. The military frequently compares its national outlook with the narrow sectional interests of its main political opponents. It has not, however, acted as a modernizing force in the key area of taxation. Only around 1 per cent of Pakistan's population pays direct taxes. This scandalous state of affairs has contributed greatly to the state's inability to provide basic services for its population. Low rates of literacy have undermined economic development and democratic consolidation.

Pakistan's experience stands out from other countries not only in the taxation field, but also with respect to the importance of external factors in shaping its development. We have seen Hilary Synott's earlier allusion to the 'heavy price Pakistan has paid for other countries' behaviour towards it'. He was referring specifically to the West's accommodation with the Zia regime and its encouragement of the launching of an international *jihad* from Pakistan's soil in the service of its Cold War strategic rivalry with the Soviet Union. The 'blowback' of militancy from the latter development has been a key destabilizing factor. One could in fact deepen the historical analysis and see the undermining of democracy in Pakistan's formative years as being in part the result of a Western accommodation with the emerging power of the army. As early as the mid 1950s, it was in receipt of an aid package of $500 million. US support bolstered Ayub Khan's first martial law, just as much as it was later to sustain Zia's grip on power. Another constant in the US-Pakistan relationship is Washington's frustration at Pakistani 'ingratitude'. The prevalence of current anti-American sentiment is well established. A Pew Research Center survey after Osama bin Laden's killing revealed that only 12 per cent of respondents had a positive view of the United States. Five decades earlier, a similar state of affairs prevailed. The Americans had funnelled aid to Ayub Khan in the late 1950s to assist economic 'take-off', and in the context of Pakistan's aligned status with US security pacts, designed to isolate the Soviet Union. When the United States for the first time supplied weapons on a large scale to India following its defeat in the October 1962 war with China, there were not only protests in the Pakistan National Assembly but also an invasion of the USIS library grounds in Karachi and the stoning of Flashman's Hotel in Rawalpindi, which was well known for its Western clientele.[43]

The burden of history is even greater with respect to Pakistan's relations with New Delhi than it is with Washington. The mistrust between Congress and the Muslim League in late colonial India culminated in the division of the subcontinent. Partition, however, internationalized this mistrust as it was accompanied by massacres, migrations, disputes over the division of assets and by the first of the Indo-Pakistan wars over the former Princely State of Jammu and Kashmir.[44] Further conflicts and proxy wars have intensified this trust deficit. Increasing Indian influence in Afghanistan since 2001 has heightened Islamabad's fears that this will imperil security in the restive resource-rich Balochistan province. While reflecting on domestic instabilities and crises, the *Whither Pakistan* report disingenuously ignores this. Yet it could be argued that India, as the emerging South Asian *hegemon*, could have done more to alleviate Pakistan's security concerns. The trust deficit has continued to hinder relations between Pakistan and India. Numerous writers have argued that their normalization will unlock the key to democratic consolidation within Pakistan itself and to regional stability, not just in terms of ending proxy conflicts but also in avoiding a nuclear arms race. While the security of Pakistan's strategic assets has exercised minds in the West, India has had to adopt a new strategic doctrine ('Cold Start') to respond to the nuclear umbrella of its rival and the prospect of the unpunished use of Islamist proxies.[45]

Pakistan's anxiety and bitterness regarding India has found its 'permanent fixation' in the struggle over Kashmir. The former Princely State's existential importance to the subcontinent's two 'distant' neighbours, however, has repeatedly thwarted attempts at resolution of a conflict which is the oldest dispute on the UN's agenda. In the eyes of some analysts, Pakistan's enduring conflict with India has in fact been a calamitous blunder. This has not only increased Indian resolve regarding Kashmir, and created a Frankenstein's monster of empowered radical Islamist groups, but has overshadowed the provision of basic services for its citizenry, thus imperilling internal security.[46]

Afghanistan and China have also influenced Pakistan's domestic development. The 'blowback' effects of Pakistan's use as a staging post for the *jihad* against the Soviet occupation of Afghanistan are now widely acknowledged with respect to establishing a *jihadist* landscape in Pakistan. The Kashmir conflict, as we have noted in passing with respect to the Punjab Taliban, has also played a role. Less understood is the impact of Afghan migration in the 1980s, as it was a key factor both in the rapid urbanization of this decade and in the creation of the conditions for ethnic conflict and violence in the port city of Karachi, Pakistan's leading city and melting pot.

Commentary on the strained relationship between Pakistan and Afghanistan in the Musharraf era frequently overlooked the longer-term tensions in the relations between the countries and the fact that Pakistan had deployed Islamic proxies as 'strategic assets' in its western neighbour long before the creation of the Afghan Taliban. Kabul refused in 1947 to accept the colonial treaty which established the Durand Line boundary between the two neighbours. It also expressed support for the Pakhtunistan demand and voted against Pakistan's admission to the United Nations. Afghanistan can be a source of future crisis, or else assist in the stabilizing of the region. Similarly, Pakistan could be a conflict-maker or a peace-broker as the momentum increases in the transfer of security responsibility from NATO to the Afghan National Army.

China is conventionally regarded in Pakistan as the country's 'all-weather' ally. Chinese reliability is juxtaposed alongside the troubled relationship with the US. Significantly, as relations between Islamabad and Washington reached an all-time low in the wake of the Osama bin Laden affair, Prime Minister Yousaf Raza Gilani took advantage of the 60th anniversary of the establishment of Sino-Pakistan diplomatic relations to visit Beijing. He not only received verbal assurances that China and Pakistan would take 'bilateral ties to a higher plane', but promises to accelerate the supply of 50 new JF-17 Thunder Combat jets under a co-production agreement. Gilani's visit, which included a meeting with China's President Hu Jintao, strengthened those in Pakistan who advocate ever closer ties with Beijing. China has in fact replaced the EU as Pakistan's second largest trading partner. However, Sino-Pakistan trade, at around an annual figure of $7 billion, still lags far behind that between India and China, which was projected to increase to $100 billion per annum by the end of 2012. Moreover, by 2010 Pakistan was running a trade deficit of over $4 billion. China, as the leading investor in Pakistan, exerts increasing influence. The extent to which this would be able to replace that of the US and its allies is, however, open to question. While relying on China as its principal future economic and military guarantor would rid Pakistan of the historical baggage of its US link, it would perpetuate the state's dependency on external strategic interests and further complicate relations with India.[47]

Tensions in centre-province relations have been another persisting feature of Pakistan's development. Resentments arising from 'Pakistanization' around the use of Urdu as a national lingua franca initiated the separatist movement in East Bengal in the early post-independence period. There were also economic resentments over the distribution of foreign exchange earned by the region's jute industry. Similar resentments over the centre's appropriation of natural resources followed the development of the gas industry in Balochistan. Water disputes have also emerged as a source of conflict between provinces such as Punjab and Sindh. The identification of the army's interests with those of the

Punjab has led elites from other provinces to talk about the 'Punjabization' of Pakistan.[48]

As early as 1948, the military was drawn into conflict with Baloch tribes. Discontent in 1958 and 1962 led to further clashes. These were the prelude to the major conflict in 1973–7, which saw some 70,000 troops pitted against tribal insurgents. The casualty figures in the recent campaigns against the Taliban in Swat and FATA in 2009–10 are dwarfed by the loss of some 5,000 Baloch civilians and 3,500 troops.[49] The bloodiest conflict of all involving the army and civilians was, of course, that in 1971 in East Pakistan which preceded the break-up of the state. The armed assault, codenamed Operation Searchlight, designed to regain control of the province wracked by a civil disobedience movement and earned its commander, General Tikka Khan, the epithet 'the Butcher of Bengal'.[50] His subsequent rehabilitation provided a figleaf of legitimacy to state terrorism in the name of national security.

The current government of President Zardari, as part of its self-proclaimed politics of reconciliation, has attempted to address some of the long-standing provincial resentments over the distribution of central funds and long-held demands for devolution of power. The mounting security crisis in Balochistan, together with problems between the executive and the judiciary, has overshadowed the important changes arising from the 18th Amendment and the agreement on the 7th National Financial Commission Award. The latter not only broke new ground in its consensual agreement, but increased the overall provincial share of the national budget and that of the 'smaller' provinces relative to Punjab. The 18th Amendment met long-term Pakhtun aspirations by renaming the North West Frontier Province, Khyber-Pakhtunkhwa. It also decentralized power through the removal of the Concurrent List, in which federal law had prevailed over provincial legislation. The implications of these concessions for provincial sentiment have yet to be fully worked out. The anxiety is that they have come too late to reconcile Balochistan, and that the years of decline in governance mean that there is now insufficient administrative capacity to implement effectively the devolution of power to the provinces.

The fifth overarching historical theme involves the role of Islam. Pakistan was created in the name of religion. Nonetheless, the freedom struggle bequeathed an ambiguous legacy with respect to the role of Islam in Pakistan's public life. Would Pakistan form a homeland for North Indian Muslims, or an Islamic state? These questions have remained unresolved, and as a result have constituted part of what might be termed Pakistan's 'identity crisis'. This also involves the relative roles of ethnic, linguistic and national allegiances.[51]

The long-term trend for Pakistan society has been to become more religiously conservative. This is the legacy not so much of the state-sponsored Islamization of the Zia era as of the reformist activities of such organizations as *Tablighi Jamaat*, *Jamaat-i-Islami* and *Tanzim-e-Islami*. Conservatism should not of course be confused with extremism, which is limited to small groups of individuals. Support for militancy rests not just on educational indoctrination, but on a sense of injustice arising from disillusionment with the country's judicial system and resentment at the widespread socio-economic inequalities. Adherence to a 'secular' vision for Pakistan is a minority view held only by small numbers of the Western-educated elite. The circumstances attending the rise of a *jihadist* mind-set and sub-culture, as we have seen, have dominated much contemporary study of Pakistan. It is important to bear in mind that there was a long-established tradition of *jihadist* activity in the future Pakistan areas of the subcontinent which even pre-dated the colonial era. Furthermore, sectarianism, which has been identified as a breeding ground for militant recruitment, again has historical roots which run far deeper than the Zia-ul-Haq era, which is the focus of much contemporary study. It is also important, however, not to overlook the established pluralist traditions of Islam embodied in the Sufi influence in the Pakistan areas.

The five major themes above are purposely addressed within a chronological framework. This counteracts a teleological understanding of Pakistan's development by revealing the significance of historical contingencies. Despite the inheritance of 'Viceregalism' from the colonial era,[52] authoritarianism was not an inevitable outcome, but was contingent on a number of key developments in the 1950s. Chapter 1 provides insights into the land and people of Pakistan. It also seeks to make the reader aware of longer-term economic, environmental and demographic challenges which are lost sight of in the preoccupation with current security challenges. This is followed by Chapter 2's thematic account of the first decade of Pakistan's development. This period is now increasingly seen as important for providing a template for the state's future struggles to consolidate democracy and to craft a political system which meets the aspirations of the smaller provinces and national communities. Chapter 3 examines the rule of Pakistan's first military leader, Ayub Khan. It focuses on the response he provided to the state's foundational problems and on his legacies for the army's future relations both with civilians and with Islamist allies. Chapter 4 covers the period of Zulfiqar Ali Bhutto, arguing that this was a missed opportunity for establishing Pakistan on a new path of democracy. It explains the failure of this potential turning point not only in terms of Bhutto's own personality and the institutional weakness of the Pakistan Peoples' Party which he had founded, but in terms of underlying socio-economic and political problems which went unaddressed. Chapter 5 examines the career and legacies arising from Bhutto's nemesis, Zia-ul-Haq. It acknowledges the negative legacies of his rule, but cautions that not all of Pakistan's contemporary ills can be laid at Zia's door. While Zia's instrumental use of Islam was notorious, most of Pakistan's rulers from the time of Jinnah onwards have used Islam and Islamist groups to underpin their domestic power and advance Pakistan's strategic interests. Chapter 6 explains why democracy was not consolidated in the decade which followed Zia's death. It points out that much of its politics remained stuck in the past rather than being forward looking as a struggle was fought out between Bhuttoist and Ziaist forces. Chapter 7 moves to the contemporary era with a reflection on the successes and failures of the Musharraf regime. Some of Pakistan's problems can be seen as arising from the new international circumstances post 9/11. The chapter also cautions the need to adopt a longer-term perspective on this period. Chapter 8 examines the Zardari presidency in terms of both contemporary challenges and longer-term historical continuities. It makes a preliminary assessment of the impact of Abbottabad on civil-military relations. Finally, the Epilogue seeks to move beyond current security crises to consider Pakistan's longer-term demographic, environmental and infrastructural challenges and prospects.

1

PAKISTAN

LAND, PEOPLE, SOCIETY

This chapter examines the impact of Pakistan's location and natural environment on its development. It also traces the challenges posed by a society which has seen its population double every generation. Finally it examines the impact of social structures and beliefs in shaping the state's evolution since independence. In the course of this study it will thus address such questions as 'Is Pakistan a prisoner of its geography?' 'What are the sources of pluralism in Pakistan?' 'How has migration impacted on political developments?' 'In what ways has Islam affected the psyche of the nation?'

The Geo-Political Context

Pakistan's sensitive geo-political situation to the east of the Persian Gulf and in close proximity to Russia, China and India has given rise to its being termed a 'garrison state' in which the military role is inevitably 'over-developed'.[1] Critics of militarism have seen the army as turning to its advantage enmity with India and regional Western strategic concerns, firstly derived from the Cold War and latterly the 'War on Terror' to transform Pakistan into a permanent 'insecurity state'. The cost of the army's positioning and repositioning itself as the state's predominant institution has been Pakistan's 'neo-vassal status'.[2]

The fact that Pakistan was carved out of the British Indian Empire has meant that its history has been profoundly influenced by relations with its mighty neighbour. Indian attitudes have been coloured by the fact that Pakistan is seen as a secessionist state; while in Pakistan there has been the abiding fear that India will seek to undo the 1947 Partition. This intensified with the breakaway of its eastern wing to form Bangladesh in 1971. Pakistan had emerged in 1947 with its eastern and western wings divided by over 1,000 miles of Indian territory. While this 'geographical absurdity' by no means condemned it to division (see Chapter 2 for the impact of Pakistan's statecraft) the remoteness of Dhaka from the federal capital first in Karachi and then later in Islamabad intensified the sense of marginality of the Bengali political elites. 'I feel a peculiar sensation when I come from Dacca to Karachi', the Bengal Chief Minister Ataur Rahman Khan declared early in 1956; 'I feel physically, apart from mental feeling, that I am living here in a foreign country. I did not feel as much when I went to Zurich, to Geneva...or London as much as I feel here in my own country that I am in a foreign land'.[3] This perception was materially based in the different topographies, landholding structures and population densities of the two wings and the fact that over 1 in 5 of East Pakistan's population was non-Muslim, whereas the figures for West Pakistan were less than 1 in 30. The loss of the eastern wing profoundly transformed Pakistan in terms of its demography. It also encouraged the country to look more to the Middle East than to South Asia as its neighbourhood region in cultural and economic terms. It was not fully recognized at the time but the federal government's use of Islamic irregulars (*razakars*) drawn from the Urdu-speaking Bihari population in East Pakistan in 1971 encouraged notions of Islamic militants' value as 'strategic assets' in the enduring rivalry with India.[4] Pakistan was greatly weakened in relation to India by the loss of its eastern wing, but this did not abate their enduring rivalry, which was rooted in the Kashmir issue.

While Pakistan's territorial dispute with India over Kashmir has symbolized the distrust between the two countries over the past six decades, it also inherited another disputed border with Afghanistan. In July 1949 the Afghan parliament formally renounced the Durand Line border which the British had negotiated with Amir Abdur Rahman Khan in 1893 to demarcate the frontier of the Raj. Kabul laid claim to the territories it had 'lost' to Pakistan. This was a serious threat because of Pakistan's immediate post-Partition weakness and because it occurred in the context of Afghanistan's support for ethnic Pakhtun nationalists across the Durand Line in Pakistan, who sought to create their own Pakhtunistan state. The date of 31 August was earmarked in Afghanistan as the official annual celebration of a 'Greater Pakhtunistan Day'. The goal of a Greater Pakhtunistan was designed not only to increase the power of the Afghan state, by absorbing a Pakhtunistan area carved out of Pakistan, but to cement the ethnic dominance of Pakhtuns within it at the expense of Hazaras, Uzbeks and Tajiks. Kabul's posture exacerbated Pakistan's insecurity, which was already fevered by the 1947–8 clash with India over Kashmir. The geo-political imperative for a strong military received further encouragement. Within less than a decade of independence, Pakistan and Afghanistan became part of competing Cold War alliance systems within the region. Pakistan became a member of the US Central Treaty Organization (CENTO). Although India and Afghanistan retained the fiction of non-alignment, they received increasing amounts of aid from the USSR. Soviet assistance encouraged closer ties between Kabul and New Delhi, adding a further antagonistic element to Pakistan-Afghanistan relations.

During the Cold War and the post 9/11 'War on Terror', Pakistan has found itself in the front line of an international conflict because of its geo-strategic location. Pakistan's support was vital in the October 2001 war which removed the Taliban regime from power. It also became an important ally as NATO battled to contain the Taliban-led insurgency from 2006 onwards. By 2010–11, around 40 per cent of all fuel and 80 per cent of all containerized cargo for Western forces was passing through the country.

Some authors have gone so far as to declare that Pakistan has been a 'prisoner of its geography'. The region's geo-politics since the 1980s have brought Pakistan economic benefits, but high costs in terms of internal instability arising from the 'blowback effects' of weaponization, the influx of Afghan refugees and the support afforded to militant and sectarian expressions of Islam. The US strategy of encouraging *jihad* in Soviet-occupied Afghanistan in the early 1980s did not initiate the Pakistan state's alliances with Islamic proxies, but it profoundly influenced their development: firstly by introducing large numbers of foreign fighters into the region; secondly by flooding weapons into the country; thirdly by increasing the power and influence of Pakistan's ISI and its links with militant groups; fourthly by providing a template which Pakistan was to adopt in its strategic aims to dominate post-Soviet Afghanistan and to 'wear down' India in Kashmir.

Since 9/11 Pakistan has feared encirclement as a result of growing Indian development assistance to Afghanistan, which it had hoped to dominate itself. By the end of 2007, India was second only to the US in the provision of aid. Moreover non-Pakhtun minorities which have traditionally looked to India for support had gained a measure of power in Hamid Karzai's regime. The resentment this generated fuelled the growing Taliban insurgency, for since the foundation of the modern Afghan state in the mid-eighteenth century it has been ruled by Pakhtuns, with the exception of the brief Tajik hold on power during the reign of Habibullah II and the post-Soviet presidency of Burhanuddin Rabbani. Pakistan has seen the Pakhtuns as its natural allies in Afghanistan following the decline of an irredentist Pakhtunistan threat. The policy of securing influence in Afghanistan through the backing of Pakhtun Islamic militants pre-dates the 1979 Soviet invasion, but received major Western and Saudi backing at that juncture. It has persisted to the present day with Islamabad seeing its strategic interests being served through successive Pakhtun groups of Islamist and Deobandi militant clients, ranging from Gulbuddin Hekmetyar, Mullah Omar and the Taliban to the Haqqanis at the time of the post-2005 Taliban insurgency against the government of President Hamid Karzai.

The Tribal Areas, which comprise the seven protected agencies of Bajaur, Khyber, Kurram, Mohmand, Orakzai and North and South Waziristan, form a 280-mile wedge of mountainous land along this sensitive eastern border with Afghanistan. Relations between Afghanistan and Pakistan have frequently been uneasy in this region. Contemporary Afghanistan presents itself as the victim of repeated cross-border incursions by Islamic militants based in this region, but it has not always been the case of one-way traffic. The Pakistan army for example had to repel major Afghan incursions into Bajaur in 1961.

Pakistan has continued the colonial strategy of regarding the Tribal Areas bordering Afghanistan as a 'buffer zone' in which rule was indirect, with stability being provided by the Political Agent working through tribal *jirgas*. Further legacies were the provision for the imposition of collective punishments under the Frontier Crimes Regulation and the absence of a permanent military presence in the tribal heartland. Another historical inheritance which pre-dated the colonial era was the raising of tribal revolt by charismatic Muslim leaders in the Pakhtun tribal areas abutting Afghanistan. This tradition can be linked as far back as the *jihad* against Sikh rule led by Sayyid Ahmed Barelvi (1786–1831). The Hadda Mullah's *jihads* against the British in 1893 and 1897 were in response to colonial encroachment into the region. Hadda Mullah and his successors fused religious revivalism with the allegiances arising from the traditional Sufi ties between *pirs* and their *murids*. *Pirs'* influence in Pakhtun society relied not just on their sanctity and learning, but on the ability to act as neutral mediators in factional and tribal disputes. Revolts continued in this region down to the end of the colonial era, including the campaigns by the Faqir of Ipi. Shortly after independence, with support from Kabul, he was to become involved in the secessionist Pakhtunistan movement.

The *jihads* against the British were waged by armed bands (*lashkars)* comprising *murids, talibs* (students) and local villagers. What is important for understanding the insurgencies in contemporary Pakistan is not only the long history of tribal resistance in the name of Islam to the encroachment of the modern state, but the fact that firstly colonial-era *jihads* were marked by a combination of both tribal motivations and Islamic objectives; secondly that the non-administered Tribal Areas summed up in the phrase *Yaghistan* (land of the rebellious) formed an ideal staging ground for armed mobilization; thirdly that the *mullahs* of the Tribal Areas maintained connections with Deoband, which had sought their support for the Pan-Islamic cause during the First World War.[5] These elements of continuity coexist with the disjunctions in the Tribal Areas arising from the Afghan conflict, which led to population movements and the presence of foreign militants.

The unanticipated ramifications of inducting Pakistani troops into the area in pursuit of 'foreign militants' linked with Al-Qaeda will be discussed later in the volume. Suffice it to say here that home-grown militancy directed increasingly not against the Afghanistan state, but Pakistan itself, can be explained in part by the region's continued isolation from political and socio-economic change elsewhere in the country. The sixth Five Year Plan declared the Federally Administered Tribal Areas (FATA) to be the least developed area of Pakistan, with an adult literacy rate of just 15 per cent. This has perpetuated extreme social conservatism and a history of sporadic uprisings against state encroachment led by unifying Islamic leaders. Despite a dramatic increase in educational expenditure from 2005, militancy and state counter-insurgency measures, with their attendant population displacement, resulted in the FATA annual school census report for 2009–10 revealing a dropout rate in government primary schools of 63 per cent among boys and 77 per cent among girls.[6]

Pakistan's geo-political location provides economic possibilities as well as strategic dangers. Pakistan could form an important hub for trade and energy transmission if regional relations were improved, with the country providing interconnecting links between Iran, Afghanistan and India. New Delhi has pulled out of the Iran-Pakistan gas pipeline project[7] because of US disquiet, which became institutionalized in the June 2010 Comprehensive Iran Sanctions, Accountability and Disinvestment Act. It is signed up however to the Turkmenistan-Afghanistan-Pakistan-India (TAPI) natural gas pipeline project which was agreed at Ashgabat in December 2010. This could eventually supply 30 billion cubic metres of gas a year from the Caspian Sea region. The pipeline would have to cross strategically sensitive areas of southeastern Afghanistan, including Helmand and Balochistan. It would however not only provide transit route fees of up to $160 million a year, equivalent to half of its national revenue, and jobs for Afghanistan, but clean fuel for both Pakistan and India.[8] US state department officials have termed TAPI's route as a 'stabilizing corridor' which would link regional neighbours together in 'economic growth and prosperity'.[9] This has been echoed by an eminent Pakistani security expert, who sees TAPI as having the 'potential for reshaping the security discourse in South Asia' away from conflicting geo-political rivalries to mutually beneficial 'geo-economics'.[10]

Climate and Natural Resources

Pakistan's location also makes it vulnerable to the vagaries of the annual monsoon. Its economy can still be affected by the failure of the monsoon or, as the 2010 floods demonstrated, by exceptional monsoon rainfall. The earlier major flooding of 1993 almost completely depleted the country's financial reserves. The 2010 floods posed huge problems for an already flagging economy. The rural population of south Punjab and Sindh is vulnerable to inundation from the mighty Indus River, while those inhabiting the Frontier and the Tribal Areas can fall victim to flash floods emanating from the Kabul River and its tributaries. Deforestation has increased these risks.

Drought, however, could also be caused by climate change. Indeed there may already be anything between a 10 and 15 per cent decrease in annual rainfall amounts in the country's coastal belt and plains. Issues of water management and disputes over water both between provinces, as for example between Sindh and Punjab, and between India and Pakistan are likely to become increasingly important. Diseases arising from inadequate water supply and sanitation according to some estimates already bring, along with human costs, economic costs of over Rs 100 billion a year.[11] Around 600 children die each day from waterborne diseases.

Inefficient water use and management alongside rising population will, according to some experts, mean that Pakistan could be 'running dry' by 2025, with an annual shortfall of anything up to 100 billion cubic metres.[12] Such a scenario would have incalculable human and political costs. The 2010 Maplecroft environmental risk report ranked Pakistan 16 out of 170 countries at risk from climate change. It fell in the 'extreme' risk category, which was headed by India and Bangladesh and also included Nepal and Afghanistan from the region.[13] The year 2010 saw a new record temperature set in Pakistan of 53.5 degrees centigrade. According to some figures there is an annual temperature rise of between 0.6 and 1 degree Celsius in comparison with historical levels.

Pakistan's geographical position, as we have noted, does provide possibilities of its acting as a hub for regional trade and a supply route to Central Asia and even to India for energy. The country is rich in natural resources. Sindh contains one of the world's largest coal reserves. Balochistan has one of the world's largest copper reserves. In addition to these mineral resources, the country has developed major agricultural resources, producing the fourth highest cotton crop in the world and the fifth largest dairy production, which is increasingly exported to the Middle East. It has also developed natural gas from its fields at Sui in Balochistan. Pakistan's own energy resources are, however, unable to keep up with rising demand at a time when still over 40 per cent of households do not have access to electricity. The 2009–10 Economic Survey reported, for example, that energy shortages caused a loss of more than 2 per cent of GDP.[14] Many manufacturing firms use their own generators in an attempt to reduce the impact of unreliable supplies on their sales revenues. According to a report by a private consultant in October 2010, Pakistan needs to add a power generation capacity of about 20,000 MW in ten years at a total cost of $32 billion in order to overcome energy shortages.[15] This is a huge challenge. If this target is to be met from mainly indigenous sources, it will have political ramifications given the past failure to agree further dam schemes and hydroelectric energy supplies. Balochistan, with only around 7 per cent of the total population, is the main supplier of natural gas and also has coal and copper reserves, but some Baloch nationalists regard the province as being colonially exploited by the state, just as an earlier generation of Bengali nationalists claimed that the region's raw jute supplies were being utilized for national interests with no local benefits accruing.

Population

In any other region of the world, a state of Pakistan's size with a population of around 175 million,[16] an army of around 500,000 and a GDP of over $160 billion would be a significant power. India, however, with its 1 billion plus population, 1 million of which are in arms, and GDP eight times higher than Pakistan's, dwarfs it and in doing so perpetuates the sense of insecurity which has dogged Pakistan's history. While Pakistan cannot match India's size, military and economic might, its population and economy have grown rapidly since 1947. According to the 1951 Census the population for what now includes Bangladesh as well as Pakistan was just 73 million. Today's truncated Pakistan, with an estimated population of 185 million, is the sixth largest country in the world in terms of its population. The rate of increase is still around 2.2 per cent per annum; this compares with 1.4 per cent and 0.6 per cent respectively for its Indian and Chinese neighbours. Around half of Pakistan's people are under the age of 15. Some estimates put the population under the age of 25 as high as 100 million, making this one of the largest youth populations in the world. This youthful dynamism is a factor in the state's resilience. Youth unemployment and underemployment are also, however, linked with ethnic and Islamic militancy and with the country's high levels of violence.[17] The youth bulge could either prove a demographic dividend, helping to drive forward economic growth, or it could prove to be a time-bomb, if the state is unable to educate and utilize it.[18]

Rapid population growth has been a contributory factor to Pakistan's poor achievements in educational provision for its citizens, although they are primarily a result of the state's historically low tax levels and the privileging of defence expenditure over that on both health and education.[19] Literacy stands at around 55 per cent of the population, although this masks significant regional and gender imbalances. Only around a third of adult women are literate, while little more than a fifth participate in the labour force.[20] Women made up only 10.96 million out of a total labour force of 51.78 million in 2007–8.[21] Pakistan in 2007–8 stood 125 out of 138 countries in terms of the Gender-related Development Index, and ranked 82 out of 93 in the Gender Empowerment Measure.[22] The following year, the increasing security crisis in the Malakand division and parts of the NWFP kept girls especially away from education. According to one report perhaps as many as 80,000 girls in Swat were deprived of education.[23] Scandalously high rates of female illiteracy in the more conservative areas of Pakistan such as the Frontier and the Tribal Areas (with just 18 per cent female literacy in the former and 3 per cent in the latter) have exacerbated the failures of half-hearted government programmes of family planning. A recent report revealed that only 18 per cent of women in the countryside use a modern method of family planning.[24] Around 200,000 women are admitted to hospital each year because of unsafe abortions, at a conservatively estimated cost of $22 million.[25] A dramatic expansion of female education is essential, not only in terms of addressing gender inequalities, but because of its historical connection with the slowing of population increase. Bangladesh's better record than Pakistan in reducing fertility rates is directly attributable not only to its more effective family planning policies, which have been largely provided by NGOs (in Pakistan they account for around 13 per cent of family planning services), but to its policies designed to educate and economically empower women. According to some accounts, there is a gap of 25 per cent between the demand and supply of contraceptive services in Pakistan. Its consequences are revealed by the slow pace in the decline in fertility and the chilling statistic that 1 in 7 pregnancies end in an induced abortion.[26]

Population growth continuing at its current rate of over 2 per cent per annum could in future reach crisis proportions. Some demographers project that this will result in a population of around 335 million by the mid twenty-first century. This would make Pakistan the fourth most populous country in the world.[27] More immediately high levels of population increase poverty in the absence of policies of economic redistribution; around 1 in 5 Pakistanis continue to live beneath the poverty line. About 60 per cent of Pakistan's population subsist on less than 2 dollars a day.[28]

There are again marked regional differences in this exposure to poverty, with the poorest populations being found in the Tribal Areas, the interior of Sindh and Balochistan. It is significant to note that the areas which were most developed in the colonial era have retained their advantage since independence. There are parallels with India with respect to the former Princely States, in that there were pockets of deep poverty in some of the Princely States which acceded, while other states were 'progressive' (e.g. Mysore in the Indian context) and had similar standards of living to those of neighbouring British India districts. Khairpur and Bahawalpur were the most developed states that acceded to Pakistan, as they shared in the irrigation (the Sutlej Valley Project) and communications developments of the adjacent British provinces. The Frontier Princely States of Amb, Chitral and Dir lagged far behind the settled districts of the Frontier. Swat had a literacy rate of just 1.75 per cent in 1951.[29] Education was banned by the Nawab of Dir in case it undermined his autocratic rule by which he owned all the land in his state.[30] However, the Balochistan states with their poor communications and nomadic inhabitants were the most backward of all the states that acceded to Pakistan.[31] Kharan and Las Bela had only one middle school each for boys by 1949.[32] The disparity of socio-economic development between the Princely States and the former British provinces, together with their strategic location, complicated their integration in Pakistan. With the notable exception of Kalat, extremely low levels of political consciousness accompanied the poor social development indicators.

Even in the most prosperous areas of Pakistan, such as the Punjab, the rural areas lag behind their urban counterparts. The absence of amenities and life chances in rural Pakistan has contributed to another marked feature of the country's economic profile: that of high levels of migration. Rural-urban migration has resulted in Karachi and to a lesser extent Lahore emerging as mega-cities. Future migration trends will increase their size and those of other urban conurbations, so that by 2030 it is estimated that half of the population will live in urban centres. Nonetheless, Pakistan continues at present to have a large rural population. Agriculture still accounts for around 20 per cent of the annual GDP and provides employment for over 40 per cent of the country's labour force. The extensive production of rice and wheat is made possible because of the existence of one of the largest irrigation networks in the world, which waters around 16 million hectares of land.

Migration

Pakistan is a society on the move. Its birth was accompanied by the Partition of the subcontinent and the division of the two Muslim majority provinces of Punjab and Bengal. The Partition-related violence sparked the largest uprooting of people in the twentieth century.[33] While the two-way transfer of over 9 million Punjabis in the short period of August-December 1947 forms the iconic representation of this upheaval, migration of Muslims into Sindh continued well into the 1950s. By 1951, the Urdu-speaking UP migrants *(mohajirs)* numbered around 50 per cent of Karachi's population. As we shall see later, the creation of a UP Urdu-speaking enclave in the sands of Sindh was to have profound consequences for Pakistan's politics. The cultural and political assimilation of Punjabi-speaking migrants, unlike their Urdu counterparts in Sindh, has obscured the fact that the greatest number of migrants from India (over 5 million) came from East Punjab. They settled on the agricultural land abandoned by the outgoing Sikh farmers in the Canal Colony areas and in the towns and cities of West Punjab, where they frequently accounted for over 50 per cent of the population. The Punjabi migrants have formed a constituency for Islamist and extremist sectarian movements as well as for the mainstream factions of the Muslim League. They are also staunch upholders of the Kashmir cause, reflecting the fact that there was not only a significant influx of Kashmiri refugees into Pakistan in 1947, but the experiences of upheaval by ethnic Punjabis led them to an anti-Indian stance. The Punjabi refugee element in Pakistan's politics has been overlooked, but it in fact has formed another of the longer-term shaping factors which are not always recognized in contemporary security-driven analyses.

Since independence, internal migration has formed an important feature of Pakistan's experience and helped shape its political developments. There has been outright rural-urban migration, but also movement from the countryside to small towns, sometimes as a staging post in the migration process. While the overall population increased by 250 per cent in the period 1947–81, urban population growth was close to 400 per cent. Karachi's population had risen from under half a million in 1947 to 13 million in 2007. Lahore's population stood at 5 million, with six other cities having a population of over 1 million.[34] By 2025 it is projected that Pakistan's urban population will total over 100 million, with Karachi and Lahore both forming mega-cities of around 19 and 10 million respectively. The presence of large migrant communities in towns and cities has sustained outlooks and community networks from the rural setting rather than resulting in the emergence of a new 'modern' urban class. Small towns especially represent more of a village environment than is expected by the Western conception of an urban society. The migration of Pakhtuns throughout Pakistan, alongside the rise of the Taliban in Afghanistan, may be seen as a factor in introducing tribal cultural mores and norms into a growing 'orthodox' expression of Islam.[35]

It is impossible to understand Karachi's political turmoil in the 1990s (which by 2010 had shown dangerous signs of resurgence) without acknowledging the fact that this is not only the city of Indian migrants (*mohajirs*) but is the third largest Pakhtun city in the world and has a greater Baloch population than Quetta. Ethnic struggles for power and control over resources, in which criminal mafias play a role, have been contributory factors in the city's reputation for violence. While Karachi is the melting pot par excellence, no area of Pakistan is homogeneous, although provincial politics are frequently discussed in these terms. Around 40 per cent of the population of Balochistan is, for example, Pakhtun. There are significant Kashmiri populations in such Punjabi cities as Lahore and Sialkot. The Soviet occupation of Afghanistan brought an influx of 3 million Afghans. Internal displacement of populations has been a feature of the military operations in the Tribal Areas. Indeed one aspect behind the resurgence of violence in Karachi in 2010 was the growing number of Pakhtuns who had moved to the city from the Tribal Areas. Alongside economic migrants and victims of military conflict, the natural disaster of the 2010 floods was another factor in internal displacement. Finally, there is the little reported movement of perhaps as many as 100,000 Punjabi settlers from Balochistan as a result of the growing number of targeted killings of Punjabis in the current phase of insurgency in the province.[36]

Overseas migration has also impacted both on Pakistan's economy and its international image. During the colonial era there was considerable migration from the Punjab future heartland of Pakistan; this included Muslim Rajputs from the poorer northern areas of the province as well as Sikh Jats from its central districts. Military service was a common feature to both areas, providing exposure to lands well beyond the native home (*desh*) and creating a culture of international migration. There was also a tradition of migration from the Sylhet region of Assam (now part of Bangladesh) based on the poorer sections of its population turning to careers as *lascars* (sailors) which led them to life overseas. Independence continued the earlier pattern of migration in that most international migrations were from Punjab and East Bengal. One discontinuity was provided by the push to overseas migration for the population of Mirpur in Azad Kashmir, following the displacement created by the construction of the Mangla Dam.[37]

North America, Europe and the UK were the main centres of permanent migration, although large numbers of workers also moved for short-term contracts to the Middle East from the 1970s and 1980s. This has undoubtedly increased the size and scale of middle-class wealth in Pakistan. The psychological reactions arising from the frustrations of newly-enriched returnees has been dubbed the *Dubai chalo* (Let's go to Dubai) theme in Pakistani society.[38] Overseas Pakistanis in UAE and Saudi Arabia provide the largest inflows of remittances. In the period July 2010 to January 2011, for example, almost half of the $5.3 billion in remittances came from Pakistanis in these two areas.[39] However, pakistanis living permanently in the West also provide large sums for their homeland's foreign exchange reserves. The cultural impact of overseas migration is much less quantifiable than its economic consequences. The growing religious orthodoxy coincided with the increase of labour migration to the Gulf and Saudi Arabia in the 1970s. Assessments of the 'Arabization' of Pakistani Islam tend to focus on the Saudi export of Wahhabism in the political context of the Iranian revolution and the Soviet occupation of Afghanistan.[40] In doing so, they overlook the influence of growing numbers of migrant oil and construction workers who returned home to Pakistan, not only with increased prosperity, but commitment to a scriptural Islam in opposition to popular 'folk-Islam'.

The UK received the largest number of migrants, with the 2001 Census revealing a population of over 1 million persons with Pakistani or Bangladeshi origins.[41] The growing South Asian diaspora in the US from 1965 onwards was dominated by Indian migrants, although there was also the emergence of a professional Pakistani class, comprising engineers, academics, and especially medical practitioners. The size of the Pakistani population in the US is disputed, as US Census figures which put it at around 200,000 do not include college students or second and third generation members. If these are counted the numbers can increase to 700,000. While the Pakistani diaspora has not played as pivotal a role in national politics as have, for example, overseas Tamils through their support for LTTE, all parties have overseas branches. London and Dubai were twin poles of the PPP during the years of exile of its leader Benazir Bhutto. London has also been the residence for Baloch nationalists. The MQM is run by Altaf Hussain from its London Secretariat. Former President Musharraf launched his All-Pakistan Muslim League in London at the beginning of October 2010. Within the UK, Birmingham because of its large diaspora community is another centre of intense political activity.

The diaspora represents an important economic resource through remittances, support for the major parties and for humanitarian aid, as at the time of the 2005 earthquake and 2010 floods. The US community is the wealthiest Pakistani diaspora and provides the most in remittances (around $1.73 billion p.a. by 2007/8.)[42] Indeed periods of Pakistan's rapid economic growth in the early 1980s and again two decades later appear to have been driven in part by overseas remittances which increased consumer demand for housing and transport. The involvement in the 7 July 2005 London bombings of British-born young Muslims of Pakistani descent who had visited radical mosques in Pakistan, followed by the failed Times Square bombing in New York in May 2010, represented a more disturbing element in the ongoing diaspora-homeland connection. Further evidence came from the fact that the grey-bearded Swat Taliban spokesman, Muslim Khan, was a returned former painter and decorator from the Boston area.

Social Structure and Organization

Pakistani society is marked by vast disparities of wealth and access to basic goods and services, such as health, education and sanitation. These remain limited in an environment in which just 1 per cent of the population is directly taxed. Western donors in the wake of the 2010 floods have urged that Pakistan address this issue and mobilize more of its own resources. Much of the funding for social welfare programmes is at present dependent on international aid. To provide just one example, USAID provides around $45 million for family planning programmes which have been chronically under-funded from government sources. The political power of big landowners continues to block the introduction of an agricultural income tax and thereby improve Pakistan's woeful tax to GDP ratio of 9 per cent. In a country of some 190 million people, there are only 2.7 million registered taxpayers. Significantly, agriculture, which accounts for nearly a quarter of Pakistan's GDP, provides only 1 per cent of its tax revenues. Its favouring is to the detriment of industry, which has a tax share three times its contribution to GDP.

The failure to bring the wealthy into the tax net has undermined the consolidation of democracy and is a factor in encouraging the notion that Islamization would bring greater social justice in its wake. State-sponsored Islamization in the1980s concentrated, however, on the punitive aspects of Islamic law rather than on the encouragement of egalitarianism. Periods of rapid economic growth in the 1980s and in the early years of the twenty-first century have seen some 'trickle down' effects, with a concomitant rise in life expectancy and lifting of sections of the population out of poverty. Nonetheless, grinding poverty affects rural populations in Sindh and Balochistan.

Estimates of the incidence of poverty in Pakistan are difficult not only because of faulty survey design, but inaccuracies in the raw official data. The World Bank estimated that 28.3 per cent of the population were living below the poverty line in 2004–5. This global figure masks trends across the provinces and between urban and rural settings. The Social Policy Development Centre produced the breakdown for 2001–2 shown in Table 1.

Table 1: Poverty Incidence by Province (per cent)

			Urban		
Province	*Overall*	*Rural*	*Provincial capital*	*Large cities*	*Small cities & towns*
Punjab	26	24	18	22	43
Sindh	31	38	10	23	40
NWFP	29	27	28—41		
Balochistan	48	51	14—44		

Source: Safiya Aftab, *Journal of Conflict and Peace Studies* 1, 1 (October–December 2008), p. 70.

We shall be noting later the extent to which uneven development has played a role in undermining nation-building. Certainly, the sense of Punjabi domination of Pakistan has been generated not only by the region's association with the military, but because it is more highly developed than elsewhere, with the exception of Karachi. More recently, attention has been turned to the link between poverty and Islamic militancy.[43] Attention has been drawn to the fact that FATA, which is the most backward region of Pakistan with 60 per cent of the population living below the poverty line, a literacy rate of only 17 per cent and a per capita public expenditure of a third of the national average, have been the focus of insurgencies.[44] Another major area of militant recruitment, however, is southern Punjab. While its poorest districts. such as Dera Ghazi Khan and Muzaffargarh, lag far behind its richest, the incidence of poverty is not as great as in for example the interior of Sindh and Balochistan. Yet neither of these areas are centres for radicalization and militancy. Muzaffargarh, the lowest ranked Punjabi district in terms of the human development index, still in 2003 stood at only 59 out of 91 districts in Pakistan.[45] While poverty and unemployment may feed militancy, this can only be fully understood in terms of a complex mix of religious, sectarian, social and historical factors.

Despite the existence of much poverty and inequality, it would nevertheless be wrong to portray Pakistan as an unchanging society. Despite major failings of governance, economic growth during the past decade has resulted in the emergence of a youthful and dynamic middle class. According to some assessments there are now as many as 35 million people with a per capita income of up to $1.900.[46] There is no monolithic middle stratum of society; it is differentiated by occupation, income, family antecedents, language and gender. The 'middle classes' contain both 'modernist' and 'traditionalist' elements and are as a result not necessarily more 'Westernized' in outlook and lifestyle than the urbanized younger generation drawn from the feudal elites. Indeed, one of the most striking developments of the past decade has been the spread of the orthodox *Al-Huda* movement amongst educated middle-class Pakistani women.[47] This has promoted the Arab dress code of the full-size *abaya*. Perhaps the most unifying element of the middle classes is consumerism, as seen in the surge in sales of cars, televisions and mobile phones. One in two Pakistanis is a mobile phone subscriber, one of the highest rates in the region. Civil society groups have established a telemedicine network (Jaroka Telehealthcare) that enables health workers in remote areas to connect with doctors in major cities. In addition to expenditure on electronic durables, the middle classes have become the main users of the burgeoning private educational establishments and privately run polyclinics which have become a marked feature of the urban landscape. According to one estimate, around three-quarters of all health care is provided by the private sector.

The rise of the middle classes has also contributed to the growth of electronic media transmission, which is another marked feature of contemporary Pakistan. The days have long since passed when recourse to the BBC World Service and grainy images from the Indian Doordarshan television network were the only alternatives to the strictly controlled state broadcasting. Ease in dealing with an increasingly independent and intrusive media is becoming as much a political requirement in Pakistan as elsewhere in a media-driven world. The new cable networks have, however, strengthened existing orthodoxies in many instances, rather than interrogating them, and in the eyes of some critics have contributed to the powerful anti-Western discourse in contemporary Pakistan.[48] Increased media access has in fact provided new opportunities for the spread of conspiracy theories, which are a marked feature of Pakistani public life. According to some commentators, they reflect a widespread national malaise which, by denying the root causes of Pakistan's problems, prevents any attempts to address them. Symptomatic of the delusional world of conspiracy theories in Pakistan was the revelation by an international opinion pollster that two-thirds of Pakistanis surveyed believed that the person killed in the US operation in Abbottabad was not Osama bin Laden but a double. The former army chief General Mirza Aslam Beg not only concurred with this view, but maintained that Osama had been killed some time before in Afghanistan and the 2 May 2011 episode was a US plot to defame Pakistan.[49] Another widely believed conspiracy theory was that the raid on bin Laden was a practice run for the US seizure of Pakistan's nuclear weapons. When Hillary Clinton visited Pakistan towards the end of the month, she pointedly remarked that 'anti-Americanism and conspiracy theories will not make problems disappear'.[50]

With respect to politics, the inchoate character of the middle classes means that no single party has benefited from their development. In Lahore, middle-class voters are likely to support the Pakistan Muslim League Nawaz (PML-N). In Karachi, they divide on ethnic lines, with

Pakhtun businessmen, for example, supporting the Awami National Party (ANP), and *mohajirs* the *Muttahida Qaumi Mahaz* (MQM or United National Movement), formerly the Mohajir Qaumi Movement. More 'traditionalist' members of the middle classes throughout Pakistan are likely to vote for the Islamist party *Jamaat-i-Islami* (JI or Islamic Society) or the Deobandi party the *Jamiat-ulUlama-e-Islam* (JUI). Although tiny by Indian standards, the middle classes in Pakistan are beginning to become an important social and economic actor, even if they lack national political power because of the continued grip of the feudal elites and *biraderi* (kinship group) heads.

It is widely argued in Pakistan that the feudals' political influence has been a major factor in undermining democracy.[51] The term 'feudal' is used loosely to include the landed and tribal elites, many of whom may have interests not only in capitalist farming, but agri-businesses and urban real estate development. Moreover, not all 'feudals' can rely on the 'coercive localism' described by critics to ensure the votes of their tenants. Socio-economic changes in parts of Punjab, for example, have created circumstances not that dissimilar from India, where elites must constantly 'rejuvenate' their ties with their clients through the provision of patronage, and voters can remove incumbents in order to maximize the benefits they receive from political elites.

The Sindhi *waderos* symbolize Pakistan's 'feudal' class. They are seen as using their power to veto socio-economic reform, including education in their localities. They are also blamed for blocking land reform and rural taxation and for cornering development aid. Zulfiqar Ali Bhutto's foes argued that he had never outgrown the arbitrariness and cruelty (*zulm*) of his Sindhi feudal background.[52] Concentration on the *waderos* ignores the fact that a new landholding class has emerged in parts of Sindh as well as in Punjab in recent decades, drawn from the higher echelons of the bureaucracy and the army. It is also important to recognize that landowning alone is not the sole basis of political power in the countryside. In order to be really effective it needs to be combined with 'tribal' and *biraderi* (kinship group) leadership and with the notion of 'reputation'. This helps to explain why controls on female sexuality which could bring family 'dishonour' are frequently so savage in tribal communities. Religious sanctity is another source of rural power. The connection between Sufi shrines and power has been traced in the colonial era in the works of such writers as David Gilmartin and Sarah Ansari.[53] At the outset of the post-2008 PPP-led government both the Prime Minister, Yousaf Raza Gilani, and the Pakistan Foreign Minister, Shah Mehmood Qureshi, hailed from leading Sufi families of Multan. Recent studies have pointed to the fact that Islamists are increasingly challenging the *pirs'* influence not just on the long-established grounds of orthodox resistance to 'shrine worship', but by presenting themselves as opponents of the feudal structures in which the Sufi orders are enmeshed.[54]

Two points need to be made regarding 'tribal' and *biraderi* leadership. It is well known that the tribal heads (*sardars*) in Balochistan wield far more power than their counterparts in Khyber-Paktunkhwa. There are large tribal heads in south Punjab who are originally of Baloch descent: the Legharis represent a good example. Outside Balochistan, the greatest 'tribal influence' is wielded by the *waderos* of the interior of Sindh. The strongest *biraderi* networks are found amongst the smaller-scale landholding communities of the central Punjab. *Biraderi* networks are also important in some towns and cities. Politics in Lahore for example are dominated by the factional struggles amongst members of the Arain and Kashmiri *biraderis*.

Four major impacts of Pakistani 'feudalism' which have encouraged political authoritarianism have been identified by its critics. First, the vast economic and social gulf between the landholding elite and the rural masses has effectively depoliticized the latter. Votes are sought in an atmosphere of 'coercive localism'. The rural poor dare not oppose their landlord patrons. Second, the perpetuation of feudal power relations has contributed to a political culture of violence and combativeness rather than cooperation. Third, the parochial and personalized character of Pakistan politics is rooted in the landlords' predominance; this is a factor in the weak political institutionalization which has hindered democratic consolidation. Fourth, the landlords are concerned primarily with bolstering their local prestige rather than with pursuing a political agenda. This means that a significant fraction of the rural elite will always be prepared to lend legitimacy to authoritarian rulers. Along with a section of the *ulama*, landlords are on hand to join what has been derisively termed the Martial Law B Team.

Mohammad Waseem has recently argued, however, that it is the 'rightist' middle class rather than the feudals who undermine democracy.[55] He maintains that the absolute majority of the middle class is rightist, although lawyers, writers and intellectuals comprise a small pro-democracy element within it. The rightist element is made up of military officers and bureaucrats, engineers, architects, corporate managers, information technologists and businessmen, all of whom are intensely conservative in outlook. While he acknowledges the combative and patronage-driven characteristics of the feudals' political involvement, he sees traditional landed elites as more reflective of plural ethno-linguistic ties and as being prepared to build alliances across communities and regions. This class is attached to the Islam of *pir* and shrine, rather than that of mosque and *madrasa*. The middle class on the other hand is driven by the twin ideologies of Pakistani nationalism, with its strong anti-Indian sentiment, and scriptural Islam, which is Pan-Islamic and anti-Western in sentiment. The rightist middle class shares the state-centric, rather than people-centred vision held by the military and bureaucratic establishment. With the exception of Zulfiqar Ali Bhutto, Waseem maintains that Pakistan's authoritarian rulers have been drawn from the middle classes. Their 'stock in trade' is that democracy has been 'hijacked' by the feudals, politicians are 'corrupt' and Pakistan society is not yet fit for democracy. Waseem's views provide a useful counterpoint to the more widely held belief that the rise of the middle class in Pakistan will go hand in hand with democratization and liberalism.[56] Indeed it could be argued that Wahhabi and Deobandi puritanical interpretations of Islam especially appeal to an emerging middle class locked out of power by 'feudals' with their rhetoric of 'equality', 'brotherhood of Muslims', and claim that the implementation of the *shari'ah* will ensure social justice. As Matthew Nelson has so expertly revealed, for the landholding classes, however, a major preoccupation has been to use a combination of coercion, legal delay and political influence to circumvent the *shari'ah*'s impact on patrilineal customs of female disinheritance. For Nelson, political influence in the Punjabi rural setting lies in the ability to 'circumvent existing post-colonial laws' which have undermined the British enhancement of 'tribal custom'. He sees the resulting informal patterns of 'extra-legal political accountability' as possessing deleterious consequences for democratic consolidation.[57] His understanding not only challenges Waseem's, but those who adopt a less nuanced understanding of the lack of 'efficiency' of the district courts and see the colonial legacies for contemporary Pakistan only in narrow institutional inheritances.[58]

Language and Identity

Tariq Rahman has engagingly traced the history of the 'upstart' Urdu language, involving its gradual displacement of Persian from the middle of the nineteenth century to its blossoming as a 'badge of identity, a mark of sophistication and refinement' for elite Muslims.[59] Its journey was to culminate in it being accorded the status of Pakistan's national language, although at the time of independence only around 7 per cent of the population spoke it as a mother tongue. As we shall see in Chapter 2 the initial refusal to accord a similar status to Bengali, the language spoken by most Pakistanis in 1947, was a factor in the growing tensions between the country's eastern and western wings.

From the 1900 foundation of the Urdu Defence Association onwards, Urdu was a major symbol of Muslim political identity in colonial India. The association owed its birth to the success of partisans of Hindi, securing its recognition alongside Urdu as an official language in the United Provinces (UP). Urdu had been adopted as the official language of UP in 1858, but Hindi language activists mounted increasingly vociferous public campaigns to change this government decision. Altogether 118 memorials signed by 67,000 persons were submitted in favour of Hindi as the medium of instruction when the Commission on National Education sat in 1882. The Hindi-Urdu controversy really intensified, however, at the beginning of the next century, arising from the anti-Urdu stance of the Lieutenant Governor of the North-Western Provinces, Sir A. P. Macdonnell. During its course, both Urdu and Hindi became identified as the language of essentialized 'Muslim' and 'Hindu' religious communities. In this respect language advocacy intersected with the growing impact of socio-religious reform in North India.

Urdu was not only the mother tongue of the UP Muslim elite, but was spoken by members of the Muslim upper classes throughout India. The mass of the Muslim population, however, spoke a variety of other languages, with Punjabi and Bengali having the greatest number of users. The British had made Urdu, however, the official vernacular language in Punjab from 1854 onwards, thereby marginalizing the Punjabi mother tongue. This decision, partly taken for administrative convenience and resting on official prejudices against the 'rustic' Punjabi language, possessed profound long-term significance.[60]

Attachment to Urdu became a key component of the Muslim separatist platform in colonial India. Nonetheless, Urdu has proved much less effective in promoting a national Pakistani identity than have regional languages in articulating ethnic identity. Centralization around one language has strengthened the role of regional languages in identity politics. This is especially marked in Sindh, where the language movement emerged in resistance to the local influx of Urdu-speaking *mohajirs* as well as to the national domination by the ruling *mohajir* and later Punjabi elites.[61] It is present in most parts of Pakistan, although it is muted in Punjab, outside of its southern Seraiki-speaking belt. This arises from the colonial tradition of subsuming Punjabi to Urdu. It also reflects the fact that the Punjab has been the core of the Pakistan state. Influential segments of its inhabitants have largely been prepared to eschew cultural nationalism in favour of physical control of state political and economic power.

The rapid social mobility arising from internal migration has certainly strengthened Urdu as a common lingua franca. The process has its limitations, however, because of the politicization of language in the smaller provinces of Pakistan. Urdu itself became the focus of an ethnic identity, rather than of Pakistani nationalism, with the emergence of a *mohajir* political identity in urban Sindh early in the 1980s.

Sindhi has long been an important element in identity politics, along with other community markers relating to dress (wearing of the *ajrak* shawl), poetry and Sufism. Indeed it was Sufi poems (*kafi*) which helped to establish Sindhi linguistic traditions, despite their ancient origins. The nationalist politician and writer G. M. Syed drew on these ancient cultural traditions to support the demand for an independent Sindhi homeland, *Sindhu Desh*, in the 1970s, although the driving force of his separatist stance was the 'Punjabi-Mohajir' political domination.[62] Syed had warned even in the early 1940s that Pakistan was likely to be a Punjabi-dominated state. There was considerable resentment towards the influx of Punjabi agriculturalists following the completion of the Sukkur Barrage irrigation scheme in 1932. This was as nothing compared with the flood of Urdu-speaking refugees from India in 1947.

During the colonial era, Sindhi was standardized in the Arabic script, formerly having also been written in Nagri and Gurumukhi. Since independence, Sindhi language activists have been engaged in clashes with the state. A strong sense of Sindhi cultural identity lay behind resistance to the centralizing and Islamizing policies of Zia, as can be glimpsed in such poems as Niaz Hamayooni's 'Love for Homeland'. G. M. Syed, despite his long-term resistance to the Pakistan state, stood aloof from this movement, however, in the main because of his hostility to the PPP. Ironically, Karachi's Urdu-speakers celebrated the veteran Sindhi nationalist's 81st birthday in January 1984.

Pashto from the colonial era onwards has become an important component of Pakhtun ethnic identity, although before this Persian was the 'language of sophisticated discourse' and the moral code of Pakhtunwali undergirded identity.[63] The British imposition of Urdu as the official vernacular language encouraged the promotion of Pashto as a symbol of anti-colonial resistance by the Red Shirt movement of Khan Abdul Ghaffar Khan. Whilst the use of Pashto thereafter became central to Pakhtun identity, along with Pakhtunwali and Islam, it met with resistance from both Hindko-speaking Muslims and the Hindu-Sikh population. The Pakistan state viewed Pashto with similar suspicion as did their colonial forebears, because of Afghanistan's irredentist claims and the Afghan state's promotion of Pashto over Dari as a symbol of Pakhtun domination. During the 1950s and 1960s, the issue of Pashto was central to the aspirations of Pahktunistan secessionists. More recently, the integration of Pakhtuns into the Pakistan state has seen the rise in Urdu use, although Pashto retains its symbolic significance in identity politics and demands for greater autonomy, which culminated in the renaming of the North West Frontier Province as Khyber Pakhtunkhwa.

Tribal social structures have been more important in framing Baloch political identity than language, as Balochistan's multilingualism has limited such possibilities. Its linguistic mix resulted not only from the presence of a sizable Pashto-speaking Pakhtun population in such areas as Sibi, Zhob and Pishin, but also from the prevalence of a Brahvi-speaking Baloch ethnic group. Indeed the Khan of Kalat's family were Brahvi-speaking, but in spite of this Baloch nationalists have looked to Mir Nisar Khan, who had forged the Kalat state in the second half of the eighteenth century, as an inspiration for independent statehood. Seraiki-speaking tribes such as the Jamalis also identify themselves as Baloch. Urdu was the recognized vernacular language of the British-administered Balochistan. Since independence the Pakistan state has promoted Urdu as a vehicle for national integration. Its prevalence amongst the Baloch elite, the underdeveloped nature of Balochi as a written language and the divide between it and Brahvi have led to tribal loyalties and economic and political grievances, rather than language driving nationalist resistance to the Pakistan state.

Modernizing states' reactions to 'sub-national' political identities based on ethnicity, language and religion have been a major factor in encouraging authoritarianism not only in South Asia but throughout the developing world. Superficially, Pakistan's limited range of politically-conscious ethnic groups in comparison with India's appears less of a threat to democratic consolidation. A number of scholars have argued conversely, however, that India's complex ethnic structure has worked as an enabling factor for democracy by for example preventing the state from being captured by a single dominant ethnic group.[64]

Religion

The Pakistan state has increasingly sought to sponsor Islamization both for ideological reasons and purposes of legitimization. Such writers as Mohammad Abdul Qadeer have seen this as falling into three eras, the period from 1947 to 1971, 1972 to 1977 and 1977 to the present.[65] This periodization is too neat, although it usefully points to a continuous and intensifying process. Recent work by Hansen has added a fourth period dating from 9/11, in which Islamic social movements, increasingly in conflict with the state, have replaced its efforts to conform public life with interpretations of Islamic precepts.[66] Alongside the state's attempts to manipulate and project religion, it has established alliances with militant groups to forward regional strategic interests.[67] This process, as we shall see in later chapters, has been constant throughout Pakistan's history, although it intensified in the 1990s. Analysts have highlighted its role in the development of what has been termed Pakistan's *jihadist* landscape.[68]

Some scholars have talked of a 'lost generation' as a result of the intellectual impact of the educational reforms of the Zia era[69] and link evidences of contemporary intolerance with the success of efforts to impose a narrow orthodoxy.[70] The rise of mosque schools (*madaris*) and their possible encouragement of 'radicalization' has exercised many Western scholars since 9/11, as we shall see later.[71] This should not obscure the impact on outlooks arising from the state-sanctioned textbooks in Urdu-medium government schools which link Islam and Pakistani nationalism and have a strong anti-India bias.[72] It is also important not to confuse ever increasing signs of personal piety arising from the activities of such organizations as *Al-Huda* and *Tablighi Jamaat* (the Society for Spreading Faith) with extremism and militancy.

The latter has roots dating to the colonial era; *Al-Huda* is a recent movement aiming to educate elite women about their rights and responsibilities as 'good Muslims'. It was founded in 1994 by Dr Farhat Hashmi when she returned to Pakistan from the UK. Furthermore, as David Hansen has recently revealed, even when numerous urban Muslims may hold 'radical' views, only very small numbers of individuals engage in violent behaviour.[73]

One area which Hansen might have explored in his thesis of 'Radical Rhetoric-Moderate Behaviour' is the fact that despite increasing orthodoxy, Islamic parties have polled badly in national elections. The exception of 2002 was marked by state intervention on their behalf. Islamic parties have exerted growing leverage, but this has rested on their 'street power' and links with the military establishment, rather than their ability to convince Pakistani voters.

Divisions amongst Islamic parties have been one factor in their poor electoral showing. Feudal domination along with internal factionalism had limited their electoral impact. The JUI party attached to Deobandi Islam has become largely limited in voter support to the Pakhtun population. Its main religious opponent is the *Jamiat-ul-Ulama-e-Pakistan* (JUP or Association of the Ulama of Pakistan) which represents the Barelvi school of *ulama*. The Islamist *Jamaat-i-Islami*, founded in 1941 by Maulana Abul Ala Maududi and opposed to the Pakistan demand, is more broadly based amongst the middle- and lower-middle-class urban populations. It has spawned a radical and violent student offshoot, *Islami Jamiat-i-Tulaba* (IJT or Islamic Students' Movement), which during the Zia era captured many of Pakistan's campuses where it is now entrenched.

Sectarianism is the defining feature of contemporary Pakistani Islam. It means that Western fears of an Islamic revolution in Pakistan are overwrought. Nonetheless, sectarianism has contributed to Pakistan's growing violence as a result of the politicization and weaponization of sectarian groups. Less appreciated is the fact that sectarianism also provides a fertile soil for recruitment to radical *jihadist* movements.

Sectarianism not only involves clashes between the Sunni majority and Shia communities, who account for around 25 per cent of the population, but between puritanical Deobandis and Barelvis who represent an institutionalized Sufi Islam. The eclipse of Sufi or 'folk Islam' by scriptualist Islam is seen as a result of state and Saudi sponsorship of Deobandi and *Ahl-e-hadith* reformers. Within a generalized understanding of the eclipsing of Sufi Islam it is important to realize that there is a tradition of reformed and revivalist Islam within Naqshbandi and Chishti Sufism and that individuals can still combine attendance at shrines with orthodox outlooks.[74] A dangerous contemporary development however has been the number of violent attacks on Sufi shrines and *pirs* since 2005. In October 2008, the Swat Taliban killed a leading Barelvi figure, Pir Samiullah, and two months later exhumed his body and hung it in the square in Mingora.[75] The year 2010 witnessed bombings and suicide attacks on the most venerated shrines of Hazrat Data Ganj Bakhsh in Lahore and Baba Farid in Pakpattan; the shrine of Abdullah Shah Ghazi in Karachi was also targeted. There were numerous protests in Punjab and Sindh following the twin suicide attack on the Data shrine in Lahore at the beginning of July, which killed 45 people. While such spectacular attacks are still relatively rare, another contemporary development which is becoming increasingly apparent is the seizure of Barelvi mosques by Deobandi and *Ahl-e-Hadith* groups. According to one observer in 2007, as many as 100 mosques in Karachi alone had been seized in this way.[76]

Such violence represents a break with the past. However, Pakistan inherited from the colonial period a divided and conflicted Islamic faith tradition. Revivalism can in fact be dated even earlier to the decline of Mughal power in North India and to the writings of the eighteenth-century Delhi scholar Shah Wali-Ullah (1703–62), whose teachings against worship at Sufi shrines, for example, still have resonance today. Revivalism in Sunni Islam, however, gathered pace with the rise to power of the East India Company.

There is a rich scholarship on the spread of religious revivalism within colonial India.[77] Within the future Pakistan areas, this was most dynamic in the Punjab. The late-nineteenth-century growth in the Christian community spurred its emergence, but indigenous reformers' competitions with each other were a major factor. Both the Sikh *Singh Sabha* movement and the *Tablighi Jamaat* emerged in response to Hindu reformers' efforts to reconvert former low-caste populations. The reconversion efforts of the Arya Samaj formed part of a revivalist response which has been dubbed 'strategic syncretism', as purification of 'degraded' religious practice reflected Christian missionary attacks, especially on 'superstition' and the mistreatment of women. Religious practice and belief were to be 'rationalized' and purged of corrupt accretions in keeping with the requirements of 'modernity'.

The Muslim revival in British India produced the major organizations and movements such as the Deobandis, the Wahhabis, the Islamists and the Barelvis, which are in conflict in contemporary Pakistan. Indeed a hallmark of the revival was its competitive activism. The impact of the printing press on Islamic identity has been chronicled by Francis Robinson.[78] *Ulama* from competing schools of thought vied with each other to propagate their interpretations of Islam. Sectarianism went hand in hand with dynamism. Many publications centred on reformers' criticisms of the Sufi shrine cult and the resistance of reformist organizations to the heterodox Ahmadi movement. This shared many of the activist and revivalist features of the contemporary Islamic movements, but its founder Mirza Ghulam Ahmad (*c.* 1839–1908) outraged the orthodox by challenging the doctrine that Muhammad is the last of the prophets by claiming divine inspiration.

The Deoband movement was the most influential revivalist movement because of the strength of its educational institutions and use of the new opportunities to circulate its ideas.[79] The movement grew out of the Islamic seminary founded in the country town from which it took its name in the Saharanpur district of the United Provinces. Its geographical remoteness from the centres of British power reflected the desire of its founders Maulana Muhammad Qasim Nanotawi (1832–80) and Rashid Ahmad Gangohi (1828–1905) to distance themselves from the colonial impact. The Deobandi schools did not teach modern science or through the medium of English. Deobandis placed emphasis on personal piety and were equally opposed to Sufi and Shia Islam and to the modernist approach of Sir Saiyid Ahmad Khan (1817–98). Lahore, Jullundur and Ludhiana emerged as important centres of Deobandi influence in the colonial Punjab. A tradition of Deobandi activism focused around animosity to the Shias and Ahmadis was established among the urban lower-middle-class Muslim population. From 1929 this was institutionalized in the *Ahrar* movement. It gained in popularity by campaigns against the Ahmadis and in support of Muslim rights in the Kashmir Princely State. It could count on support in the latter movement from their large Kashmir population which resided in Lahore. The *Ahrar* were eventually to lose their influence because of their stance on the Pakistan movement, but modern militant sectarian organizations such as the *Sipah-i-Sahaba Pakistan* (SSP, the Army of the Companions of the Prophet in Pakistan) draw inspiration from the *Ahrar* and indeed find their support in the same sections of population, including Partition migrants drawn from the artisan Kashmiri, Sheikh and Arain communities.

In 1926, the Deobandi Maulana Muhammad Ilyas founded the faith movement of the *Tablighi Jamaat* (Society for Spreading Faith), which began as a missionary preaching movement seeking to renew the faith of the partly Islamicized Meo population of the Mewat region of south-eastern Punjab.[80] It now has a worldwide following of over 60 million, with its world headquarters near Dhaka and its European base at the Markazi mosque in Dewsbury. Zia greatly encouraged its activities within Pakistan, including the preaching to soldiers. Its growth in Pakistan can be gauged by the fact that the *Jamaat*'s annual meeting at Raiwind regularly draws over 1 million people. While the organization has traditionally been apolitical in outlook with its emphasis on personal reform, perpetrators of the March 2004 Madrid bombings and July 2005 London bombings have been linked with its activities.

Significantly while the Muslim separatist movement drew inspiration and leadership from those educated in Sir Saiyid's Aligarh educational establishment, the majority of the *ulama* attached to the Deobandi movement opposed the creation of Pakistan because its secular leadership and territorial nationalism clashed with their adherence to a revived Islam and to the *ummah*—the worldwide Islamic community.[81] The Pakistan movement thus relied on the Sufi leadership for its mobilizing of mass support and drew its intellectual inspiration from the modernist reformism of the Aligarh movement.

The future role of Islam in Pakistan's public life was never fully spelled out in the heat of the battle with Congress. This provided an opportunity for revivalists who had opposed Pakistan's very existence to migrate from India and to seek to Islamicize the state in terms of their particular sectarian understanding. As we shall see in the course of this study, the conflicting interpretations of Islam have dogged efforts at reform while raising sectarian tensions. Top-down state-sponsored Islamization reached its zenith in the Zia era. The attempt to 'Sunnify' the state, at a time of Shia resurgence following the Iranian revolution, stoked Shia-Sunni conflict in Pakistan. Mufti Jafar Husain in 1979 founded the Shia organization *Tehreek-i-Nifaz-i-Fiqh-Jafariya* (TNFJ, the Organization for the Implementation of Jafari Jurisprudence), to resist 'Sunnification'. In response the militant Deobandi-linked *Sipah-i-Sahaba Pakistan* (SSP) was created six years later by Maulana Haq Nawaz Jhangvi (1952–90). Haq Nawaz was influenced by the *Ahrar* tradition of activism and radical oratory. He had first come to prominence in the campaign against the Ahmadis which culminated in their being declared on-Muslims by the 30 June 1974 Constitutional Amendment. The SSP received backing not only from Deobandi institutions but from the Pakistan state, as Zia sought to contain the Shia threat which had emerged following the widespread protests against the Zakat and Ushr ordinance of 1979.

Haq Nawaz developed a powerful base in his home district as a result of the increasing tension between artisan communities, enriched by migrant remittances from the Gulf and the traditional Shia feudal elite. His murder in 1990 intensified sectarian strife and led to the creation of a splinter organization, *Lashkar-e-Jhangvi* (LeJ, the Army of Jhangvi). These organizations later became more powerful as a result of the return of Afghan veterans and the ability to use Afghanistan as a training base for their activities. Both LeJ and SSP were banned by Musharraf while he was president, but have subsequently formed important components of the 'Punjab Taliban' (see Chapter 7). The militant *Lashkar-e-Taiba* (LeT, Army of the Pure) is also Punjab-based, with its headquarters at Murdike, although it derives its inspiration from Salafist Islamic traditions. It is the military wing of the *Dawat ul-Irshad Markaz* (the Centre for Preaching and Guidance) which was founded in 1987. Its integration of missionary call to faith and commitment to *jihad* is publicized in the Urdu weekly, *Jihad Times*, and the English monthly, *Voice of Islam*. From 2005 onwards LeT extended operations from Jammu and Kashmir where it initiated *fidayin* (suicide missions) to other areas of India, culminating in the 26 November 2008 Mumbai attacks. It has been internationally linked with plans to bring down planes and to attack Heathrow airport. LeT's ability to continue to function has undermined the peace process with India. The Indian view is that it is receiving 'protection' from the Pakistan military so that it can be used in future 'proxy' operations. Some observers in Pakistan point to its ability to act independently of its former state patrons as it has become socially embedded because of public sympathy for its pro-Kashmiri cause and its charitable and humanitarian activities.

Many militants in the Pakistan and Punjab Taliban were educated in mosques and started out as activists with such mainstream Islamic parties as *Jamaat-i-Islami* (JI) and *Jamiat-ul-Ulama-e-Islam* (JUI). While the Pakistan Taliban is now pitted against the state, and organizations such as LeT and SSP are officially banned, it is important to understand that militant movements emerged in an atmosphere of official support and indeed were in some instances directly patronized by the state through its security services. Involvement in militancy was not only state-sanctioned when it involved the Kashmir *jihad*, but had wide social approval. This helps to explain why the *jihadist* culture has proved difficult to challenge post 9/11 and why even today fundraising for militant groups goes on openly and *jihadist* literature is widely available. It also explains the ambiguous stance of the mainstream Islamic parties to militant actions. JUI has distanced itself from the Pakistan Taliban, but has close ties with its former cadres in the Afghanistan Taliban.

Conclusion

This chapter has highlighted the ways in which Pakistan's geography, culture, religion and society have shaped its post-independence development. Security concerns have shaped its development, because in many respects it is a borderland state with a historical colonial legacy of contested boundaries. It can also be conceptualized as a state which has been significantly influenced both by its migrant populations and its trans-national population linkages. While Pakistan lacks the immense linguistic and religious diversity of India, it is not the monochrome society portrayed in some Western works and sought after by Islamist activists. It is at heart a plural society. The failure to acknowledge this politically and the consequences flowing from it form part of the historical narrative we will explore herein.

What also emerges from this chapter is the country's highly differentiated socio-economic development. The areas which formed Pakistan were at different stages of development at the time of the state's creation. Inherited advantages and more importantly disadvantages with respect to agricultural production, communications, education and personal rights have complicated post-independence nation-building. Similarly, the challenging regional security environment has impacted on political development. The state's response to its inheritances has shaped the history of the past six decades. It is to this that we will be turning in the following chapters. It is important to recognize however that political instability was not pre-ordained because of Pakistan's colonial inheritance. Similarly, the separation of the two wings of Pakistan by a thousand miles of Indian territory did not make the state's break-up a foregone conclusion. Political choices and responses to security challenges and inherited diversities have profoundly influenced national development.

2

UNDERSTANDING THE FAILURE OF PAKISTAN'S FIRST EXPERIMENT WITH DEMOCRACY 1947–58

Pakistan emerged amidst the traumas of Partition, but also with a great sense of expectation for both individual and collective transformation. The cultural and material life of India's Muslim population would flourish in a new democratic homeland. Within less than a decade, cynicism had replaced hope. A passive population looked to a military ruler to offer the prospect of a renewal of state and society. Where had Pakistan's first experiment with democracy gone wrong? Why had Pakistan's political trajectory differed so markedly from neighbouring India, which had inherited similar traditions and institutions from the Raj?

This chapter argues that Pakistan's political inheritances, together with the emergence of the Kashmir dispute, undermined its democratic development. The outcome was a state in which democratic consolidation was sacrificed on the altar of national security and in which centralization prevailed over the pluralist vision contained in the 1940 Lahore Resolution. Before turning to this analysis, however, we will first consider the range of explanations that has been proffered to explain the state's political trajectory in its formative decade.

Explanations for Democratic Failure

There are numerous explanations for Pakistan's democratic failure. The simplest is that which publicly justified the 1958 coup which ended the first experiment with democracy. This depicts the politicians as bringing the country to its knees through their misuse of power, corruption and factional intrigue. It conveniently ignores the fact that the army may have possessed institutional motives for intervention. Subsequent coups have similarly denied this element. Diametrically opposed to the army's explanation has been the view that the profound anti-democratic sentiments of such bureaucrats as Iskander Mirza (President 1956–8) and Ghulam Muhammad (Governor-General 1951–5) paved the way for the coup by their distrust of politicians and willingness to dismiss elected governments. It could be argued that their early career development in the colonial bureaucracy had nurtured these sentiments.[1] In many respects, Ghulam Muhammad's October 1954 dismissal of the Constituent Assembly was a major turning point in Pakistan's post-independence development. Allen McGrath, in his work on these events, is highly critical not only of Ghulam Muhammad but of Chief Justice Muhammad Munir for providing legal cover for this action.[2] M. M. Syed joins McGrath in attaching the bulk of Pakistan's democratic failure to the 'misfortune' of having such seasoned bureaucrats elevated to positions of authority.[3] Alternatively, Pakistan's failing parliamentary democracy has been attributed to the decline of the Muslim League.[4] Certainly unlike its Congress counterpart in India, having won freedom, it did not evolve as a pillar of the post-independence state. This stemmed from the fact that it was a 'latecomer' in the Pakistan areas. Without a tradition of rule or firm institutions, it had to accommodate the leading landlord elites in order to make a political breakthrough in such key provinces as Punjab. The cost in achieving freedom in this way was the strengthening of patron-client political relations, which inhibited subsequent democratisation.

Ayesha Jalal has provided the most authoritative study of Pakistan's post-independence decade. The theme which runs through her study is the contradiction between the requirements of state consolidation and political participation. Pakistan's pressing financial problems and strategic insecurities worked against the type of constitutional arrangements envisaged in the 1940 Lahore Resolution. They also meant that the Muslim League itself suffered from benign neglect. The bureaucracy and the military emerged as the main pillars of state as it grappled with the refugee crisis and hostilities with India over Kashmir. Resources were diverted from a political economy of development to a political economy of defence. The process was enabled by Pakistan's growing strategic ties with the United States. Jalal concludes her analysis of the background to the 1958 coup by maintaining that the political processes in the provinces had been curbed, but not entirely crushed during the consolidation of state authority around its non-elected institutions. The army is thus portrayed as launching a pre-emptive coup to forestall the assumption of power following national elections of Bengali-led political interests that had a different vision for Pakistan than that held by the West Pakistan establishment.[5]

Recent research on the Princely States, which formed much of the land mass of West Pakistan, provides additional evidence for Jalal's analysis. While the powerful politician Sardar Patel played a key role in the integration of the Indian Princely States, it was the bureaucracy in Pakistan which oversaw this process, with Colonel A. S. B. Shah, first Joint Secretary in the Ministry of Foreign Affairs and then Secretary of the States and Frontier Regions Ministry, playing a leading role. The emphasis on security over political development, which was present throughout Pakistan, was even more marked in the Princely States, where autocracy went unchallenged for many years in such states as Dir and Swat, or was rapidly replaced by centralized government control as in Khairpur, the short-lived Balochistan States Union and even Bahawalpur.[6]

Pakistan's post-independence failures have also been understood in terms of the ending of the temporary political unity brought by the freedom movement struggle. The resurgence of 'centrifugal' forces was encouraged by heavy-handed centralization, according to Yunas Samad. Like Jalal, he draws attention to the boost which the emerging bureaucratic-army axis received from US financial and military support. This he believes was 'crucial' when Ghulam Muhammad dissolved the Constituent Assembly.[7]

Whatever the explanations for the Pakistan Muslim League's demise, authors are agreed on its major signposts: the February 1948 Pakistan Muslim League Council decision to separate the party from the government by debarring ministers from holding any office within it; the assassination of Liaquat Ali Khan in October 1951 as he was on the point of reactivating it; the defeat of the Muslim League in the spring 1954 elections in East Pakistan; the desertion of West Punjab landlords to the Republican Party following its establishment as a 'pet' of the bureaucracy in May 1956; and finally the resignation of the bureaucrat turned Prime Minister Chaudhuri Muhammad Ali in September 1956, as it signalled the end of a Muslim League government presence at both the centre and the provinces.

These key events need to be understood in terms of a historical framework which sees political decline in terms of the administrative culture inherited from the colonial era, the Muslim League's weak institutionalization in the future Pakistan areas and the resultant recourse to centralizing solutions to the problem of state construction in a context of financial constraint and strategic insecurity. These issues form the focus of the remainder of this chapter.

Historical Inheritances

(i) The British Security State in North West India

For some writers, the army's increasingly predominant position in post-independence Pakistan had its roots in the colonial state's military recruitment policies in the late nineteenth century. These made the Punjab the main army centre. This decision accorded with the ideology of the 'martial races', but also ensured a steady stream of recruits from an area which was largely untouched by Indian nationalism.[8] The Punjab's 'loyalty' at the time of the 1857 revolt encouraged the development of strategic alliances between the British and military contractors exemplified by the Tiwanas of the Salt range region.[9] While the Punjab benefited economically from this imperial connection, a tradition of paternalist authoritarianism was established both in this province and in what later became British Balochistan and the North West Frontier Province. Rather than India and Pakistan possessing shared systems of governance from the Raj, it is argued that much of the area that became West Pakistan formed part of a British security state.[10] The requirements of maintaining political order were privileged over those of encouraging representative institutions to flourish.

Khalid bin Sayeed was the first to coin the phrase 'viceregalism' to sum up the authoritarian ethos of governance which was a legacy of colonial rule in the future Pakistan areas. Its hallmarks were paternalism, the wide discretionary powers afforded to bureaucrats and the personalization of authority. They were most clearly institutionalized in the Frontier Crimes Regulation. The British had annexed territory in this part of the subcontinent, primarily to secure the Indo-Gangetic heartland from the expanding Czarist Empire. Even when the NWFP was administratively separated from the Punjab, the strategic importance of the latter area was maintained as it had become the centre of recruitment for the Indian army. Order was the major prerequisite, not just in Punjab but throughout the future West Pakistan region. This administrative ethos survived the spread of popular representation elsewhere in India. Political participation was delayed in the Balochistan and Frontier regions. As late as 1927, the Simon Commission argued that the strategic location of the Frontier made it unsuitable for self-government. It was only after the widespread unrest of 1930–2 that the system of dyarchy introduced elsewhere in India in 1919 was extended to the Frontier. The denial of political rights explains why a section of the Pakhtun population forged close links with Congress. Right up to independence, electoral politics in Balochistan were restricted to the Quetta Municipality. This 'slow growth' in elective politics in important areas comprising contemporary Pakistan 'must be taken into account', Muhammad Waseem has argued, 'in any study of electoral democracy... especially when it is compared with India'.[11]

The bureaucratic attitudes engendered by the British security state in North West India survived until the last days of the Raj and were imbibed by leading Pakistani bureaucrats of the 1950s. They were given their freest rein in the Princely States, where security considerations were used to justify a bureaucratic and military grip on power which presaged later national developments. Yaqoob Khan Bangash has revealed that the 'creeping authoritarianism' which writers have seen preceding the first coup from around 1954 onwards existed much earlier in the former Princely States.[12] Policy in these areas was controlled by the States and Frontier Regions Ministry. Security concerns arising from tensions with India and Afghanistan overrode the desire to address the 'democratic deficit' in the former states. Democracy was 'rationed' and deployed not as part of a full process of national integration but to undermine those princes who proved awkward. 'With limited constitutional and political integration by 1954', Bangash declares, 'the princely states were not fully a constituent part of Pakistan and their subjects not full citizens of a free country'.[13] Even in the most 'progressive' states of Khairpur and Bahawalpur, which had their own elected assemblies, centrally appointed Advisors and Chief Ministers held sway rather than elected representatives.[14] Where representative politics threatened security interests in the Frontier and Balochistan states, both the bureaucracy and the Pakistan Muslim League moved to stifle it. It was telling for wider attitudes towards democracy in Pakistan that not only was the oppositional Kalat State National Party banned in 1948, but the All Pakistan States Muslim League was disavowed when it appeared too autonomous. Democratization went only as far as semi-elected Advisory Councils in Swat, Chitral and Amb. On the national stage, full powers of nomination were accorded to the Princes with respect to the States' representation in the Constituent Assembly. The government of Pakistan's stance starkly contrasted with its Indian counterpart regarding integration and democratization of the Princely States.[15] The narrow equation of 'security' with the centre's control was, however, to prove self-defeating as the thwarting of democratic activity through to the mid 1950s not only created antagonism towards the centre, but space for the flowering of ethnic and linguistic nationalism in parts of Bahawalpur and Kalat.

Bengal was the exception to the security state tradition of 'guided democracy' and although the region's more developed areas, including Calcutta, went to India at the time of the 1947 Partition, its governance culture was more conducive to the growth of democracy and civil society than in any of the other Muslim majority areas. Pakistan was to be faced with the major task of accommodating these varying colonial inheritances. One way in which this could have been achieved would have been by jettisoning viceregalism in the West Pakistan areas. The character of the freedom struggle and the chaos arising from the 1947 Partition prevented this.

(ii) The Legacy of the Freedom Struggle

Landownership had traditionally gone hand in hand with political power in North West India. In many parts of this area, land had been rapidly changing hands in the final years before colonial rule. The British demilitarization of Indian society ended this avenue of social mobility, thereby creating a more static village-based society. At the same time, the colonial state bolstered the influence of local power-holders, especially in the wake of the so-called 'conservative reaction' which followed the 1857 revolt. Despite colonial stereotypes of changeless rural India, many of the Raj's new collaborating elites were not hierarchies steeped in antiquity, but were of modern origin.

The colonial state regarded the landholders as important intermediaries. Their position was bolstered in the following ways: land transfers as a result of inheritance and indebtedness were controlled through the introduction of primogeniture and legislation which limited the opportunities for designated non-agriculturalists to acquire land permanently; existing estates were increased as land was granted in newly irrigated areas in respect of state services such as raising army recruits or breeding livestock for the army; landholders were given police and judicial powers in their localities; political constituencies were drawn to coincide with landholders' control of villages; the landholders were the gatekeepers of the local population's access to British officials; the status and prestige of leading families was enhanced through the grant of honorary awards and titles.[16] The subsequent enhancing of the landed and tribal elite was a common feature across the future West Pakistan region. In the North West Frontier Province the larger Khans were the main beneficiaries of British patronage; in the Punjab it was the large landlords, the heads of *biraderis* (kinship networks, tribes) and the Sufi religious leaders who had landholdings attached to their shrines. In Sindh, *pirs* and *waderos* were rewarded as important intermediaries, as were the tribal *sardars* in the Balochistan area.

The Muslim League in its struggle to create Pakistan acknowledged the reality of the entrenched power of local ruling elites. Rather than bypassing them, it sought to use their local influence in its political mobilization. This process has been most fully documented with respect to its breakthrough in the key Punjab region from 1944 onwards.[17] The strategic alliances it made with the elites ensured that the votes of their clients were delivered for the League in the vital 1945–6 elections, which it portrayed as a referendum on the Pakistan demand. Without the landholders' support the credibility of the Pakistan movement would have been severely compromised. Nevertheless this policy came at a cost. Landholders did not organize local League branches themselves and were reluctant to allow outsiders to do so. Muslim League membership in the Punjab stood at just 150,000; it was ever lower in Sindh with just 48,500 members. The result was that the Muslim League, in contrast to the Congress, had few local roots. This undermined party loyalty and discipline. The entry of opportunist landed elites into its ranks also inducted their local factional rivalries. Factional infighting in the Frontier League prompted an enquiry by the All-India Committee of Action in June 1944 which admitted that 'there was no organisation worth the name' in the province.[18] The Provincial Muslim Leagues in the future Pakistan areas were in reality ramshackle organizations beset by in-fighting and parochial outlooks, which were difficult to harmonize with Jinnah's all-India understanding of the Pakistan demand.

The situation in Sindh on the eve of the 1946 elections was by no means unique, but illustrates the Muslim League predicament. The *waderos* alone possessed the money and influence to secure election in their localities. But they were more concerned with winning power for themselves than advancing the Pakistan demand. By September 1945 a bitter three-way factional struggle for League tickets had broken out. 'I wish people thought less of Premier and Ministers and thought more of the paramount and vital issue confronting us', Jinnah admonished one of the leading contestants; 'I do hope the seriousness of this situation will be fully realised... The only issue before us is Pakistan versus Akhund Hindustan and if Sindh falls God help you'.[19] The British Governor, Sir Hugh Dow, sympathized. 'Jinnah dislikes them all', he wrote to the Viceroy, Lord Wavell; 'he once told me he could buy the lot of them for five *lakhs* rupees, to which I replied I could do it a lot cheaper'.[20] This reality of course does not fit well with official Muslim League portrayals of this being a golden age of idealism. It does, however, help explain why the Muslim League, unlike the Congress, was unable to act as a focus for nation-building following independence. Many of its branches existed only on paper or were weakened by factional infighting. The pyramid of branches stretching from the localities to the All-India level, which was the Congress's hallmark, was noticeably absent. The Muslim League's electoral breakthrough in 1946 masked the weak organizational base in the future Pakistan areas.

Its heartland had always lain in the provinces of UP and Bombay, where Muslims formed a minority of the total population. It was the UP's Urdu-speaking elite which had felt most acutely the cultural and economic threat arising from Hindu majoritarianism as political representation was introduced by the British. Muslims in the future Pakistan areas did not share this sense of threat. Indeed, the introduction of an element of democracy offered them the prospect of using power to redress the educational and economic 'backwardness' of their community, in the face of Hindu domination of commerce and professional life. The Unionist Party's founder, Mian Fazl-i-Husain, for example, took advantage of the British devolution of responsibility for education to reserve 40 per cent of places for Muslims in prestigious institutions like Government College Lahore and Lahore Medical College, which had previously been a Hindu preserve.

The Muslim League throughout the colonial era drew its leadership from the UP; in particular this was provided by graduates of the leading Muslim educational institution in North India, Aligarh College. Jinnah was later to dub the college the 'arsenal' of the Pakistan movement. However, in any division of the subcontinent on the basis of religious community, the UP region would be included in India. Few of the League's leaders in the future Pakistan areas had experience of government. The Punjab Muslim League never held office in the colonial era. In the Frontier, the Muslim League had only one brief experience of rule (1943–5) and was significantly not in office at the time of Pakistan's creation. The Congress emerged from the 1946 elections not only as the major party, but with a majority (19/36) of the seats reserved for Muslims.[21] The Muslim League, under the leadership of Qazi Mohammad Isa, possessed even less influence in Balochistan. Its activities were confined to the Pakhtun areas of Quetta and its neighbourhood. In the Baloch and Brahui areas, where modern politics existed at all they took the form of demands for a greater Balochistan. These were initiated in the Young Baloch movement of Abdul Aziz Kurd and crystallized in the Kalat State National Party. The Khan of Kalat, Ahmed Yar Khan, was initially supportive of the Kalat State National Party (KSNP) as it placed him at the head of a greater Balochistan movement. He was eventually to ban it, however, in 1939 when its demands for democratic reform became too clamorous. But this did not halt the KSNP's activities or growing ties with Congress. Most importantly, the tradition of scant Muslim League influence in the Balochistan region persisted down to 1947. The ending of British paramountcy and the circumstances of Kalat's accession to Pakistan were to reinvigorate the links between the Khan and Baloch nationalists.

Ashok Kapur has argued that Pakistan's slide into authoritarianism resulted not only from the Muslim League's historical shallow roots in its constituent provinces, but the character of the freedom struggle. He argues that Pakistan emerged as the legacy of British divide-and-rule policies, rather than as a result of the kind of principled mass struggle which the Congress waged for India's independence. Pakistan, he declares, 'got its separate status as a gift' not 'by any brand of nationalism; or through mass movement... or by conception of liberty, representative government, or majority rule'.[22] The implication is thus that Pakistan started out with little sense of idealism, public service or self-sacrifice. The Pakistan movement in Bengal certainly gives the lie to this rather jaundiced view. Thanks to the efforts of Abul Hashim, who had become the secretary of the Bengal Muslim League in November

1943, a broad democratic institution based on 'clarity of purpose' capable of 'fighting for liberation from all forms of oppression' had been established in the province.[23] Like the Congress, the Bengal League possessed full-time party workers whom it paid and accommodated. Primary Muslim League branches were established even in remote villages. Yet ironically this platform was dismantled rather than built on after independence and was even threatened during the heat of the freedom struggle by the more conservative Muslim League members. Their misgivings were voiced in the newspaper *Azad*, which denounced Hashim and his fellow workers as communists. As we shall see in a later chapter, the Muslim League's post-independence demise in Bengal was rooted both in its inability to deliver the hoped-for transformation and its recapture by the old guard Khawaja faction.

The freedom struggle in the other Muslim majority provinces was mired, however, both by factional infighting, which was at its worst in Sind, and by competing understandings of the Pakistan demand. For landowners, it represented the protection of their interests from future Congress rule committed to agrarian reform. For Muslim bureaucrats and army officers, it opened up the prospect for rapid promotion. Businessmen saw the new homeland as an opportunity for reducing, if not completely removing, the Hindu domination of trade and industry across North India. For the religious classes, Pakistan represented an opportunity to implement their particular vision of Islam. In Bengal, Hashim's supporters believed they were fighting to achieve a sovereign East Pakistan state in which agrarian relations would be transformed. These conflicting understandings meant that unity could only be achieved around the towering charismatic personality of Jinnah and by falling back on a negative basis for unity. Hostility was primarily directed against the Congress and its leadership. Pakistani nationalism took on its abiding negative characteristics. Muslim opponents of the League as well as the Hindu 'other' were demonized. Mock funerals were conducted for Khizr Tiwana, the Unionist leader, during the Muslim League Direct Action against his ministry in February 1947. In the previous year's elections, its campaigners had declared that anyone who voted against the League was a *kafir* and would not be buried in a Muslim graveyard.

A political culture of intolerance was thus a gift to the new Pakistan state from the freedom struggle. It was rapidly seen at work. The Congress government of the Frontier was dismissed within two weeks of independence. Opposition to the Muslim League was increasingly seen as unpatriotic. In October 1950, for example, Liaquat Ali Khan declared that 'the formation of new political parties in opposition to the Muslim League is against the interest of Pakistan'.[24]

Attempts to establish a centralized state around the predominance of the Muslim League and the unifying symbols of Urdu and Islam, however, created tensions with regional ethno-linguistic groups. As we shall see later, they not only encouraged authoritarianism, but ultimately strained the Pakistan state to breaking point. Centralization in post-independence Pakistan was justified in terms of the need for unity in the face of threats from India and Afghanistan. Recourse to centralization was not simply a response to Pakistan's pressing problems. It too can be linked back to the characteristics of the freedom struggle.

The All-India Muslim League, although it conducted the Pakistan movement in terms of the need to protect Muslim minority rights from Hindu majoritarianism, was itself a highly centralized body. Its more 'representative' institutions, the Council and the provincial branches, were increasingly subject to the authority of bodies nominated by the president such as the Working Committee and, from December 1943, the Committee of Action. Moreover, the AIML was not only increasingly centralized, but remained dominated by members from the Muslim minority areas, rather than the future Pakistan areas. Bengal, with its 33 million Muslims, possessed just ten more members on the Council than the UP with its 7 million. The dominance of politicians from Bombay and UP even after the introduction of the new AIML Constitution in February 1938 was to have important post-independence repercussions. These migrants to the new state in 1947 had no local parliamentary constituency, although they could continue to wield power through the League organization and through their dominant position in the bureaucracy. Mohammad Waseem has neatly stated: 'Recourse to elections was considered suicidal by the migrant-led government at Karachi because there was no way it could win elections and return to power in the Centre. Elections were considered dysfunctional for the political system of Pakistan in the immediate post-independence period'.[25] Attitudes in favour of authoritarianism had thus been conditioned by the nature of the freedom movement. They were further encouraged by the chaotic conditions in the aftermath of Partition.

(iii) The Legacy of Partition

Pakistan's creation was accompanied by mass migrations and communal massacres. The exact death toll will never be known, although the figure is likely to lie between 200,000 and 1 million fatalities. There were 9 million refugees in the Punjab region alone, which was divided between the two successor states to the Raj. Pakistan bore the hallmarks of a refugee state, in that a tenth of its population were enumerated as Partition migrants by the 1951 Census.

Ayesha Jalal was the first to link the perpetuation of a viceregal tradition with the exigencies of Partition.[26] She argued that scarce government resources were diverted from building representative institutions to seeking administrative and military solutions to the refugee problem and the emerging conflict with India over Kashmir. The priority of building up the armed forces was spelled out by Liaquat Ali Khan in a broadcast to the nation on 8 October 1948: 'The defence of the State is our foremost consideration... and has dominated all other governmental activities. We will not grudge any amount on the defence of our country.[27] In fact the years 1947–50 saw up to 70 per cent of the national income being allocated to defence.[28] The weakness of the Pakistan army at the time of independence had been brought home by the fact that almost 500 British officers had been employed to make up for the shortfall of qualified Pakistanis. Indeed some in Pakistan saw the British Commander-in-Chief Sir Douglas Gracey's reluctance to commit Pakistan's troops to assist the tribesmen in the Srinagar valley as a 'missed opportunity' for a lasting military solution to the Kashmir issue.

The aftermath of Partition also encouraged authoritarianism by creating tensions between the provinces and the centre regarding refugee resettlement. This will be examined later in the chapter. Suffice it to say here that the downfall of the Sindhi Prime Minister Muhammad Ayub Khuhro over this issue not only strengthened Sindhi sentiment against the centre, but also encouraged the precedent of executive action against elected representatives which boded ill for the future.

Finally the traumas of Partition have impacted on both the Indian and Pakistan states' longer-term responses to sub-national movements. Neither New Delhi nor Islamabad has been prepared to countenance another Partition. This has resulted in the violent suppression of ethnonationalist movements. India has managed these challenges better than Pakistan, but in Kashmir, the North East and the Punjab region it has resorted to naked force. Pakistan has less successfully attempted to counter regional nationalist movements in East Bengal, Balochistan and in Sindh. This manifestation of what has been termed the 'fearful state' in South Asia will be examined in more detail later in this text.

The dispute between Pakistan and India over Kashmir in 1947–8 can also be seen as part of the unfinished business of Partition. The end of colonial rule had profound implications for the patchwork of Princely States spread across the subcontinent. As rulers of nominally independent territories, the princes had direct treaty relations with the British Crown, but their apprehensions concerning their future relations with a self-governing India had increased in the 1930s because Congress had encouraged the States' peoples' Conference movements for political reform. The princes' predicament worsened as the British departure approached. Significantly the greatest problems arose in such states as Jammu and Kashmir and Hyderabad, which had rulers drawn from a religious community different from the majority of their population. The former was to be the most significant for India and Pakistan's enduring rivalry because it symbolized the two states' competing conceptions of national identity. The decision of Hari Singh to accede to India in return for the airlifting of Indian troops to the Kashmir valley to thwart a tribal invasion resulted in hostilities between India and Pakistan, United Nations' intervention and a de facto division of Jammu and Kashmir in January 1949 along the ceasefire line.

The conflicting interpretations of these events continue to dominate scholarship in contemporary India and Pakistan. The intention here is not to repeat the arguments concerning the 'legality' of the instrument of accession, or the roles of Mountbatten and Nehru in events; in particular Nehru's waning commitment to the Security Council Resolution of April 1948 that the dispute should be 'decided' through democratic method of free and impartial plebiscite. It is rather to highlight the ways in which the Jammu and Kashmir dispute impacted on the emergence of militarism and authoritarianism in Pakistan.

The starting point is to acknowledge that Kashmir came to symbolize the rivalries and mistrust between Pakistan and its Indian neighbour after Partition. The mass migrations and disputes over the division of assets soured relations which already had a history of conflict in the Congress-Muslim struggle in colonial India. It was however the dispute over Kashmir which went to the heart of the ideological foundations of both states and set Indo-Pakistan relations on a basis of inter-state rivalry. The external Indian threat hastened the emergence of the military-bureaucratic combine in Pakistan. This was greatly strengthened during the Ayub era and was further institutionalized during the Zia and Musharraf periods. Nonetheless, the roots lay in the first decade of independence.

Without the heightening of India's perceived threat following the 1947–8 conflict, it is possible that Pakistan might not have militarily aligned itself with the US, as Washington in the Cold War context sought assistance for the policing of the Middle East and the Soviet Union. By the mid 1950s, however, Pakistan had embarked on what was to become a chequered relationship with the US. This was marked by differing strategic outlooks; Pakistan remained resolutely Indo-Centric, while Washington had broader regional and international interests. Pakistan's role as the US's 'eastern anchor' was formalized when it joined the South East Asia Treaty Organisation (SEATO) in September 1954 and two years later the Central Treaty Organisation (CENTO). These treaties were followed by US financial and military aid which strengthened the army's position vis-à-vis other state institutions. A template for the Pakistan polity was laid down, arising from its security concerns, in which democratic governance would always play second fiddle to the military and a centralized bureaucracy.

The Jammu and Kashmir dispute also marked the beginning of another long-running theme in Pakistan's history. This was the state's use of *jihadist* forces to achieve strategic goals in its drive against India. Pakhtun tribesmen loyal to the Pir of Manki Sharif were assisted in their invasion of Kashmir by irregular Pakistani troops. This began a tradition of covert Pakistan state support for *jihadist* groups. Much contemporary writing links the state's patronizing of such forces to military regimes and in particular the Zia era (1977–88). It is however much more deep-rooted than this.

Throughout the initial months of Pakistan's birth pangs, the ailing Jinnah was the mainstay of the new state. The central cabinet was even more docile than the Working Committee of the AIML had formerly been. Its members were not only handpicked by the *Quaid*, but he chaired their meetings and was authorized to overrule their decisions. Jinnah held the Evacuation and Refugee Rehabilitation and State and Frontier Regions portfolio under his direct control, thus establishing a tradition in which the holder of the highest office in the land would not merely be a constitutional figurehead. Nevertheless, despite his immense prestige as the country's founding father and the multiple crises at its birth, Jinnah never exceeded the limits of his authority as Governor-General laid down by the Indian Independence Act. This was to contrast markedly with the later actions of Governor-General Ghulam Muhammad (1951–5) and President Iskander Mirza (1956–8). Jinnah's death at the age of 72 on 12 September 1948 shocked the nation and marked the passing of an epoch in Indian Muslim history.

The Collapse of Democracy

By the early 1950s, the constitution-making process had reached a serious impasse, and as power passed incrementally from the politicians to the bureaucracy and the military, a mode of 'institutional path dependency' emerged that stymied any genuine efforts at building national and provincial administrations that would be accountable and democratic.[29] The high water mark of these developments was the summary dismissal of the Constituent Assembly in October 1954 by Governor-General Ghulam Mohammad and the creation of the One Unit scheme the following year, which established a unified West Pakistan province by dissolving the historic provinces 'in order to pre-empt any possibility of a Bengali-controlled centre'.[30] Thereafter the mould was set of an authoritarian military-bureaucratic polity in which nation-building was to be imposed rather than evolve and where Islam would function as a surrogate for political legitimacy. In sum, Pakistan was predestined for a collision course between 'state consolidation and construction' and 'the social dynamics underlying [its] political processes'.[31]

One Unit was heralded as being the inevitable consequence of 'the essential oneness and indivisibility of West Pakistan'.[32] In reality it made provincial-level politics in the western wing even more unstable and fractious than in the past, as those leaders who could not be bought off from the now defunct smaller provinces rallied against Punjabi domination. At the same time, One Unit was seen in East Bengal for what it was intended to achieve, to prevent thorough inter-wing parity, the majority Bengali population implementing its interests in national politics. Provincial-level politics fed into national politics, which came to be increasingly marked by opportunism, shifting and unstable coalitions. This was epitomized for example by Suhrawardy's reversal of his opposition to One Unit once he had become national Prime Minister in 1956. The politicians became increasingly discredited. The bureaucracy and the military were emboldened to take more effective power into their own hands, hastening the demise of even a façade of democracy.

One major reason why centralization was to succeed against the interests of provincial autonomy was the gradual emergence of Punjab as the core of the new state. Before 1947 Punjabi political leadership had been quintessentially provincialist, arguing against a unitary post-colonial India. Even in the early post-Partition period, the Nawab of Mamdot sought to use the provincial card against the centre on the refugee issue. His great rival and eventual successor as Prime Minister, Mian Mumtaz Daultana, vacillated between being the centre's man and the champion of Punjabi interests. His controversial role in the anti-Ahmadi movement in March 1953 led to his dismissal and a two-month period of martial law, which could be seen as the decisive moment in the subordination of elected politicians to executive power. The army had been called into action to restore law and order on other occasions, for example following the East Pakistan language riots of 1952, but this was its first experience of running the civil administration. The Lahore martial law thus marked another milestone on the road to the shifting of power from the politicians to the military and bureaucratic oligarchy within Pakistan. The turn of events questions an easy assumption that the interests of the Punjab and centre were always identical. In Yunas Samad's words, 'centrifugal forces' existed as much in Lahore as in other provincial capitals.[33] Punjabi particularism was however ultimately to lose its potency precisely because the province secured a dominant voice at the centre.

The army's rapid restoration of order in Lahore failed to save either Daultana's provincial government or Nazimuddin's national government. Daultana was dismissed on 23 March, being replaced by his long-time rival Firoz Khan Noon, who was at that time Governor of East Pakistan. Less than a month elapsed before the anti-Ahmadi agitation received its second victim, as in a defining moment in Pakistan's history Governor-General Ghulam Mohammad dismissed the national government of Khwaja Nazimuddin.

However, in the topsy-turvy world of Pakistani and Punjabi politics, all was not yet lost for Daultana. Ironically he re-emerged as the centre's ally in the Punjab, while Noon was expelled from the Muslim League and reinvented himself as a Republican. The circumstances for these reversals of fortunes arose from the dissolution of the first Constituent Assembly and the need for 'reliable' Punjabi representatives in its successor. Noon objected early in May 1955 to the attempt by the Pakistan Muslim League Parliamentary Board to select the majority of Punjabi representatives to the Constituent Assembly. He made his stand on the issue of Punjabi rights. This touched a popular chord as by no means were all Punjabi politicians happy with the submergence of their province into the One Unit West Pakistan which was to come into existence in October 1955. Its expected beneficiaries were those politicians allied to the centre. Noon's stance led to his dismissal. The Punjab League split between his supporters and those of Daultana who backed the centre. The latter group was rewarded when Abdul Hamid Dasti was installed as chief minister.[34] The seeds were however sown for the future emergence of the Republican Party, which was to elbow the Muslim League aside in the new West Pakistan Province and contribute to the growing instability at the centre.

The Republican Party which emerged in the province in May 1956 was a prototype of future pro-establishment parties such as the Convention Muslim League and more recently the PML-Q. Henceforth, as the new state was increasingly fashioned in the image of 'Punjabistan',[35] a section of its leadership comprising large landowners and *biraderi* heads willingly acceded to the centrist design of the military and the bureaucracy in return for Punjabi hegemony. This saw a gradual marginalization of *mohajir* influence, which was to gather pace following Ayub's coup. It was to be symbolized by the shifting of the Federal capital from the *mohajir* stronghold of Karachi to the new city of Islamabad deep in the Punjab. Such a turnabout was accomplished not only because of the demographic, military and strategic importance that Punjab now occupied and the establishment leanings of the traditional landowning elites; it was also the direct consequence of the division of the province itself, which set in motion a certain dynamic by which its fortunes became intimately tied to the ideological survival of the state.

To appreciate this it is necessary to recognise that three-quarters of all the Pakistan Partition refugees were Punjabis, although they did not adopt the *mohajir* label. Unlike the *mohajirs*, they were 'acute' migrants who had fled from East to West Punjab accompanied by levels and intensity of violence that forever coloured their imagination. This violence, moreover, was especially virulent in some Muslim majority districts (e.g. Gurdaspur, Ferozepur) that were expected to become part of Pakistan. Their exclusion from Pakistan, which provided an Indian land route to Jammu and Kashmir, created a deep sense of injustice about the fairness of the British demarcation of the new international boundary. In contrast to *mohajirs*, the assimilation of Punjabi refugees was largely an untroubled affair because culturally and linguistically they shared a common heritage and eventually settled in areas of the economy where direct competition with indigenous inhabitants was avoided.[36] Cooperation between East and West Punjab authorities, moreover, in the patterns of settlement enabled whole communities to relocate together in re-establishing the familiar bonds of *biraderi*. However, while the refugees were relatively easily assimilated into broader Punjabi society, their revanchist outlook made them a 'safe constituency for martial law governments, or as a lobby for right wing parties in pursuit of anti-India or Pan-Islamic parties'.[37] The Kashmiri element of refugees settled in Sialkot and Lahore were especially committed to the Pakistan state's approach to the dispute with India. East Punjab refugees, generally because of their experiences during partition, were sympathetic to the Kashmir cause.

The gradual melding of Pakistan and Punjab identities had its longer-term historical roots in the colonial state's decision to make Urdu rather than Punjabi the official language of government.[38] Attitudes in contemporary Pakistan, aside from those of language activists, mirror Orientalist caricatures of Punjabi as a 'rustic' language suitable only for use in the home. The process was thus set before the refugee influx for a neutralization of a potential Punjabi ethnic question in Pakistan. The Punjabi-military-bureaucratic combine has been further strengthened by the historical tradition of political opportunism amongst the region's landed elites. A section of the landed elite is always readily available, as we have already noted, to form a 'King's Party' for military leaders. Finally the legacies of colonial educational development and military recruitment policies, under the aegis of the martial races mythology, ensured a high Punjabi representation in the army (80 per cent) and civil service, which has from the 1950s tightened its grip on the state. Punjab has thus become the backbone of the Pakistan state.

Not surprisingly, the most sustained resistance to this polity was to come from ethnic mobilizations in provinces excluded from the new power structure. These initially occurred in the North West Frontier Province, Balochistan and Sindh. Even more disruptive for Pakistan's political development, however, were Bengalis' responses to the centre's attempts to deny them majority democratic power in national political life.

North West Frontier Province

The centre had much to fear from Pakhtun nationalism, given the Muslim League's historic marginality in Frontier politics and the threat of Afghan irredentism. Kabul did not accept the Durand Line as a national border and claimed areas of Balochistan and the NWFP. There was also the possibility that the state of Dir might accede to Afghanistan. While this danger was averted, the Pakistan authorities throughout the first decade of independence were chary of pressing democratization on its Nawab. Dir, along with the other Frontier States of Chitral, Swat and Amb, were not included in the One Unit Scheme. The Pakistan state largely succeeded in countering the Afghan irredentist challenge in the opening decade of independence, although not before the precedent had been set for the dismissal of the popularly elected Congress government. A combination of co-option and reliance on a strong local ally thereafter secured the centre's interests. The Kashmiri Muslim League leader in the Frontier, Khan Abdul Qaiyum, proved a reliable ally. His success stemmed both from the powerful backing of the administrative machinery and the introduction of rural development programmes. Qaiyum's abolition of the *jagirdari* system in 1949 was in keeping with his earlier Congressite career. Along with the repression of the Red Shirts in the wake of the 'Hazara plot'[39] it ensured that Abdul Ghaffar Khan was unable to reverse the setback to the movement caused by Jinnah's dismissal of his younger brother's Congress ministry within eight days of independence. Qaiyum dealt as resolutely with former Muslim League colleagues who opposed his will. Pir Manki, who founded the Awami Muslim League, was externed from the province from June 1949 onwards.

Qaiyum's firm grip banished the threat of Afghan irredentist claims based on the Pakhtunistan slogan. His agrarian reform measures, however, invariably created dissensions amongst the large Khans who were the Frontier League's traditional supporters. The dissidents amongst the old guard were led by Khan Ibrahim Khan of Jaghra and Mohammad Yusuf Khattak. But unlike their landlord counterparts in Punjab and Sindh, they could not readily call up reinforcements from the centre to support their group interests. Qaiyum's steadying influence in a strategically vital region bordering Kashmir and Afghanistan was working too much in its interests to be undermined.

The One Unit scheme invariably created centre-province tensions in the Frontier. These were surprisingly less acute than in Sindh, despite the colonial legacy of a well-developed Pakhtun political consciousness. An important reason for this was the co-option of Dr Khan Sahib at the centre, which muted the opposition of Abdul Ghaffar Khan and his followers. The centre eventually turned, however, to Ayub Khan's brother, Sardar Bahadur Khan, the former Pakistan Minister of Communications, to oversee the transition to the One Unit. A safe pair of hands was particularly welcome at this stage, for growing hostility within the Frontier to the One Unit scheme was matched by hostile signals emanating from Kabul.

Balochistan

If the Frontier was a relative success story for the centre in the opening decade of independence, Balochistan was the reverse. The post-independence tradition of tribal insurgency and military intervention which has dominated the region dates back to the ending of British paramountcy in Kalat. The Khan immediately created two houses of parliament which were elected on a restricted franchise in order to ascertain their views on the issue of accession to Pakistan. The KSNP, which emerged as the leading group in the lower house, led the opposition to this. The Pakistan government increased the pressure on Kalat through encouraging the accession of Las Bela and Kharan, whose rulers disputed the Khan's claim to suzerainty over them. The Khan's decision to accede possibly prevented a 'police action' as Pakistan troops had been detached to Kharan, Las Bela and Makran. Baloch nationalists have subsequently always alleged that the accession in March 1948 was made under duress. The Khan's younger brother, Prince Abdul Karim, formed the Baloch National Liberation Committee and briefly launched operations against the Pakistan army.

The accession was followed closely by the Pakistan state impressing its influence on Kalat. The Khan was forced to accept its nominee as his Prime Minister in July 1948. Khan Bahudur Mohammad Zarif Khan was a seasoned bureaucrat whose loyalties lay with the Pakistan authorities not the Khan. He oversaw the merging of Kalat with Kharan, Las Bela and Makran in the 1952 Balochistan States Union.

The Khan's agreement was secured when his privy purse was increased. Instead of an elected council, the centre's appointee as Prime Minister headed the new arrangement. The centralizing policies of the Pakistan state were viewed with disquiet by nationalist groups in the state and in Balochistan province. The Khan himself was stirred into action in 1954 when reports circulated that the Balochistan States Union would be merged with Balochistan. This was all part of the drive to prepare for the One Unit scheme with the single province of West Pakistan. When this came into effect in October 1955, Kalat was reduced to the status of an administrative district. The death of the 'historic' state of Kalat completed the merging of Baloch and Kalat nationalism. This went back as far as the 1920s, but had grown apace since the accession of Kalat to Pakistan. Its future hallmark of bouts of armed resistance was established when Prince Farim provoked a second tribal uprising in 1958. The Khan of Kalat was arrested and stripped of his pension. The insurgency was continued at a low level by Sher Mohammad Marri who set up guerrilla camps in the areas around Jhalawan and Bugti. When martial law was introduced by Ayub, the prevailing situation in Balochistan formed one of its pretexts.

Sindh

Sarah Ansari has revealed how Sindhi dissatisfaction with the prospect of a future Punjab-dominated Pakistan had emerged in the late colonial era, primarily as a result of an influx of Punjabi settlers to cultivate the lands newly irrigated by the Sukkur Barrage. The sense of a uniquely Sindhi Muslim identity lay uneasily beneath the surface of support for the Pakistan demand. The arrival of Partition migrants and the decision in July 1948 to separate administratively Karachi, the new federal capital of Pakistan, from Sindh strengthened sentiment against the centre. This was initially articulated not by the well-known Sindhi nationalist G. M. Syed, but by M. A. Khuhro, the first Muslim League Prime Minister of Sindh. Khuhro clashed with the centre not only over the issue of foot-dragging with respect to taking refugees from Punjab, but over his ultimately unsuccessful attempts to halt the exodus of non-Muslims from Karachi.[40] His supporters in the Assembly bitterly complained that they were dubbed 'provincialist' when they attempted to safeguard Sindhi interests, but 'In West Punjab, Punjabis [had not allowed] anyone else but the refugees from East Punjab. Was [that] not provincialism?'[41] Khuhro's dismissal by Jinnah on 27 April 1948 on charges of 'mal-administration, gross misconduct of his duties and responsibilities and corruption' was well received by the refugee lobby. But it nevertheless signalled a further setback for Pakistan's democratic development.

Khuhro used his influence in the Sindh Muslim League, despite his disqualification from politics, both to undermine the ministries which followed and to argue for provincial rights. In March 1951 he briefly returned to power, only to be dismissed once again after less than 8 months in office in a flurry of corruption charges. Ghulam Muhammad, in a rehearsal for his later dismissal of the Constituent Assembly, dissolved the Sindh Assembly and introduced direct rule. Normal political life resumed following elections in May 1953, but by this time the unedifying spectacle of factional infighting and of mounting social tension as the refugee influx continued unabated had emboldened G. M. Syed. During an Assembly debate the following September, he maintained that Sindhis were a distinct nationality and 'deserved equal treatment with other nationalities in the country'. He also criticized the centre for the inadequate representation of Sindhis in the Constituent Assembly, the absence of compensation for the loss of Karachi, extreme central interference in the provincial government's 'disposal and arrangement of her internal affairs', insufficient representation for Sindh in the services and not enough help by the centre for refugees in Sindh.[42]

In yet another political twist, Khuhro was once again rehabilitated as the centre needed him to muster support for the One Unit scheme. The incumbent, Abdus Sattar Pirzada, lacked the wiles and power to overcome the 'Security for Sindh' common front which had been formed in March 1954 to oppose the merger plans.[43] Pirzada was accordingly ditched and Khuhro freed from the PRODA (Public and Representative Offices (Disqualification) Act) disqualifications by Ghulam Muhammad. The fact that Khuhro was neither a member of the Sindh Assembly nor of the Muslim League was now conveniently overlooked as he was appointed Prime Minister for the third time only in order to oversee the extinction of his province. The strength of Sindhi opinion against One Unit meant that things were much trickier than in neighbouring Punjab. Khuhro turned to the trusted technique of involving such opponents as Ghulam Ali Talpur and Pir Ilahi Baksh in conspiracy charges. Representatives were intimidated by a heavy police presence which surrounded the Sindh Assembly Building, and legal cases were used to silence opposition. These methods ensured that the One Unit resolution was bulldozed through and that the Khuhro group was elected to the new Constituent Assembly in June 1955. While the centre thus got its way, the politicization of Sindhi ethnicity continued apace.

East Bengal

The momentum of the freedom movement could have been utilized in East Bengal to establish an effective ruling party within the framework of a participant parliamentary democracy. Instead there was decay in the League's structure and an increasing sense of alienation of its population from the centre, despite the fact that Pakistan had three Bengali Prime Ministers in Nazimuddin, Bogra and Suhrawardy during its formative decade.

The reorganization of the East Bengal Muslim League in May 1948 strengthened the influence of the conservative Khawaja faction. This was seen as more loyal to the centre than the progressives who had pushed the Dacca old guard to one side during the final stages of the freedom struggle. The restoration of the old guard represented a shift in power from the Bengali-speaking leaders who were rooted in the countryside to the urban *ashraf* Urdu-speaking elite. It superficially strengthened the one nation, one culture policy. But in reality, the pursuit of this Pakistanization programme undermined the very process of nation-building it was designed to serve. A minor example was provided in July 1948 when protests forced the Director of Broadcasting to end the highly unpopular practice of introducing Arabic and Persian words and phrases into the Bengali news bulletins of Radio Pakistan Dhaka.[44]

The Constituent Assembly's initial rejection of Bengali as a state language, coupled with a refusal to hold sessions in Dhaka, led to growing protests within Pakistan's eastern wing. Another source of discontent involved the posting of large numbers of Punjabi officials to East Pakistan. At street level the economic dislocation arising from the cessation of trade with West Bengal was another early source of anti-centre sentiment. West Pakistan's leaders refused to accord any legitimacy to Bengali grievances. They were at best dismissed as inspired by misguided provincialism; at worst they were seen as evidence of the existence of an Indian fifth column in Dhaka. These attitudes were expressed as early as January 1948, during a tour by the Federal Communications Minister Abdur Rab Nishtar. 'Regional patriotism [is] simply repugnant to Islam', he declared to a gathering at Parbatipar; 'Pakistan was established on the basis that Muslims were one nation and the tendency to think in terms of Bengali, Punjabi and Bihari would undermine the very foundations of Pakistan... These disruptive ideas [are] being spread by enemies of Pakistan who [are] working as fifth columnists amongst the Muslims'.[45] The fact that Hindu members of the Constituent Assembly had supported the Bengali language cause, as had Calcutta-based Bengali papers, was seen as evidence by the West Pakistan elite that the demands emanating from the eastern wing were Indian-inspired.

The language movement re-emerged in East Bengal early in 1952 following the publication of the Interim Report on the constitution which declared Urdu as the national language. Nazimuddin's tactless handling of the language issue intensified the protests. The death of four student demonstrators in clashes with the police at the Dhaka University Campus on 21 February marked an important milestone on the Muslim League's road to ruin within the province.[46] It was far easier for the police to destroy the memorial (Shahid Minar) erected to the martyrs than it was for the government either in Karachi or Dhaka to quell growing Bengali cultural and political self-assertion. This was heightened every year on 21 February, which was celebrated as a day of mourning and protest known as *shahid dibas* or martyrs' day.[47]

The language issue coincided with a growing feeling that West Pakistan was colonially exploiting East Bengal. The economic disparity between the two wings at the time of independence[48] widened during the first decade as industrial production and infrastructural development in West Pakistan outpaced that in the east. The greatest Bengali criticism, however, was reserved for the transfer of resources from east to west through the diversion of foreign exchange earnings.[49] This evidence for what was called 'internal colonialism' was to feed into demands for political autonomy and ultimately separatism.

The growing utilization of foreign exchange earned by East Bengal jute exports for West Pakistan development projects was at the heart of 'internal colonialism' charges. Even before this, jute became a divisive issue. The setback to the jute trade with India following the Pakistan government's unilateral refusal to devalue its currency against the

US dollar in September 1949 was the initial bone of contention. The resulting downturn in trade intensified Bengali discontent. The Pakistan government's establishment of a Jute Board in an attempt to stabilize prices gave a further twist to the crisis, as it was dominated by West Pakistanis. In the 1954 East Bengal elections, therefore, the jute issue constituted an important element in the opposition's election programme.

Along with the language and economic issues, the process of Constitution-making impacted unfavourably on provincial-centre relations. At the same time disputes between the two wings, over such issues as joint versus separate electorates, held up the overall process to the detriment of national democratic consolidation. As we have seen earlier, the One Unit Scheme was an attempt to stymie the Bengali democratic majority. The 1950 Interim Report had first denied this. Bengali counter-proposals raised the issues that were eventually to result in separation. These were expressed at a Grand National Convention held in November 1950 in Dhaka under the auspices of the newly founded Awami League. They included the proposal for a United States of Pakistan, consisting of the Eastern and Western Regions with a parliament elected under a joint electorate system in which only defence and foreign affairs should be reserved for the centre, and even then there should be regional Defence Units and a Regional Foreign Office in the Eastern Wing. Any new taxation items would only be added following the consent of the regions. The Six Points programme of the Awami League, which led to the break-up of Pakistan in 1971, was more or less the reformulation of this 1950 position.[50]

Even within the East Bengal Assembly, the Interim Report met with severe opposition. This was not confined to the Awami League, but also included some East Bengal Muslim League members. The party, however, was increasingly saddled with the image of representing the West Pakistan establishment's interests. The demise of the Bengal Muslim League dealt a blow to political stability not only in the eastern wing, but in All-Pakistan politics. The language disturbances in February 1952 sealed its fate. The opposition parties, including the octogenarian Fazlul Huq's Krishak Sramik Party, coalesced with the Awami League. Huq's reputation and still formidable oratorical skills propelled him to the forefront of the opposition United Front which was formed to contest the 1954 provincial elections, although his party lacked the institutional strength of Suhrawardy's Awami League.

The Front campaigned on a 21-Point Manifesto which had as its centrepiece a call for regional autonomy, which left only defence, foreign affairs and currency to the centre. Support from non-elite groups was sought by including calls for 'fair' agricultural prices and for a removal of income disparities between the high- and low-paid salariat. Such demands were extremely popular in a climate of inflation and distress resulting from the collapse of the Korean War boom. Finally, by calling for the nationalization of the jute industry, the Front struck at the leading symbol of East Bengal's 'colonial' status. The 21-Point Manifesto was presented to the people as a 'Charter of freedom'.[51] All later opposition programmes were merely shorter versions of this seminal document.[52]

The East Pakistan 1954 elections turned into a rout for the Muslim League, which was so closely identified with the centre. It was reduced to just 10 seats in an assembly of 309; the United Front, which had polled 65.6 per cent of the vote, had secured 223 seats.[53] The electors had rejected the contemporary manifestation of the Muslim League, but had in fact expressed their support for many of its pre-independence policies. They were voting in many respects for the future of East Bengal as originally envisaged by the Lahore Resolution. The centre's refusal to countenance such a development, however, drove the Bengalis further down the path of complete separation.

Huq's government was summarily dismissed after little over a month in office, following charges of both pro-Communist and pro-Indian leanings. The howls of protest were partly stilled because of the undeniable deterioration in the law and order situation during its brief tenure. This climaxed in the riots at the Adamjee jute mills, which claimed 400 victims and were only suppressed by the army's intervention.[54] The question whether *agents provocateurs* were behind the labour disturbances remains an unsolved mystery.

The Governor's rule was lifted only on the eve of the Constituent Assembly elections in return for Fazlul Huq's Krishak Sramik support for Bogra at the centre in his tussle with Suhrawardy for the post of Pakistan's Prime Minister. Huq's split with the Awami League earlier in April 1955 made him all too ready to oblige. The League-Krishak Sramik coalition at the centre enabled a United Front government (minus the Awami League) to assume power in Dhaka under the leadership of Abu Husain Sarkar.

In a classic case of poacher turning gamekeeper, Fazlul Huq was now installed as Governor of East Pakistan. He unsuccessfully attempted to sustain Sarkar in office. However, by the end of August 1956 he was so isolated in the Assembly that he had no choice but to quit. This opened the way for the formation of an Awami League Government led by Ataur Rahman Khan. The change of ministry in East Pakistan inevitably had a knock-on effect in the Constituent Assembly. Chaudri Mohammad Ali's Muslim League-United Front Government at the centre was now replaced by a Suhrawardy ministry comprising the Awami League and the Republican Party. Suhrawardy's national assumption of power created deep strains within the Awami League's ranks, especially on the issue of foreign policy, with the provincial leadership seeking an outright condemnation of the pro-Western approach in the fevered atmosphere generated by the Suez affair. Indeed, demands from disgruntled Awami Leaguers for provincial autonomy intensified rather than slackened as a result of Suhrawardy's assumption of national leadership. The ideological clash between the Suhrawardy and Bhashani groups led the latter to form a new national opposition party in July 1957. Its West Pakistan support was drawn from such long-time dissidents as Mian Iftikharuddin, Ghaffar Khan, G. M. Syed and Abdul Majid Sindhi. The grouping was called the National Awami Party and it campaigned on a five-point programme. This called for the abolition of One Unit, a neutral foreign policy, regional autonomy, early elections based on joint electorates and the implementation of 14 unfulfilled items of the 21-Point Manifesto.[55]

The emergence of the National Awami Party reduced Suhrawrady's usefulness to the Karachi establishment. It also imperilled Ataur Rahman's Awami League government in Dhaka. In another of the bewildering about-turns of Bengali politics, the National Awami Party first unseated Rahman on 18 June by remaining neutral in a vote, then immediately afterwards brought down the government of his successor Sarkar. A further brief period of presidential rule ensued, before an Awami League ministry returned to office in August 1958 supported by the National Awami Party, but not in coalition with it. The chaotic and opportunistic political manoeuvrings discredited democracy. In a debate on 21 September, verbal assaults turned into physical blows which resulted in the death of the Deputy Speaker. This disgraceful episode would not alone have guaranteed army intervention, but it was to provide a useful pretext for Ayub and Mirza's coup in the early hours of 8 October 1958.

Conclusion

The term democracy is often used loosely, but there is a world of difference between what may be termed 'procedural' and 'social' democracy. The former comes down to little more than the holding of regular ballots, while the latter implies a participatory element in the exercise of power and the removal of social inequalities. In its absence, only lip-service to democracy can be paid. Pakistan during the period 1947–58 displayed aspects of a 'procedural' democracy, with elections at provincial if not the national level based on a universal franchise. But it did not possess any of the characteristics of a 'social' democracy which it could be argued were necessary to consolidate the transition from colonial rule. Limited attempts at land reform in Sindh and Punjab were thwarted by the landowning elites whose power had been entrenched during the British period. Politicians such as Mamdot and Khuhro protected group interests by adopting the language of provincial rights directed against the centre. An opportunity was lost to accompany political independence with social transformation. This could have formed an important step towards the achievement of a participatory democracy.

The post-independence decade was marked by bewildering twists and turns, especially when the gaze is diverted from national to provincial-level politics. Nevertheless it is possible to see firstly how patterns of politics and administration inherited from the colonial era continued to have an impact long after the British departure; secondly to discern the importance of legacies from the freedom movement and the painful partition process which also militated against democratic consolidation. Certainly the Muslim League's weak political institutionalization in the future Pakistan areas prevented it from playing a similar consolidating role to that of the Congress in India.[56] Thirdly, it is clear that Pakistan's precarious strategic position and its subsequent responses impacted on domestic political developments by shifting the state's reliance from the politicians to the army and the bureaucracy for the exercise of authority. From the mid 1950s onwards, Pakistan embarked on a creeping centralization and authoritarianism which culminated in the country's first military coup. Far from being a decade of promise and democratic consolidation, Pakistan's initial period of independence became the formative years for the creation of a path of dependency that has been responsible for the country's subsequent thwarted democratization, military interventions and post-military withdrawal crises.[57]

3

AYUB'S PAKISTAN

THE END OF THE BEGINNING

The chairlift at Nathia Gali which provides fine views over the Neelum River in Kashmir, even with the deteriorating security situation, remains a tourist attraction. It forms part of the national park which is called Ayubia in honour of Pakistan's first ruling general. Few of the younger generation of now mainly Pakistani tourists who view its splendours have much interest, however, in Ayub or his legacy. This popular lack of interest is matched at a scholarly level,[1] yet on closer consideration it is evident that the Ayub regime (1958–69) still casts its shadow over contemporary Pakistan.

This chapter has a threefold aim: firstly to reveal Ayub's impact on Pakistan's foundational problems with respect to authoritarian traditions of governance, political institutionalization, centre-province relations, and the role of Islam in public life; secondly to explain how the army expanded its reach into Pakistan's polity and society; and thirdly to reveal how both diplomacy and the patronage of Islamic groups were deployed to counteract India's predominance in the enduring rivalry between the two states.

Ayub, Governance and Depoliticization

Ayub reinvigorated the viceregal tradition inherited from the British. He famously asserted that democracy was not suited to the 'genius of the people'. His distrust of the political class had intensified during the year he spent as Minister for Defence, following Ghulam Muhammad's dismissal of the Constituent Assembly in October 1954.[2] Indeed, he blamed the 'unruly' politicians for Pakistan's ills. In his first broadcast as Chief Martial Law Administrator on 8 October 1958, Ayub delivered a withering attack on the politicians, claiming that they had waged 'a ceaseless and bitter war against each other regardless of the ill effects on the country, just to whet their appetites and satisfy their base demands'. There had been no limit 'to the depth of their baseness, chicanery, deceit and degradation'.[3] Ayub's paternalistic solicitude for the 'real people' of Pakistan, on the other hand, the rural classes, came straight out of the British lexicon for the security state in North-West India. Typical of his sentiments echoing British paternalism were such descriptions of rural dwellers as 'by nature patriotic and good people' who were 'tolerant and patient and can rise to great heights when well led'.[4]

The much-vaunted Basic Democracy scheme[5] which Ayub promulgated on the first anniversary of the coup, reintroduced nineteenth-century colonial ideas of political tutelage through indirect elections and official nomination of representatives. At the union council and committee level of the Basic Democracies system, the government could nominate up to one-third of the members. One report into the workings of the Basic Democracies scheme revealed that 85 per cent of the items for discussion at union council meetings were initiated by government officials.[6] The 80,000 Basic Democrats collectively formed the electoral college which affirmed Ayub as President in the January 1960 ballot. Following the introduction of the 1962 Constitution, the Basic Democrats were also the electorate for the national and provincial assemblies.

As in the British era, the elite civil service formed the backbone of a system of governance which privileged administration over popular participation. Ayub in fact was to rely more on the Civil Service of Pakistan (CSP) than later military rulers. The screening process to purge it of 'corrupt' elements initiated under Martial Law Regulation no. 61 was half-hearted at best. The CSP played an increasingly important part in his regime as a result of the central role accorded to Commissioners and Deputy Commissioners in the Basic Democracies scheme and the control over development funds which they acquired under the Rural Works Programme. Leading bureaucrats such as Altaf Gauhar and Akhter Husain acted as Ayub's key advisers.

Pakistan's already weakly institutionalized political system was dealt a further blow by the Ayub regime. This initially banned parties, and even when Ayub began the civilianization of his rule, the indirect elections to the newly constituted National and Provincial Assemblies in 1962 were held on a 'partyless' basis. This further entrenched the power of the local landholders and *biraderi* heads who were inimical to the development of grassroots political organization. Ayub reluctantly legalized party organization in the July 1962 Political Parties Act. Even then, the political system bore his imprint in that the Convention Muslim League emerged as a pro-regime party, just as the PML(Q) was to do, a little over a generation later. Ayub became its President in December 1963.

Freedom of expression and of individual political activity was circumscribed. The notion of accountability and the banning of 'corrupt' politicians from elective office, which had been introduced by Liaquat in 1949, was greatly extended. Ayub introduced the Public Offices (Disqualification) Order (PODO) and the Elective Bodies (Disqualification) Order (EBDO) respectively in March and August 1959. Those accused had the option of trial by a tribunal for 'misconduct' or voluntary withdrawal from public life. Persons found guilty under EBDO were to be automatically disqualified from membership of any elective body until after 31 December 1966. At the most conservative estimate, 400 political leaders were disqualified.[7] Muhammad Waseem has maintained that EBDO 'turned out to be one of the strongest arms in the hand of the Ayub Government' and that its stifling of meaningful opposition helps to explain the longevity of the Ayub system.[8]

Censorship further undermined the opposition. Ayub not only used the Public Safety Ordinances already on the statute book to control news items, but in 1963 promulgated the Press and Publications Ordinance, 'to make the press conform to recognised principles of journalism and patriotism'.[9] A tighter grip on news management followed in 1964 when the supposedly independent National Press Trust was established. It acquired ownership of such former radical papers as the *Pakistan Times* and transformed them into government mouthpieces. 'Sycophancy and servility' replaced a true 'patriotism' born of honest reporting. Altaf Gauhar, in his role as Central Information Secretary, was the virtual 'Editor-in-Chief' of over 1,500 publications.[10] Ayub's actions not only undermined resistance to his particular brand of authoritarianism, but hampered the long-term development of civil society. The Press and Publications Ordinance was repealed in 1988 and the National Press Trust was only dismantled in 1996.

Centre-Province Relations

Ayub favoured a centralized state. Despite his otherwise considerable constitutional tinkering, he significantly made no effort to modify the One Unit Scheme. The 1962 Constitution devolved some additional powers to the provinces, such as control over industries and railways, but hedged around this so much that little in reality was conceded.[11] Political centralization was to be accompanied by cultural integration. The biggest challenge involved the de-emphasizing of the distinctiveness of Bengali. The 1959 report of the Commission on National Education recorded that:

> Urdu and Bengali [should be brought] nearer to each other by increasing the common element in their vocabularies and by putting such common elements to extensive use.[12]

Ayub suggested that this task could be better promoted by introducing the Roman script for all Pakistan's languages. This idea was abandoned because of public opposition, but government institutions such as the Central Boards of Urdu and Bengali worked to integrate the languages. In this atmosphere, the central government played down the 100th anniversary celebrations of the birth of the great Bengali poet Rabindranath Tagore (1861–1941) and later banned the broadcasting of his poetry. Activists retaliated by changing street signs and name plates from Urdu to Bengali throughout Dhaka.

While Urdu continued to be stressed as the national building block, Ayub's regime saw the pushing to one side of the *mohajirs* in favour of the Punjabis. Pakhtuns, in part because of military recruitment, came to form a junior partner in an increasingly Punjabi-dominated state. The new locus of power in Pakistan was symbolized by the decision to shift the federal capital from Karachi to the new city of Islamabad, deep in the Punjab beside the Margalla Hills and adjacent to the army headquarters at Rawalpindi. The movement of Central Government personnel began as early as September 1960, with civil servants and their families being temporarily housed in the cantonment town at Chaklala while the construction work at Islamabad was carried out.

Mohajir resentment was to develop slowly during the following decades and eventually to focus on a new ethnic political identity which challenged the state the *mohajirs* had helped construct. During the Ayub regime, the greatest resentment, however, was to be expressed by Sindhi and Bengali leaders whose communities had next to no influence in the powerful bureaucracy and army. The rapid but uneven economic development of the 1960s compounded this sense of alienation. By the time of the mass mobilizations in 1969 which forced Ayub to step aside, the seeds for the major conflict in East Pakistan had been sown. They were to bring a bitter harvest in the short-lived regime of his successor, Yahya Khan. The key to Pakistan's survival lay not through a strong centre, but in developing consociational-type arrangements of power-sharing based on the acceptance of cultural pluralism. The advent of military rule on top of inherited traditions of viceregalism and political intolerance precluded such a course of action, with tragic circumstances.

(i) Sindh

The Ayub regime increased the alienation of the Sindhi political elite. The leading nationalist figure G. M. Syed fell foul of the 'accountability' process launched under the new EBDO and PODO dispensation. He was imprisoned for eight years from October 1966. During this period, he wrote a number of books including one on the poetry of Shah Abdul Latif Bhittai, who was the symbol of Sindhi identity and whose verses were later to inspire the 1983 rebellion against Zia. Many Sindhis resented the increasing allocation of land made available through the construction of the Ghulam Muhammad Barrage near Hyderabad to Punjabi army officers and bureaucrats.[13] The fears of the subordination of Sindh to Punjab in a future Pakistan state which G. M. Syed had inveighed against through the columns of his newspaper *Qurbani (Sacrifice)* in 1946 appeared to be materializing.[14]

The pill was not sugared by growing prosperity. The Sindhi elite missed out on the fruits of Ayub's self-styled 'decade of development'. This saw annual rates of economic growth of over 5 per cent, but was accompanied by a staggering concentration of wealth in the hands of Gujarati-speaking Khojas and Punjabi businessmen from Chiniot. Significantly, there were no native Sindhis in the notorious 'twenty-two' families which came to control 66 per cent of all industrial assets, 79 per cent of insurance funds and 80 per cent of bank assets.[15] Ayub's strategy of channelling resources to a tiny entrepreneurial elite in pursuit of his private sector-led development strategy was to bring about his downfall. The Sindhi-speaking Zulfiqar Ali Bhutto coordinated the protests of students, workers and lawyers which broke out in West Punjab in November 1968. Ayub eventually stepped down on 25 March 1969 leaving a legacy of enhanced class and regional inequalities in an already fractured state.

It was not so much the economy, however, as the fate of the Sindhi language that became a focus for growing resentment within the province. In 1959 a Report on National Education suggested that Urdu should be introduced as the medium of instruction from Class 6 upwards. This move designed to increase national integration had the reverse effect. There were province-wide protests at the reduction of Sindhi's educational importance. Ayub suspended the decision, but this did not prevent a continuing decline in the number of primary schools teaching in Sindhi. In all around 30 schools were closed down.[16] This was seen as a conspiracy by Sindhi nationalists who took up other issues including the replacement of Sindhi by Urdu on public buildings such as railway stations. They also claimed that Sindhi publications were hampered by being denied lucrative advertising revenue, that writers were discouraged and that there was a reduction in Sindhi radio broadcasts. Bitter disputes accompanied the decision in June 1965 by the Hyderabad Municipal Corporation to make Urdu its working language. The following year Sindhi language activists at the University of Sindh, Hyderabad unleashed a campaign, in retaliation, to adopt Sindhi as the language of instruction and examination. Their arrest by the Urdu-speaking Commissioner for Hyderabad Division, Masroor Hasan Khan not only exacerbated Sindhi-*Mohajir* tensions, but provided a further focus for the alienation of Sindhis from Ayub's regime.[17]

(ii) Bengal

The Bengali political elite had been alienated since Pakistan's inception. The Ayub era fatefully increased this. Ayub's coup may well have been designed to pre-empt a Bengali challenge to the interests and policies of the West Pakistan establishment. It is therefore unsurprising both that his regime increased the already palpable sense of marginality which many Bengali politicians shared and that leading figures, such as Maulana Bhashani, Sheikh Mujibur Rahman and Hamidul Huq Chowdhury fell foul of the EBDO restrictions. Alienation spread much more widely as was evidenced by the fact that less than one in two of those eligible cast their vote in the election of Basic Democrats. When the veteran politician Suhrawardhy was arrested on 30 January 1962, there were violent student protests in Dhaka. Ayub, who was in the city to chair a Governor's conference, was a virtual prisoner in the President's House for the last three days of his visit.[18] Units of the Punjab regiment had to be despatched to bring peace to the university campus. In contrast to these violent protests, tumultuous crowds in Dhaka and Chittagong greeted the 71-year-old Miss Fatima Jinnah who was Ayub's challenger in the 1965 presidential elections. Ayub won the polls in East Pakistan as elsewhere, but had clearly lost the people.

The increasingly radical demands of Bengali nationalists were reflected in the Awami League's 6-Point Programme (May 1966). This called for the establishment of full provincial autonomy in East Pakistan on the basis of the Lahore Resolution. The centre was left only with responsibility for defence and foreign affairs. Even with respect to the latter, following the eastern wing's sense of defencelessness at the time of the 1965 war with India, demands were made for the creation of a separate militia or paramilitary force in East Pakistan.[19] Ayub's attempt to take the wind out of the sails of the 6-Point Programme by involving the Awami League leader Sheikh Mujibur Rahman in the celebrated Agartala conspiracy case badly backfired. The charges brought in open court that he and his 50 or so co-defendants had sought Indian help to achieve secession provided the perfect platform to expound Bengali autonomist views. The prosecution's bungling, although Mujib had indeed met with Indian officials, put the Ayub regime on the back foot. The case was dropped, providing Ayub with one of his most serious and humiliating reversals. Mujib was now parleyed within a round table conference, to the backdrop of mounting disturbances in the eastern wing. They contributed to Ayub's resignation, but his successor was not to learn from this lesson that it was better to seek to co-opt Bengali aspirations, rather than to confront them.

Power in Ayub's Pakistan lay not with the official apparatus of the Basic Democrats, nor after 1962 with the Convention Muslim League, but rather with the army and the bureaucracy. In these unelected pillars of the state, Bengalis were historically under-represented. Hence the very nature of Ayub's regime, whatever its intentions, was bound to marginalize Bengali interests. Official figures confirm this, with Bengalis providing just 5 per cent of the Army Officer Corps and around

30 per cent of the elite cadre of the CSP. Bengalis were not only as a result under-represented in the Central Secretariat, but on the commissions of inquiry which littered the Ayub years.[20] This not only meant that Bengali interests went unheard and unsupported, but that the regime's awareness of conditions in the eastern wing was undermined. The lack of expert advice from Bengali civil servants was compounded by the fact that, as a high-ranking army officer informed the American Consul-General in January 1963, 'East Pakistanis in the Cabinet are men of no particular stature and competence and are only trying to please Ayub and say what they think he might like to hear'.[21]

The rapid economic growth of the Ayub era, rather than creating the basis for a modernized and strong Pakistan state, undermined national unity because of its differential impacts. The rate of economic growth in the eastern wing lagged far behind that in West Pakistan.[22] This stemmed from the fact that the majority of private firms which provided the economic motor for growth were based in West Pakistan. Their owners on climatic, cultural and infrastructural grounds were reluctant to set up in the East. They had received the lion's share of credit facilitated through the Pakistan Industrial Development Bank and the Pakistan Industrial and Credit and Investment Corporation. Ayub stepped up public sector investment in East Pakistan in a bid to reduce former disparities, but growth in this sector was relatively sluggish. The whole thrust of his economic policy was thus unintentionally to accentuate inter-wing disparities.

Demands for regional Bengali autonomy became entwined with the notion that the two wings of the country possessed two distinct economies with different needs and requirements. This was recognized to a certain extent by Ayub with the creation of separate Industrial Development Corporations and Water and Power Development Authorities for West and East Pakistan. Significantly, the 6-Point Programme went much further than this and included the provisions that East Pakistan should raise its own taxes, mint its own currency and operate its own foreign exchange account. The latter demand rested on the long-term resentment that the foreign exchange generated from the export of raw jute accrued to West Pakistan. A grievance more specific to the Ayub era was that profits from industries set up by West Pakistan businesses were repatriated to the western wing of the country. In the case of the Fauji Foundation's rice, flour and jute mills in East Pakistan, the profits were reinvested in welfare projects in the main Punjab recruitment areas.[23] This naturally fuelled claims of the 'Punjabization' of Pakistan.

The Role of Islam

Ayub did not toy with Islam as a form of legitimization as some politicians had done earlier in the decade. Modernization was to be the hallmark and justification of his regime. This involved not just economic development and an attempt, albeit half-hearted, at land reform,[24] but modernization of Islam itself. The 1962 Constitution significantly dropped the title 'Islamic' from the Republic of Pakistan title. Another significant change was the rewording of the Repugnancy Clause. This dropped the earlier direct reference to the Quran and Sunnah and merely stated that no law should be enacted which was repugnant to Islam, thereby encouraging the modernist conception of *ijtihad*.[25] In a further decisive move, Ayub sought to introduce 'secular' influence into the functioning of marriage and inheritance through the Muslim Family Laws Ordinance. Finally, he attempted to introduce state management of the endowed properties attached to mosques and shrines, through the West Pakistan Auqaf Properties Ordinance.

A variety of motives have been attributed to this attempt to resolve the ambiguities surrounding the future role of Islam in the Pakistan state, in favour of a modernist approach. Undoubtedly, Ayub imbibed not only a Pakistan nationalist outlook, but a modernist approach to Islam through his education at Aligarh. He was also of course part of what has been termed the 'British' generation of army officers, which was to adopt a very different attitude to Islam than that of the 'Pakistani' generation of the Zia era. Ayub's modernist Islam was practical and based on common sense rather than any theological interpretation. It was summed up in the sentiment, 'It is a great injustice to both life and religion to impose on twentieth century man the condition that he must go back several centuries in order to prove his bona fides as a true Muslim'.[26] Personal observation confirmed him in the view that the *mullahs* were no better than the politicians he so detested, in that they were covetous of 'wealth and power and did not stop short of any mischief'.[27] Yet rather than emerging as a latter-day Kemal Ataturk, Ayub was soon forced to backtrack in the face of resistance from Islamist groups. Ironically, he turned to the traditionalist Islam of the Sufi shrines. He was supported by Pir Dewal Sharif and many of the prominent *sajjada nashins*. By the end of his regime, the role of Islam in Pakistan's public life was as unresolved as it had ever been.

The *ulama* opposed the 1962 Constitutional changes and were also unhappy with the composition of the Islamic Advisory Committee which Ayub had established to assist the National Assembly in framing laws based on Islamic concepts. He was forced to retreat on the name of the country. The First Constitutional Amendment Act of 1963 restored the name 'Islamic Republic of Pakistan'. When the Political Parties Act legalized political organizations, JI swung onto the offensive. Maulana Maududi fired off volleys of criticism at the anti-Islamic features of the Ayub regime. Even before the ban on political activities had been formally lifted, he organized a meeting of fifty *ulama* from the two wings of the country to condemn the Muslim Family Laws Ordinance. To counter attempts in the National Assembly to repeal it, Ayub provided constitutional cover which protected it from judicial scrutiny. Similar safeguards were built in at the time of the 1973 Constitution, by which time the Muslim Family Laws Ordinance had become both a totem for women's rights and the *bête noire* of the Islamists. Maududi, however, continued his attack on the Ayub government. The Central Council of JI which met in Lahore during the first week of August 1962 passed a series of resolutions which condemned among other things the official Advisory Council of Islamic Ideology, the Muslim Family Laws, the Pakistan Arts Council, the Girl Guides and the Blue Birds, the construction of cinemas and the importation of books critical to Islam.[28]

Less than a generation later, JI was to be temporarily at the heart of Zia's martial law regime, rather than pitched against the army. We will be examining later the emergence of what has been termed the 'Mullah-Military' complex. Farzana Shaikh has argued that for all Ayub's modernism and 'ambitious programme of economic and social reform', he helped make room for this development:[29] firstly, by turning to Islam as ethnic and class divisions threatened his regime; secondly, by emphasizing that Pakistan was both a Muslim territorial homeland and a fortress of Islam in which the army played a guardianship role; thirdly, as we shall see later in this chapter, by working with religiously motivated irregular forces to advance Pakistan's strategic objectives in Kashmir. Shaikh sees the 1965 war with India as being a crucial turning point with respect to these inheritances from Ayub's rule. It was then, she declares, that he for the first time bound Islam, Pakistan identity and the army together in a common defence against 'India aggression'.[30]

Another reading of Ayub's legacy would be to see it revealing how Islamist groups had gained sufficient street power by the 1950s to challenge even authoritarian regimes. Ayub, like later rulers, was to fight shy of a conflict with these groups; but appeasing them, as Zulfiqar Ali Bhutto was later to discover, only emboldened resistance. Another feature which had longer-term implications can also be discerned. This was the willingness of Islamist groups to ally with the political opposition in the name of advancing democracy. They were thus able to increase their influence. JI joined the National Democratic Front which Suhrawardhy launched on 4 October 1962, although its bedfellows included the Awami League, the NAP and the KSP, along with more congenial allies such as the Council Muslim League. The latter had been founded by old-style Muslim Leaguers who opposed Ayub and were hostile to the formation of the Convention Muslim League as his supporters club. JI revealed its greatest flexibility when it threw its weight behind Fatima Jinnah at the time of the 1965 presidential contest. In different circumstances, the prospect of a female head of state would have been considered an anathema.

The Rise of Milbus Under Ayub

Ayesha Siddiqa has shed new light on the army's entrenched role in Pakistan's business and industrial life. She utilizes the term 'Milbus' to conceptualize this. She sees Indonesia and Turkey as other key examples of armed forces' intrusion into the state's economy. The rise of Milbus has led to the army being conceived as a pressure group with its own agenda and motives for intervention in the political process. The Ayub era saw the extension of the army's 'colonization' of the Pakistan society and polity. This was rooted in the colonial practice of providing grants of land for ex-servicemen in the newly irrigated areas of West Punjab and Sindh. It was not until 1954, however, with the establishment of the Fauji Foundation, that servicemen's welfare funds began to be diverted into large-scale commercial activities. By the beginning of the twenty-first century the Fauji Foundation numbered among the largest business conglomerates in Pakistan. Throughout its formative development during Ayub's power, it was exempt from taxation.

The army's expanding role in the economy was facilitated both by the fact of martial law itself, which weakened the political elite and civil society, and by the importance which Ayub attached to a private sector-led economic growth. This strategy was encouraged by the Western countries such as the US and West Germany which provided copious amounts of development aid.[31] The business class could hardly complain in any case, because it was in receipt of the same kind of tax breaks as were afforded to the enterprises run by the Fauji Foundation. Islamist opposition to Ayub focused on the criticism of his modernization programme, not on his economic policies. Indeed JI saw free enterprise as being a fundamental Islamic economic objective.[32] The result of all these factors was that the development of Milibus was given a free rein.

The Fauji Foundation became heavily involved in industrial units in the tobacco, sugar and textile industries. It ran for example a textile factory in Jhelum, a sugar mill at Tando Mohammad Khan in Sindh, and the Khyber Tobacco Company in Mardan.[33] We have already noted that it was active in the eastern wing with establishments in Dhaka and Chittagong.

Alongside these developments, the army involved itself in infrastructural activities. The most famous was the construction by the Frontier Works Organisation of the 805 km Karakoram Highway linking Pakistan and China. The Frontier Works Organisation, which was established in 1966, has grown to be the largest contractor for road construction in Pakistan. It also manages toll collection on all of the country's motorways.

The Ayub era also saw the beginnings of the welfare structure, which has become a hallmark of the army's corporate interests. Profits generated by the Fauji Foundation were ploughed into the construction of schools, and hospitals for the use of military personnel. From these beginnings had grown an enterprise which by the early twenty-first century ran 90 schools and colleges with an enrolment of about 40,000 students, 11 hospitals and 23 medical centres.[34]

While these were new developments, the Ayub regime also saw an extension of the earlier policy of rewarding servicemen with agricultural land. This was acreage brought into production in Sindh through the construction of the Kotri, Guddu and Ghulam Muhammad dams. The amount of land set aside in this way has been approximated at anything between 300,000 and 1 million acres.[35] Senior generals including Ayub (247 acres), Muhammad Musa (250 acres) and Umrao Khan (246 acres) benefited the most, but even lieutenants to majors were assured of allocations of up to 100 acres.[36] This encouraged the creation of a military agriculturalist class and helped cement links between the army and sections of the feudal elite who when necessary could make up the numbers as the Martial Law B Team.

Ayub initiated the policy of the induction of army officers into the bureaucracy which was to be greatly expanded by Zia and Musharraf. This policy was not simply a reward system. It was based on the army's self-perception that it was the most effective state institution. The practice of calling on the army to undertake routine civilian administrative tasks has persisted. In Nawaz Sharif's second government, for example, the army was deployed during the much delayed 1998 Census and to root out 'ghost schools' among the 56,000 government-funded primary schools.[37] By the end of 1959, 53 army officers held civilian administrative positions.[38] Lieutenant-General Azam Khan was the most influential of these. In his role as Minister for Rehabilitation, he relieved Karachi's serious refugee housing situation by pushing through in a six-month period the new Korangi housing development of some 15,000 dwellings. He was later to serve as Governor of East Pakistan.

The army's expansion into many areas of Pakistan's public life brought corruption in its wake. It also encouraged nepotism and what Hasan-Askari Rizvi has termed 'authoritarian clientelism'. These were the very aspects of the political process which had been earlier condemned by Ayub. As later under Zia and Musharraf, the army was not required to undergo the process of 'accountability' that was imposed on civilians. Some of the worst episodes of corruption involved Ayub's own family, although much of this took place after his sons Akhtar and Gohar had retired from the army.[39]

In sum, Pakistan's first martial law period marked the formative years of the military's penetration into the economy. The senior officers were the main beneficiaries, but the lower ranks also received the rewards for service in terms of social welfare and land acquisition. The army as an institution embarked upon the creation of an economic empire which was to strengthen both its capacity and motivation for further political intervention. In Ayesha Siddiqa's words:

> Militaries that develop deep economic interests or have a pervasive presence in the economy shrink from giving up political control. In fact, the tendency is to establish the organization's hegemony in the state and society. The military's hegemonic control is noticeable in the cases of Pakistan, Indonesia and Turkey.[40]

While many of Ayub's other legacies have been forgotten, in this respect his regime represents a major watershed.

The Enduring Rivalry with India

Most scholars agree that the 1965 war with India marked the downturn in Ayub's fortunes. His decision to accept a ceasefire on 22 September shocked a populace fed on a diet of victory reports. It also created a breach between him and his Foreign Minister, Zulfiqar Ali Bhutto, who finally resigned in June 1966 to emerge as the leader of the growing opposition. The Tashkent Declaration in January 1966, which set the terms of a post-war settlement and saw Pakistan accept the pre-war status quo, was greeted with rioting in Lahore by students and Kashmiri migrants. For the latter, the British High Commissioner at the time, Sir Morrice James, has noted: 'Ayub had betrayed the nation and had inexcusably lost face to Indians'.[41] Shortly afterwards, Maulana Maududi joined other opposition figures in a press conference in the city in which Ayub was accused of 'unpardonable weakness' in purchasing peace at the cost of national honour and betraying the 'just cause' of Kashmir.

Two other important legacies of the conflict are less reported. Firstly, it created the sense of US betrayal which was the beginning of a chequered relationship between the two allies that persists to today. Secondly, it marked a further stage in the Pakistan state's use of irregular Islamic forces. This was undertaken by Ayub, as we shall see, on tactical rather than ideological grounds. It nevertheless helped to pave the way for the link-up between the military and *jihadist* groups which was to pay well in the 1980s, but come back to haunt the state during the first decade of the twenty-first century.

Ayub, as we have seen in the previous chapter, played an important role in the forging of close military and diplomatic ties with the US in the mid-1950s. The army had institutionally benefited from these at the expense of the democratic process. Pakistan saw the US as a guarantor in any conflict with India, although the US had wider Cold War strategic interests. When Ayub visited the US on a state visit in 1961, President Kennedy in his welcome address at Andrews air force base fulsomely described Pakistan as 'a friend of immediacy and constancy'.[42] Many in Pakistan were to feel that these were empty words of praise when the chips were down in 1965.

Even before the outbreak of hostilities with India, Zulfiqar Ali Bhutto, the young charismatic Foreign Minister, was advising Ayub to tilt towards China. He subsequently took the credit for this manoeuvre, although Ayub in the wake of the U-2 spy crisis with the Soviet Union[43] had already felt let down by the US and was reconsidering his long-established foreign policy doctrine. The most significant turning point had been the October 1962 Sino-Indian war. Firstly, it raised the prospect of alliance with China on the basis of the old adage that an enemy of an enemy should be a friend; secondly, it had created disquiet in Islamabad because, in the wake of India's defeat, the United States and Britain agreed to supply New Delhi with $120 million of emergency military aid. The view from Islamabad was that the expansion of the Indian army would be directed at Pakistan, rather than China. It added the need for urgency to those, such as Zulfiqar Ali Bhutto, who advocated a military solution of the Kashmir dispute. Thirdly, it reinforced Pakistan sentiment that India was militarily weak, with limited fighting capability. This sentiment was further strengthened by the fighting between Indian and Pakistani troops in the Rann of Kutch coastal border during the first week of April 1965.[44] Pakistan claimed the northern section of the salt marsh, peopled only by flamingoes and wild donkeys; India the whole of the 8,400 square miles of territory.

Pakistan's diplomatic realignments and planning for a new conflict with India occurred against the backdrop of popular protests about US arms sales to India, which culminated in an invasion of the USIS library grounds in Karachi[45] and the stoning of government and army vehicles in Rawalpindi along with the Flashman's Hotel.[46] Even more disquieting for Washington were reports of a growing anti-US sentiment among the junior ranks of the Pakistan army.[47]

Anti-Americanism was to be intensified by its arms embargo from 8 September during the war with India. The lack of spare parts for tanks and aircraft undoubtedly had an effect on Ayub's decision on 23 September to respond to the unanimous United Nations Security Council Resolution for a ceasefire. The US stance at this crucial time still feeds into contemporary popular animosities to Washington. American perfidy is contrasted with the diplomatic support from Beijing[48] and its arms agreement with Pakistan in the wake of the conflict. America only agreed to provide spare parts again in April 1967 and then these were to be purchased on a cash only basis.

There is growing literature on the infiltration into Kashmir which resulted in the 17-day second Indo-Pakistan war. This has focused on such issues as, firstly, Zulfiqar Ali Bhutto's involvement in the genesis of the strategy which became codenamed as Operation Gibraltar;[49] secondly, the motives for the military irredentism involving Kashmir which are often broken down to strategic and self-interest factors;[50] thirdly, the reasons why the hoped-for general uprising of the Kashmiri Muslim population failed to materialize. Here the emphasis is on why Pakistan misread popular attitudes in Kashmir in the wake of the 1963 disturbances around the celebrated disappearance and reappearance of the sacred relic of the Prophet Muhammad's hair from the Hazratbal shrine on the banks of the Upper Dal Lake in Srinagar.[51] Most recently a number of works have emphasized that Ayub's use of irregular Islamic militants in Operation Gibraltar marked a further step in the state's fateful strategic alliances with *jihadist* groups.[52] It is to this issue that we shall now turn.

Operation Gibraltar headquarters were based at the Pakistani Hill Station of Murree under the command of Major General Akhtar Hussain Malik. The six raiding parties which were to advance over the ceasefire line on 5 August were named after famous Muslim military commanders. The infiltrators planned to destroy infrastructure and hit military targets. Their actions were expected to result in a spontaneous uprising of the Kashmiri Muslim population. The bulk of the task forces comprised volunteer Islamic fighters (*mujahadin*) who had been recruited from the Pakistan-controlled Azad Kashmir region and the border Punjabi city of Sialkot, which had a large Kashmiri refugee population. The remainder comprised regular Pakistan forces drawn from the Azad Kashmir Rifles, the Northern Light Infantry and the Special Services Group Commandos. The irregulars were initially trained in May 1965 by instructors from the 19th Baluch Regiment at Attock. They were then moved to such localities as Kotli, Nikial, Tarkundi and Bher in Azad Kashmir. Swami interestingly points out that the training which was carried out by personnel of the Azad Kashmir Rifles was in camps later to be used to instruct the cadre for the 1989 *jihad*.[53]

The army's later engagement with *mujahadin* and *jihadist* groups was to occur on a much larger scale and in a different international environment. Its own changing composition and prolonged interaction with such groups also meant that there was a greater ideological commitment to the *mujahadin* cause. In 1965, their use was primarily tactical, although it did not prevent, from the Pakistan viewpoint, a disastrous escalation of the Indian response into the Punjab theatre. However, even at this earlier stage, there were officers committed to models of Muslim soldierhood and of creating an army committed to a 'nationalist state ideology', as had been evidenced by the 1951 Rawalpindi Conspiracy.[54] This point is often overlooked in analysis of the contemporary nexus between sections of the army and Islamic groups. Neither the failure of Operation Gibraltar nor the fully-fledged military follow-up in Operation Grand Slam ended Pakistani military irredentism. The covert conflict in Kashmir continued during Ayub's quiet years of retirement in Islamabad and reached new intensity during the eras of his military successors, Zia and Musharraf.

Conclusion

Despite its many unique characteristics, the Ayub era may be best viewed as a hinge period, between the emergence of the Pakistan security state amidst the chaos of Partition and its solidification under later military rulers. It saw both the formative period of Milbus and the beginnings of the nexus between the army and Islamic groups. Ayub retained the commitment to a centralized state and cultural integration which had been a feature of the early years of state construction. Again, however, this was a transitional era from one in which the state was largely a *mohajir* enterprise to that of Punjabi domination, with the Pakhtun a junior partner. The Sindhi and Bengali elites were shut out of power. Attempts at cultural integration further alienated them. The sense of a Punjab-dominated state was also encouraged by the uneven economic development. Ayub's rule had been marked by a decade of high rates of growth, but growing inequality. National integration was consequently more imperilled at the close of his regime than at its outset. Moreover, the corruption and political chaos, which he had pledged to end in 1958, remained undiminished.

Although Ayub sought to modernize the Pakistan state and society, he was unable to resolve decisively the role of Islam in public life. He had to abandon a number of initiatives, including dropping 'Islamic' from the country's title. He was increasingly on the defensive in the face of opposition from the *ulama*, seeking ultimately support from the traditional Islam of the shrines which had always been the target of modernist reformers. His weakness stemmed from the growth in Islamic influence during the preceding years and his regime's lack of legitimacy. Islamists joined hands with liberals, ethnic nationalists and students initially in the 1965 presidential election campaign and later in the mass mobilization which four years later forced Ayub to step aside. This pattern was to be repeated less than a decade later in the Pakistan National Alliance movement against Zulfiqar Ali Bhutto, which culminated in Pakistan's second bout of martial law. As we shall see in the next chapter, Bhutto had been presented with the opportunity to forge the rump Pakistan state on a fresh basis, following the military debacle in the Bangladesh war. The reasons for his failure remain a major issue of controversy in contemporary Pakistan.

4

BHUTTO'S PAKISTAN

A MISSED OPPORTUNITY

On 20 December 1971, Zulfiqar Ali Bhutto formally replaced Yahya Khan as President and Chief Martial Law Administrator of Pakistan. Following the lifting of Martial Law and the National Assembly's approval of a new Constitution, he became Prime Minister in August 1973. During the following four years he held power in a regime which remains a source both of controversy and of definition for contemporary Pakistan. Bhutto was presented with an opportunity to set Pakistan on a new footing with respect to civilian supremacy over the military, political institutionalization, centre-state relations and the role of Islam in public life.

Lying behind all of these were even more transformative possibilities for the empowerment of subordinate groups who had been excluded by the state oligarchy and its allies throughout Pakistan's existence. These groups, which included emergent middle classes, industrial labour and small landholders and tenant farmers, had been radicalized by the Ayub regime's overseeing of an elite consolidation of economic and political power at a time of rapid socio-economic transformation, arising from the effects of industrialization, the Green Revolution and resultant large-scale rural-urban migration. Bhutto had not created these circumstances, nor had he formed the movement which eventually swept Ayub from power. He had rather intuitively sensed the new political wave and positioned himself to ride it to power. Once he had achieved political ascendancy, however, he failed to harness the new populist forces, but returned to the time-honoured parochial politics and co-option of elites. Bhutto's ambivalence to the status quo meant that he faced hostility from the established elites at the same time as disappointing the newly politicized. This created the circumstances for his removal. The injustice surrounding his eventual execution in April 1979 recovered his standing with the subordinate classes and sustained 'Bhuttoism' sufficiently to propel his daughter to power.

Zulfiqar Ali Bhutto's charismatic appeal for the poor was based however not just on the modern possibilities for conscientization he offered, summed up more in the 1970 election cry for *musawat* (equality) than in the famous call for *roti, kapra aur makaan* (food, clothing and shelter). It also had more traditional roots. Even before his death Bhutto had on occasion spoken of himself in mystical Sufi terms, declaring to his audiences that there were 'two Bhuttos', one of which resided in each of his hearers in an inseparable bond.[1]

This chapter explains why the Bhutto era was a mere civilian interlude, rather than a decisive break with Pakistan's past. It looks at how his regime tackled the long-term problems of state construction and identity formation and why his populist approach was not best suited to resolve them. There is also the need, however, to consider whether the situation he inherited from the discredited Yahya Khan provided challenges as well as opportunities for the restructuring of the Pakistan state. It is to the legacies of Yahya Khan's debacle in East Pakistan that we will first turn.

Bhutto's Inheritance from the Break-up of Pakistan

Such scholars as Hasan-Askari Rizvi have pointed out how the military debacle and the break-up of the country provided Bhutto with a major advantage in asserting civilian primacy over the army.[2] While the full details of the government-appointed Hamadur Rahman Commission were not circulated, the press was full of criticisms of the army and its top leadership. Pakistan's initiating air attacks on north-west India on 3 December 1971 was criticized as it legitimized India's intended intervention in East Pakistan in support of the Bengali Mukhti Bahini freedom-fighter forces. The performance of the Pakistani air force in East Pakistan was castigated, as there was virtually no air cover for the troops. The army commander Lieutenant-General Niazi was censored for his failure to halt the Indian advance and ultimately for his unconditional surrender in Dhaka on 16 December. The greatest criticism of all was reserved for Yayha, both for his poor leadership performance as Pakistan president from March 1969 onwards and for his moral turpitude.

Yahya had made a series of disastrous blunders, including the miscalling of the outcome of the 1970 National Assembly elections;[3] the partisan attitude he adopted to the tense negotiations for power-sharing between the Awami League and the Pakistan People's Party after the polls, in which the former had a majority in the National Assembly, although it had failed to win a single seat in West Pakistan; the preference for the application of force, rather than uncomfortable negotiation with Sheikh Mujibur Rahman; and the sleep-walking into war with India in the period from the brutal military crackdown in East Pakistan on 25 March.[4] The likelihood of an independent Bangladesh was increased as around 7 million people fled to India, thereby internationalizing the crisis in East Pakistan.

Almost until the eve of the military catastrophe, the West Pakistan populace had been fed a diet of military successes. This made defeat seem almost incomprehensible and the result of treachery. Yahya and his advisors were seen as traitors. This sentiment was summed up in the banner headline of an Urdu paper published in Lahore which screamed '*Aik awaz, aik élan: Qaum ka katil Yahya Khan*' (One voice, one declaration: Yahya Khan is the murderer of the nation).[5] Pakistan had not fallen apart because of Bengali primordialism or Indian machinations. The primary responsibility lay in Islamabad: chauvinism had compounded folly in the dangerous denial of Bengali democratic urges.

The Pakistan army's traditional unity cracked in these circumstances. A delegation of junior officers led by Colonel Aleem Afridi demanded Yahya's removal in a meeting with the Chief of the General Staff, Lieutenant-General Gul Hassan. This provided the backdrop for Bhutto's recall from New York where he had been putting Pakistan's case to the UN and his installation as president. The army was not only divided, but defeated and demoralized. No civilian since at least the early 1950s had faced an army as bowed as it was in 1971. The military defeat to the Indian enemy was hard enough to take, as during the course of the two-week war Pakistan lost half its navy, a third of the army and a quarter of its air force.[6] But it was rubbed in by the fact that over

90,000 comrades in arms languished in Indian prison camps for two years following Niazi's surrender at the Dhaka racecourse. Niazi in his memoir has mounted a spirited defence of his role, maintaining that the 'Eastern Garrison was used as an expendable pawn in a game of power-politics' in which the villains were Yahya, Bhutto and Mujib.[7]

Altogether 29 senior officers were relieved of their duties within the first four months of Bhutto's assumption of power, including the Chief of Army Staff, Lieutenant-General Gul Hassan Khan. However, while the military collapse provided the opportunity for asserting civilian supremacy, it also created a dilemma for Bhutto. Paradoxically he needed a strong army. He toyed for a while with the possibility of a 'People's Army', but was eventually to devote a disproportionate portion of the state's resources to the army's re-equipment. A key component of the populist message which had propelled him to power in West Pakistan was a resolute anti-Indian approach. He had thrilled audiences when he had declaimed the need for a thousand-year war with India to reclaim Kashmir. He had been heavily involved in the planning of Operation Gibraltar and in the country's diplomatic realignment designed to enable Pakistan to wrest Kashmir militarily from India. Nevertheless, rather than being censured for Pakistan's failure in the 1965 war, he had been feted as the champion of the country's interests following his resignation as Foreign Minister in June 1966. Huge crowds greeted him as he journeyed by train from Rawalpindi to his native Larkana. Such an acclamation encouraged his decision to form the Pakistan People's Party 15 months later. Its credo included an 'independent foreign policy', for which read continuing resistance to India, as well as a 'socialist pattern of economy'. Hostility to alternative visions of Pakistan's future had been an element in his stand-off with Sheikh Mujibur Rahman following the PPP triumph in West Pakistan in the 1970 general elections. The stalemate enabled the army to implement the crackdown which plunged the country into civil war. The massacres in Dhaka ensured the 'mutiny' of the East Bengal Regiment under Major Zia-ur-Rahman.

Even if Bhutto had been less hawkish, prospects for better relations with India were highly unpromising in the wake of the emergence of Bangladesh. The sense of being faced by a hostile neighbour intent on undoing the partition had always been present. India's actions during the civil war in support of the *Mukhti Bahini* and its subsequent military intervention greatly magnified these fears. The asymmetric power relations between the two rivals were furthermore greatly pronounced. Belligerence over Kashmir might have to be put to one side while Pakistan licked its wounds, but it was hardly likely to go away. Yet in the 1970s, as in contemporary Pakistan, a normalization of relations with India was a necessity for domestic democratic consolidation.

The bifurcation of Pakistan presented Bhutto with another important challenge. How should the country be ideologically reconstructed? The emergence of Bangladesh dealt a body blow to the Two Nation Theory, which had provided the official underpinning for the Pakistan demand and the state's construction. The Bengali elites had shown that a common adherence to Islam was insufficient to keep them in the federation, when their separate linguistic and economic interests were threatened by 'Punjabi imperialism'. Bhutto, because of his Sindhi background, was at one level well placed to re-craft a Pakistani identity based on pluralism rather than its former centralizing adherence to one language and one religion. As we shall see later in the chapter, he did strengthen Sindhi identity, but at the cost of further strain with the *mohajirs*. While he was personally liberal, he still felt compelled to talk in terms of 'Islamic socialism' even at the height of the PPP's radical phase in 1970. As his regime moved away from its radical roots and came under more pressure from the status quo he increasingly made concessions to Islamist groups. The 1973 Constitution, which came into operation on 14 August, included the declaration that Islam was the state religion and stipulated that only Muslims could hold the offices of president and prime minister.

Bhutto also sought to forge ties with the Muslim world, if not to attempt to lead it. The latter was essayed when he held a successful Islamic summit in Lahore in February 1974. By bringing together on the same platform Yasser Arafat, King Faisal of Saudi Arabia, Colonel Qaddafi and Presidents Assad, Sadat and Boumedienne, Bhutto ensured that the world spotlight fell on Pakistan. Lahore with its Mughal splendours and historic place in the Pakistan movement provided the perfect backdrop. The euphoria in the crowd which packed the new Qaddafi stadium to hear the Libyan leader declaim that Pakistan was the 'citadel of Islam in Asia' and 'our resources are your resources'[8] lifted any lingering gloom from the debacle of December 1971. The summit was designed not only to restore national pride and boost the economy with oil and monetary support. It also reflected the fact that the loss of the eastern wing had impacted profoundly both on Pakistan's demographic profile and its geo-political outlook.

Pakistan lost one sixth of its territory with the emergence of Bangladesh. It also lost the significant Hindu minority population which resided in the eastern wing. Henceforth it was an overwhelmingly Muslim country, with the minorities together totalling just 3 per cent of the population. Bhutto sought not only to adjust to these new circumstances, but to make a virtue out of them. As he acknowledged in a speech, 'the severance of our eastern wing... has significantly altered our geographic focus... It is [in West Asia] that our primary concern must henceforth lie'.[9] He directed Pakistan more towards the Islamic cultural world and encouraged increased trade and investment with the Organisation of the Islamic Conference states (OIC). Pakistan's economic and cultural moorings turned away from South Asia and towards West Asia. Bhutto's nemesis, Zia-ul-Haq, accelerated this shift. By 1981 over 30 per cent of both Pakistan's exports and imports were with OIC states. At the same time, Pakistan was receiving up to a quarter (some $100 million) of total Saudi aid.[10] Pakistan increasingly resembled a Middle Eastern rather than a South Asian society as Saudi-funded mosques and religious schools mushroomed. It is unlikely that this transformation, which was to be accompanied by Zia's state-sponsored process of Islamization, would have been as dramatic without the breakaway of the pluralistic eastern wing.

The new contours of the post-1971 Pakistan state presaged Punjabi domination. In the United Pakistan, the Punjab had possessed an educational, infrastructural and economic advantage over the other regions, which was compounded by its connection with the army. It did not, however, possess a demographic majority. As we have seen in earlier chapters, a dominant theme in politics had been the attempts by the West Pakistan increasingly Punjabi-dominated establishment to get round this factor. The loss of East Pakistan removed this demographic constraint. Punjab now accounted for over 56 per cent of the population, as well as 65 per cent of food grain production and 52 per cent of manufacturing output. It was the uncontested power centre of the rump Pakistan state. Its first leader however was a Sindhi. This offered the prospect for establishing a new decentralized and plural politics which could banish fears of Punjabi domination. How Bhutto dealt with the issue of centre-province relations will form the focus of our next section.

Bhutto and Centre-Province Relations

Bhutto came from a minority province. Both during the anti-Ayub campaign and then at the time of the country's first national elections in 1970, overseen by Yahya Khan, he had often expressed sentiments in favour of provincial autonomy. This raised hopes that Pakistan's long-standing problem of composing differences between the centre and the provinces might be finally resolved. The 1973 Constitution granted more provincial autonomy than Pakistan's earlier constitutions. It also created a Council of Common Interest to resolve economic disputes between the federating units. Nevertheless, the list of concurrent subjects and the powers of the centre to intervene in the provinces remained considerable. The Constitution's almost universal approval in the National Assembly on 10 April 1973 reflected the fact that it was less centralist than the interim presidential system, which had operated since Ayub's fall and was seen as the best deal on offer. Nevertheless, Bhutto's dismissal of the NAP-led provincial government in Balochistan just two months earlier questioned whether the Bhutto era would see any more willingness to shift power from the centre to the provinces than during its predecessors'. Before turning to the conflict in Balochistan, which was to signal a turning point more generally for the Bhutto regime, we will briefly assess the impact on Sindh arising from Bhutto's premiership.

Sindhis had been traditionally under-represented in Pakistan's bureaucracy and business elite. The Ayub regime had led to a further diminution in the educational importance of Sindhi. The Sindh Chief Minister, Sardar Mumtaz Ali Bhutto, saw the opportunity to reverse this, with his cousin in office in Islamabad. He introduced legislation in July 1972 which not only made Sindhi a compulsory language from the lowest level of education, but which provided for the progressive use of Sindhi in the courts, administration and legislature. The *mohajir* elite, which already felt under pressure from Punjabi competitors, reacted angrily. Its mouthpiece *Jang* proclaimed the death of Urdu. Violence led to a curfew being introduced in Hyderabad and Karachi and the army being called in. The conflict was diffused following Zulfiqar Ali Bhutto's intervention, which postponed for 12 years the need for officials to know Sindhi. The increased bitterness between Sindhis and *mohajirs* was not abated, however, because the federal government introduced a new reservation policy for public service posts which tilted the balance in respect of Sindh's provincial quota in favour of the rural, predominantly Sindhi-educated class.[11] Moreover the quota system in public sector employment was extended to educational places and was enforced through domicile documents. Their forgery meant that wealthy Sindhi students encroached still further on the already limited *mohajir* urban quota. The All-Pakistan Mohajir Students' Organization (APMSO), the direct precursor of the MQM, came into being in 1978 because of the educational quota and domicile issues.

Zulfiqar Ali Bhutto was not the first, nor was he to be the last, Pakistan ruler to use the state's coercive power to suppress Baloch nationalism. However, the confrontation which claimed at least 9,000 lives not only dealt a blow to hopes for a new era of decentralization in Pakistan, but opened the way for the army to return as a major player in politics. Indeed in his testament from his 'stinking death cell', Bhutto claimed that the army overrode his plans for a withdrawal because the generals wanted to 'spread their tentacles throughout Balochistan'.[12]

Baloch long-term grievances were in some respects similar to those of Bhutto's native Sindhis, in that they centred both around under-representation in state structures and a sense of status displacement as a result of the migration of 'outsiders' into the province, in this case Pakhtuns and Punjabis. Like the Bengalis in pre-1971 Pakistan, the Baloch also felt marginalized in economic development with their region's natural resources being exploited for national rather than local interests. The immediate catalyst for the tribal insurgency in Balochistan however was Bhutto's unwillingness to allow a rival party in power in the region, as he increasingly began to extend his own authority. This was also to see him dismiss the NAP government in the NWFP.[13] In February 1975, the NAP was banned on the grounds that it was working against the integrity of the Pakistan state.

The background to the dismissal of Ataullah Khan Mengel's government in Balochistan remains controversial. The pretext was the discovery of weapons in the Iraqi Embassy in Islamabad, which were claimed to be part of a gun-running operation for separatists within Balochistan. Bhutto had also intervened in Baloch tribal politics in an attempt to make use of the traditional rivalries between the Bugtis and Jamotes and the Mengel-led government.[14] A tribal insurgency following Mengel's dismissal escalated into a full-scale military conflict. At the height of the fighting, the Pakistan air force received assistance from the Shah of Iran, who had his own 'Baloch problem'.[15] In all, 55,000 Baloch were pitted against 70,000 Pakistani troops[16] in a conflict whose memory continues to contribute to nationalist demands.

Bhutto and Political Institutionalization

The dismissal of the NAP government in Balochistan was symptomatic of growing authoritarianism. This was evidenced not just in Bhutto's dealings with rival parties, but within the ranks of his own Pakistan People's Party (PPP). When this was founded in Lahore in November 1967, there were high hopes that the prevailing pattern of weakly institutionalized parties might be ended, thereby removing one of the long-term barriers to political development. Ideas rather than clientelism and patronage appeared to be the order of the day when the party's foundation meeting document set out its progressive credo, declaring that 'the people...are not willing to tolerate the present conditions much longer. They want a new system based on justice and attached to the essential interests of the toiling millions. Only a new party can discharge this responsibility'.[17] These ideas were later to be given fuller expression in the concept of Islamic *musawaat* and to be popularized by such writers as Hanif Ramay. While Bhutto's charismatic leadership was a crucial factor in the PPP's success in the 1970 national elections, its progressive ideals summed up in the phrase '*roti, kapra aur makan*' ('food, clothes and shelter') were an important vote winner that enabled it to capture 81 out of the 138 West Pakistan seats.

In the words of Kenneth Jones, the PPP support represented 'a tide of opinion in favour of systemic change'. 'It had been a vote for a party and its programme... not for specific individuals'.[18] Nevertheless, half of the election tickets in Punjab had been allocated to members of the traditional elite, 'who already had long political careers behind them'.[19] Many of the PPP's most 'programmatically committed social groups' were outside the legislature. This state of affairs was to set up tensions between the Punjab party cell and those MLAs whose allegiance was personal to Bhutto. This helps explain the factionalism which dominated the PPP's history in this period. Ministerialist views were expressed in such PPP publications as *Musawat* and *Nusrat*, while the more radical organizational wing of the party had its position represented in the daily *Azad* and the weekly *Dehqan* and *Al-Fatah*.[20] The PPP party organization in Punjab fought an increasingly rearguard action from its Mozang Road headquarters in Lahore. The Chief Minister G. M. Khar had his rival base at Temple Road. Bhutto further exacerbated the divisions by seeking to bolster his power through internal factional manipulation. Rather than transcending Pakistan's traditional personality-based politics and establishing a new intraparty democratization, the PPP increasingly exemplified the old-style approach. What was new was the increasing use of firearms from 1972 onwards, as factional groups became engaged in increasingly bitter internal conflicts.

Party-building, instead of proceeding along the lines of elected institutions and formal structures, revolved around patronage. The PPP's growing organizational weakness coincided with Bhutto's rapprochement with traditional power elites who had feared being swept away at the time of its triumph in the western wing in the 1970 elections. Even before Bhutto had become president, an elite 'quiet counter-revolution' of tenant evictions aided by the police and bureaucracy had begun in the countryside.[21] This was designed to nip in the bud any hopes of PPP leftists that the election victory would usher in a *Kisan-Mazdur Raj*. Rather than backing the left wing, Bhutto sought to control it to reduce resistance to his assumption of power. This set a precedent for his later dealings with established power-holders at the expense of PPP radicals. J. A. Rahim, who had drafted the PPP foundation documents, was removed from his cabinet and party positions in July 1974 and badly beaten by FSF members after he had the temerity to voice public disagreement with Bhutto. The comprehensive PPP reorganization of December 1976 emphasized personal loyalties over effective institutionalization. The increasingly autocratic Bhutto selected the higher office-bearers, his secretariat, and even appointed figures at the district level and below. The PPP's progressive founding members were one by one marginalized; sycophancy replaced creative thought as the key to influence.

The PPP increasingly looked like any other party, as it inducted opportunist landowners to gather votes and found itself the victim of their factional rivalries. In the Punjab, for example, the PPP government of Ghulam Mustafa Khar relied on time-honoured policies of involving rivals in legal cases. In this way, Khar marginalized and then purged the supporters of his rival Sheikh Rashid. Even more worrying were reports of abductions and political murders of Khar's opponents. His government became known as *danda* (stick) *raj* rather than an *awami* (people's) *raj*. Khar's hatchet-man, Iftikhar Ahmed Tari, was reputed to have criminal connections and became a reviled figure. Khar was eventually forced from office in March 1974, but this stemmed neither the erosion of the PPP's popularity nor the growing domination of the rural elite in its ranks. This was exemplified by the emergence in mid-1975 of Nawab Sadiq Hussain Qureshi as the Punjab Chief Minister.

Personal rivalries not only in Punjab but also in the Frontier and Sindh spilled over into violence. Bhutto noted in a memo in August 1973, 'Pistols to the right of us, pistols to the left of us, pistols all around us. This seems to be the motto of the party. For the most trivial of things pistols are drawn and flashed'.[22] Bhutto was not an innocent bystander in this and was prepared to use threats of violence to get his way. This was to expose him to charges concerning the death of Nawab Muhammad Ahmad Khan, which provided Zia with an opportunity to hang the former prime minister.[23]

Bhutto responded to the mounting disorder, which his political style helped generate, by increasing the stifling of political expression through banning the NAP, and the use of Section 144 of the Penal Code, the High Treason Act, Prevention of Anti-National Activities Ordinance and the Press and Publications Ordinance. Rather than introducing a new era, his regime seemed identical in these respects to those of his predecessors, Ayub and Yahya. It completed the alienation of the intellectuals and students who had vested their hopes in the party's formation. Fears that Bhutto was attempting to establish a one-party system were reinforced by his purging and politicization of the bureaucracy and his creation of the Federal Security Force and the People's Guards.[24]

Hindsight has reinforced the view that Bhutto's greatest weakness in office was his failure to regard political opposition as legitimate and to institutionalize his own party. In the words of William Milam:

> The most far-reaching long-term impact was the myopic refusal of Bhutto... to transform the (PPP) from a collection of opposition interests centred upon its charismatic leader to an institutionalized party—in other words, into a real political party. The PPP remained undemocratic in its structure, based on patronage, or clientelism, rather than merit or distinction. This may have preordained the return of the Army to its self-appointed political role as protector of the state.[25]

Bhutto and Islam

Bhutto's liberalism meant that he was never going to entertain seriously the idea of using Islam as an ideological glue in the wake of the discrediting of the Two Nation Theory. Bhuttoism, however, was too inchoate to be an effective substitute. Just as his regime was marked by creeping authoritarianism, it was also marked by the opening of space for the Islamic redefinition of Pakistan. This was not just in response to his personal excesses, but resulted from his efforts to restore Pakistani pride by linking it more firmly to the Islamic world.

The need for Pakistan to develop closer links with the Middle East and to break its dependency on the West was a constant refrain of his regime. Pakistan thus left the Commonwealth (30 January 1972) and the SEATO security Pact (8 November 1972). We have already noted the holding of the 1974 Islamic summit in Lahore. Financial support from two of the participants, Saudi Arabia and Libya, was to be important in Bhutto's quest to secure nuclear weapons. From the mid-1960s onwards, he had argued for this even if it meant that the people had to 'eat grass or leaves'. It was not until January 1972, however, that Bhutto made the decision to produce a nuclear weapon. This predated India's nuclear test by two years. Bhutto's decision was motivated by the need both to deter India's military superiority after the Bangladesh war and to restore Pakistan's place in the world after the defeat. It was not of course until after his fall that Pakistan eventually acquired its 'Islamic' bomb.

While closer ties with the Islamic world were all well and good for Pakistan's economic position and its clandestine nuclear ambitions, money from the oil-rich Middle East also flowed into the coffers of his would-be political opponents. The export of labour to the Gulf region further encouraged the spread of Islamist ideas. Within two months of the closing ceremony of the Islamic summit, an eight-party coalition of the *ulama* known as the All Parties *Tereek Khatm-e-Nabawat* (TKN, Movement for the Finality of the Prophethood) Action Committee led by Maulana Muhammad Yusaf Binnawri launched a hundred-day campaign against the Ahmadi community. We have noted earlier that the 1953 campaign had failed to achieve the goal of stripping them of their Islamic status. Amidst mounting violence in the state's Punjab heartland, Bhutto however conceded this demand by means of the Second Amendment of the 1973 Constitution. This action not only weakened his position with respect to further Islamic demands but, in the words of Farzana Shaikh, 'established a precedent that enabled a political institution (the National Assembly) elected through a secular process (elections), formally to arrogate to itself the authority to pronounce on matters of faith pertaining to individual citizens'.[26] This measure opened the way for discrimination against the Ahmadis during the Zia era.

Bhutto had thrown the Ahmadis to the wolves to strengthen his own Islamic credentials and rebut allegations that his party had been funded by Ahmadis. His capitulation, however, did not forestall Islamic attacks on his regime. Significantly, a number of participants in the agitation, such as Maulana Haq Nawaz Jhangvi, were to go on a decade later to play leading roles in the rise of sectarian militancy in Pakistan.[27]

Bhutto, like Ayub before him, turned to Sufism as an alternative source of Islamic legitimacy. He patronized the shrine of the Sindhi saint Lal Shahbaz Qalandar. Bhutto's endeavours however did not even prevent some local *pirs* in rural Punjab and Sindh from joining the campaign for the Introduction of a Prophetic Order, *Nizam-i-Mustafa*, which was organized by the *ulama* against him. The call for a vague but Islamically just social order carried resonance amongst the small-town traders in Punjab who were not only attracted by the religious appeals of the *ulama* and Islamist parties, but had been alienated by the economic reforms of the Bhutto regime. His labour reforms had made life difficult for small-scale manufacturers, while the nationalization of the *ghee*, cotton and rice-husking trades had hit the small traders, merchants and shopkeepers, many of whom were partition migrants. In addition to this lower middle class group, the PPP's working-class constituency had also been hit by rising fuel prices in the wake of the oil shock.

The PPP faced a coalition of the disillusioned poor and those whose vested interests had been threatened by its reforms. Unsurprisingly a wide range of parties stretching from the left to the Islamic right came together under the umbrella of the Pakistan National Alliance (PNA) to contest the March 1977 elections against the Bhutto regime. Much of the manpower for the campaign came from the Islamic parties. Just as in the later Iranian revolution, mosques became mobilization centres because the government dared not ban assemblies within them. Financial support, again as in Iran, came from bazaar merchants who were closely linked to the local *mullahs*. The persistent allegations that Bhutto had rigged the polls to ensure victory formed the background for continuing agitation by the PNA. Bhutto sought to halt this by making further concessions to his Islamic opponents. They included such measures as the prohibition of gambling, the closing of wine stores and night clubs and the designation of Friday as the weekly holiday instead of Sunday. He also promised to enforce Islamic moral codes. This new Puritanism could not, however, break the deadlock between the government and the PNA. The bloodless coup of 5 July removed Bhutto from power. It opened the way for a much more thoroughgoing Islamization than Bhutto had been forced to concede.

Bhutto and the Army

Bhutto's initial purge of army officers had put the military on the back foot. His moves to create competing forces in the shape of the Federal Security Force and the People's Guards were a source of resentment. Indeed on one occasion he inspected a guard of honour of the People's Guards rather than a regular army contingent.[28] The Federal Security Force (FSF) was designed to assist the police in the maintenance of law and order, but Bhutto's critics termed it a private army. This had some justification as the FSF was used to harass the regime's NAP and JI opponents. The army's displeasure was seen in its refusal to provide training or to place tanks and other heavy equipment at the FSF's disposal. Significantly one of the first actions of the Zia regime was to disband it.[29]

Further resentment arose over the slow pace of repatriation of prisoners of war from India. This was a factor in the abortive plotting by a number of army and air force officers to overthrow Bhutto in March-April 1973. However, 11 of the 35 defendants were acquitted and just two life sentences were passed.[30] The delay in repatriation was the result of Bhutto's drawn-out post-war diplomacy with both India and Bangladesh. This was designed to ensure that any notion of a Tashkent-type 'sell-out' was avoided. Bhutto's grandstanding at the Simla conference with Indira Gandhi in July 1972 enabled him to claim that he 'had won the peace'. Certainly there was no Indian hoped-for explicit no-war pact, or final solution to the Kashmir dispute. Bhutto was also able to face off JI, which had been running a vigorous '*Bangladesh-Na Manzur*' ('No Recognition of Bangladesh') campaign.[31] It was however cold comfort to the officers and men in the Indian camps at such places as Jubblepur and Calcutta, confronted with a 'monotonous' vegetarian diet.[32] Their release had to wait until August 1973.

Bhutto's wariness of the army was seen in the measures he introduced to forestall future military intervention. He reduced the tenure of the Chiefs of Staff to three years. He also sought to dilute the army chief's power, by creating a permanent post of Chairman, Joint Chiefs of Staff Committee. The third schedule of the 1973 Constitution contained an oath which serving members of the military were to take forswearing political activities of any kind. Article 245 defined high treason as any attempt to abrogate or subvert the Constitution, 'by the use of force or show of force or by other unconstitutional means'. Within a month of the Constitution being enacted, a law was passed enforcing the death sentence or life imprisonment for those found guilty of attempting to subvert it. As Hasan-Askiri Rizvi has noted, 'No previous Constitution provided such...safeguards'.[33] Bhutto mistakenly thought that he had further shored up his position when he promoted the apolitical and apparently pliant General Zia-ul-Haq to the post of Chief of Army Staff in March 1976.

We have already drawn attention to how Bhutto unintentionally perpetuated the conditions for military intervention, through his failure to institutionalize the PPP and his use of the army to suppress legitimate Baloch demands. His need for a strong force to confront India was a further factor in weakening his endeavours to assert civilian supremacy. As we have noted above, Indian hopes that a truncated Pakistan would now accept its regional hegemony were dashed by the Simla conference. The Indian nuclear explosion in the Rajasthan desert in May 1974 further strengthened Bhutto's resolve. Despite the PPP's initial commitment to what might be termed human developmental goals, the traditional policy of directing scarce resources to the army was maintained. Pakistan's defence expenditure rose by over 200 per cent during the Bhutto era. Throughout this period $8 per citizen was being spent on the armed forces.[34] The distortion to the economy can be seen in the fact that Pakistan's spending on defence was almost twice as great a percentage of its GNP as was India's. For the period 1971–80 Pakistan's weapons bill stood at $1.54 billion. China had taken the lead in the early Bhutto period, supplying tanks, naval vessels and combat aircraft. But the US became a major source of military hardware following the lifting of its arms embargo in 1975. The Chinese also constructed a tank repair factory at Taxila and an air force repair facility at nearby Kamra.

Every dollar Pakistan spent on arms reduced funding for education, healthcare and housing. It also led to growing budget deficits. Attempts to reduce these by curbing food subsidies as in April 1974 cost the government further support amongst those people who had been attracted by its promises in 1970. As we shall see in the final section of this chapter, Bhutto was eventually faced with a fatal combination of failing to meet the expectations of his poorer supporters while ruffling the feathers of better-off opponents.

While the Bhutto government followed the pattern of earlier regimes regarding defence allocation, it did not repeat the use of Islamic proxies in the enduring rivalry with India over Kashmir. A number of explanations have been provided for this factor. They range from Bhutto's ongoing problems with Islamists in domestic politics to wider strategic considerations.[35] Nor did Bhutto succumb to the temptation of pitting Islamists against the forces of ethnic nationalism in Balochistan. Only with respect to the renewed Pakhtunistan threat is there evidence of the development of tentative ties with such figures as Gulbuddin Hekmatyar, who had taken refuge in Pakistan.[36]

In a pattern which was to be repeated in the 1990s, civilian politicians approached the army to intervene against their detested opponents. In 1972 during the Sindhi language disturbances and again in 1973, the army was approached by right-wing and Islamist groups calling on it to remove Bhutto. The pressures for intervention were however much greater during the PNA agitation. The weakly institutionalized PPP lacked the coherence to counter them. As the protesters became increasingly violent, the police and FSF struggled to contain them. Bhutto had to declare martial law in the worst affected areas of the Lahore and Hyderabad districts and the Karachi division.

This limited martial law paved the way for Bhutto's ousting. A more middle-class pattern of recruitment in the officer corps (a process greatly increased during the Zia era) made the army more sympathetic to the PNA's call for the establishment of *Nizam-i-Mustafa*. According to the account of General Arif, Zia's Chief of Staff after the coup, the politicization of the Corps Commanders as a result of their frequent meetings with both Zia and Bhutto also played a role.[37] Perhaps most important was the fear of disunity in the army's own ranks following the refusal of three brigadiers to fire on those protesting in Lahore against 'election riggers and cheats'.[38] Arif concludes his narrative with the time-honoured justification for military intervention in Pakistan, that of the absence of 'reconciliation, accommodation and tolerance among the quarrelling politicians'.[39]

The coup was greeted calmly, perhaps because its implications were not fully appreciated at the time. Zia in his maiden address promised elections within 90 days. Bhutto was released from protective custody after three weeks. More importantly, its bloodless character indicated the exhaustion of Bhutto's populism.

Bhutto's Populism: Hopes and Dashed Expectations

Bhutto's meteoric rise in popularity from 1967 onwards owed much to the hope he brought of a dramatic break with Pakistan's past. He held out for the masses the prospect of economic as well as political empowerment. If this had been achieved, it would have provided him with an infinitely stronger safeguard against military intervention than that arising from constitutional niceties and the shallow trappings of the FSF. Bhutto's land reforms, nationalization measures and labour laws did not, however, transform Pakistan for good. They merely added to the number of enemies generated by his combative political style.

A number of explanations have been provided for the failure of Bhutto's populism. Some focus on his personal failures and on the logical inconsistency of a hugely privileged Sindhi feudal landowner preaching the virtues of socialism.[40] Others maintain that, if Bhutto's rule had been properly institutionalized, reforms could have been better implemented. To these we must add the factor that just as his attempts to rein in the military came up sharp against Pakistan's geo-political insecurity vis-à-vis both Afghanistan and India, so attempts to reduce Pakistan's glaring economic inequalities were made more difficult by the inflationary pressures generated by the 1973 Arab-Israeli War. For the man in the street, the rhetoric of egalitarianism sounded increasingly hollow when confronted with annual price rises of 20 per cent.

Bhutto's 1972 land reforms were more radical than Ayub's, but they did not meet his 1970 election aspiration to remove the 'remaining vestiges of feudalism'. The maximum land ceilings were still 150 acres for irrigated and 300 acres for un-irrigated land. Intra-family land transfers were still allowed and individual ceilings could be increased if evidence of agricultural improvements, including the use of tractors and tube-wells, were provided. This meant that, as in Ayub's 1959 reforms, little land was available for redistribution. The fact that Bhutto's reforms removed any compensation for owners meant that they retained their most fertile holdings, leaving poor quality land to be distributed to landless tenants and small peasant owners. To make matters worse, as in 1959 there were numerous instances of fictitious transfers. Ironically, rather than signalling a shift in the rural balance of power, the reforms encouraged many Punjabi landlords to enter the PPP's ranks in order to safeguard their position. The PPP's weak institutionalization enabled them to take up leading roles. Despite his populist rhetoric, Bhutto liberally distributed election tickets to landlords at the time of the 1977 polls. This further disillusioned the PPP rank and file.

Significantly, in an admission of the failings of the reforms, Bhutto announced more stringent measures on the eve of the 1977 elections. Ceilings were lowered to 100 acres of irrigated land and 200 acres of un-irrigated land. This still hardly represented an agrarian revolution. Nevertheless, the measures were suspended with the introduction of martial law on 5 July.

Bhutto's labour reforms, which were also introduced in 1972, were more far reaching, thanks in part to the radical influence of Muhammad Hanif, the Minister for Labour. Union power was increased with the establishment of Works Councils and special Labour Courts for the adjudication of industrial disputes. A compulsory system of shop stewards was established in factories. Employers were called upon to provide subsidized housing and education to matriculation level for at least one child of every employee. The state also held out the promise of old age pensions and insurance against injury.[41]

For some PPP activists even these measures were insufficient and they demanded the introduction of a minimum wage and the labour laws' extension to pieceworkers. The newly emboldened workers became embroiled in a number of strikes and *gheraos* (lock-ins) which further hit production in many of the poorly managed new nationalized industries. There was a bloody conflict between strikers and some employers in Karachi, which was only ended when the army was called in. This precipitated a break between Bhutto and a number of PPP radicals. Lower-middle-class PPP supporters who owned small enterprises were hit by the cost of pension and medical benefits for workers. They also chafed under the workers' new participation in management structures. Some small-scale enterprises, as for example those in the Sialkot sports goods industry, sought to circumvent the reforms by reverting to a home-based decentralized production.[42] Business confidence was in fact hit, not just in the small-units sector of the economy. There was rising unemployment for workers whose lives were already being made miserable by the spiralling prices of goods. Ironically, the improved conditions which some sections of the working class experienced during the Bhutto years owed far more to government encouragement of labour migration to the Gulf than to its vaunted reform programme.

Labour reform had gone hand in hand with a far-reaching nationalization programme. This encompassed the banks and life insurance companies, large heavy industry such as engineering, chemicals and iron and steel, but also small-scale consumer industries such as the ghee, rice husking and cotton trading industries. We have already noted that their owners, along with small-scale traders and merchants, were at the forefront of the anti-Bhutto campaign. Nationalization was intended to 'eliminate, once and for all, poverty and discrimination in Pakistan'.[43] This tall claim was impossible to fulfil, not just because there were a myriad of other causes of poverty and discrimination, but because of the fact that many of the newly nationalized industries were badly managed. Moreover, the threat of further nationalization led to a flight of capital and skills out of the country. The resulting decline in private sector investment meant that the high rates of economic growth of the Ayub era were replaced by near stagnation.

Nationalization also brought increased corruption and clientelism in its wake. This occurred both at individual and political level. The PPP's vastly increased resource base further encouraged the process of substituting patronage for political institutionalization. The support of the large landholders who were opportunistically joining its ranks was facilitated by cheap credit from the newly nationalized banks. A precedent was set in which successive governments used loans from government-controlled institutions to buy support. By the mid-1990s, the scale of defaults had reached the staggering level of Rs 108 billion. The bad loans threatened the liquidity ratios of nationalized banks, undermined Pakistan's credibility with international financial institutions and fed into a culture of endemic corruption.

The unintended effects of Bhutto's reforms were to expose the PPP to disunity and clientelism, to create powerful enemies amongst the rural and urban elites and to fail to create the conditions for a more just society, capable of supporting a democratic system of government. This populist period can be variously described as a 'heroic failure', 'missed opportunity' or as merely a replay of Pakistan's traditional personality-centred politics, in an albeit more exaggerated form. The immediate fruits of the socio-economic reforms were displayed during the 1977 elections and their chaotic aftermath, which brought down the curtain on the Bhutto theatricals.

Bhutto also moved to nationalize educational institutions. The only exemption was those schools and colleges under the direct control of foreign missionaries. Nationalization was seen as the necessary instrument for 'Preparing Pakistan's educational sector for meeting the demands of a modern and dynamic society'.[44] The linkage of education with empowerment was made explicit by the introduction on 1 October 1972 of free, but not compulsory, education for all children up to the age of 13. Bhutto was to maintain that these educational reforms were his greatest achievement. As with other measures, however, they failed to take account of the complex and interlocking causes of deprivation in Pakistan. Poor parents could not allow their children to take up the offer of free education as they needed them to work to supplement meagre household incomes. Indeed around two-thirds of all young adults were forced to work. A staggering 39.5 per cent of the total labour force was made up of children in 1971.[45] The rate of educational enrolment in these circumstances hardly surprisingly only increased by 5 per cent over 1972–4, taking into consideration population growth. The nationalized schools and colleges experienced falling standards to the chagrin of the urban middle classes. Once again, the PPP government was creating enemies without effecting the sweeping changes of its rhetorical discourses.

Conclusion

Bhutto had sought to transform Pakistan. His rule witnessed tumultuous events, but at its close much remained the same. Despite the claim that he would abolish feudalism, the large Punjabi and Sindhi landowners continued to wield power. The promise to empower the poor had achieved only limited success. Politics remained in the thrall of patron-client ties in which personality counted for more than ideology or party institutionalization. The party system displayed instability and immaturity, rather than vitality and development, thereby opening the door for military intervention. Within a few years of the army's defeat and demoralization at Dhaka, it had been allowed back into public life to aid civil authority. It was soon in receipt of the swollen budgetary allocations which had distorted Pakistan's economy since independence. Its institutional recovery and re-emergence as a domestic political power contrasts sharply with that of other demoralized forces such as the Greek colonels (after the 1974 Turkish invasion of Cyprus) or the Argentine junta after the 1982 Malvinas/Falklands War.

Bhutto had not only been unable to restructure civil-military relations, but he had failed to resolve once and for all the tensions between the centre and the provinces. Hopes for a new beginning had collapsed because of his own authoritarian tendencies and a threatening regional security environment. Centralization was turned to as in the past, in an attempt to shore up the state. While Punjabis were dealt an even more favourable hand after 1971, Sindhis emerged for a short time as successful players in the Bhutto political dispensation.

Despite his 'secular' predilections, Bhutto made concessions to Islamist demands. The 1973 Constitution denied the possibility of attaining the highest offices in the land to non-Muslim citizens of Pakistan. Just two decades after Pakistan had experienced its first martial law administration in Lahore following anti-Ahmadhi riots, the *ulama* succeeded in the goal of removing the community's Islamic status. In its dying days, the Bhutto regime made further concessions which opened the way for Zia's more wide-ranging state-sponsored Islamization. The vulnerability of such a powerful figure as Bhutto revealed how the loss of the eastern wing, with its large non-Muslim minority, had strengthened the influence of the Islamist groups.

Bhutto ultimately remained committed to Pakistan's long-established notions that a strong army and a unitary state were crucial to its survival. He also returned to a concept of politics that was founded on patronage and vertical rather than horizontal networks of mobilization. The outcome was, in Mohammad Waseem's words, the 'degeneration' of the PPP into yet another 'Statist' political party at the service of the oligarchy.[46] Bhutto's failure to transform Pakistan was not however inevitable. Through the force of his personality, popular support and the demoralization of the army, he had been afforded a unique opportunity to set Pakistan on a new course. He had, however, undermined the very individuals and institutions which might have brought about reformist change and defended him from the vested interests which felt threatened by the prospect of popular democracy. The circumstances of his re-arrest by Zia, trial and eventual execution have led wider sections of Pakistan society to gloss over his foibles and failings and burnish a Bhutto myth. He is revered as a martyr and a *pir* especially in Sindh, where the execution of the country's first Sindhi prime minister by Punjabi generals evokes strong nationalist overtones. Ultimately, Bhutto's career was not just a personal, a family or a Sindhi tragedy; it was rather a tragedy for the Pakistan nation which witnessed a second missed chance for democratization. As Kenneth Jones has argued, 'the progressive deterioration of the PPP... reproduced the experience of the Muslim League after 1947'.[47] He goes on perceptively to declare that:

> Both periods of decline followed periods of unity and electoral success produced by a mass movement strategy which focused both on a dominant leader… and on a strategy that combined nationalism with a radical social programme. Both the League and the PPP were essentially loose coalitions of diverse and competing interests and both parties had difficulties in maintaining their organizational boundaries or finding mechanisms to solve internal disputes. For both parties, the accession to power corroded party organization and ended any pretence at party unity. As particularistic cleavages began to re-emerge, so too did the pattern of playing off powerful interprovincial interests, one against the other, and in both cases this ultimately redounded to the advantage of the rural notables and the bureaucracy.[48]

It was to be another decade before a third opportunity for democratization presented itself. The PPP under the leadership of its founder's daughter Benazir Bhutto was to re-emerge as the challenger to the establishment's interests. The possibilities for a major re-alignment of power were however far less promising than they had been in the heady days of 1970–1. Zulfiqar Ali Bhutto's name remained a stirring popular memory, but the possibilities for socio-economic transformation and democratic consolidation were more distant than they had been in the late 1960s and early 1970s.

5

ZIA AND THE QUEST FOR PAKISTAN'S STABILITY

Zia-ul-Haq's rule (1977–88) strengthened presidential authority and the army's entrenched political and economic role. It also bequeathed the doleful legacies of the 'kalashnikov culture', the linkage between the military and Islamic extremists and increased sectarianism. Many of the mosque schools which mushroomed in this era were highly sectarian in outlook as well as committed to a trans-national *jihadist* outlook. Successive post-Zia governments have been unable to rein in the radical *madaris* and their militants.

Less remarked upon, but equally portentous for Pakistan's future stability, was the continued underfunding of social welfare, despite a period of remittance and investment-fuelled growth. Pakistan still outperformed India at this time in terms of economic growth (with growth rates of over 6 per cent in the Zia era) and per capita income. But its uneven development and lack of human capital investment meant that it was more poorly equipped than India to take advantage of the rapidly approaching late-twentieth-century spread of globalization. The neglect of human development was accompanied by a further weakening of such important state institutions as the civil service, the universities and the courts. Zia's rule also coincided with an onslaught on civil society and an attempt to write Jinnah's pluralist vision of Pakistan out of the history books.

This doleful inheritance has been so profound that writers have been tempted to blame all Pakistan's ills on Zia's rule. We have already seen, however, that there were longer-term influences at work which have contributed to its contemporary crisis. Moreover, it is important to understand Pakistan's second martial law ruler as being shaped by cultural and economic currents as well as leading the country singlehandedly onto a new path of development.

Pakistan at the Time of Zia's Rule

Bhutto had threatened established interests and tantalized the masses with the glimpse of a more egalitarian society. But the impact of his reforms had been largely cosmetic. His land reforms, according to one estimate, had released just 1 per cent of the cultivable land to the tenants.[1] Rather than destroy feudalism, Bhutto ultimately accommodated himself with the landed elite. Zia thus inherited a situation in which, as throughout Pakistan's history, a section of the landed class would be available to lend legitimacy to an authoritarian regime. Bhutto had also alienated the business classes through his nationalisation programmes. Zia returned to the private enterprise approach of Ayub and sought to co-opt those who had recently lost out. The most striking example of this was the Sharif family's Ittefaq business group. Nawaz Sharif began his political rise to prominence under Zia, which was to see him twice become Pakistan's Prime Minister in the 1990s. His political role for many years exemplified the army's success in neutralizing the PPP influence in Punjab, through appeal to a combination of the Islamically-inclined lower middle class, the trader-merchant groups, the business and industrial elites and finally a fraction of the feudal class.

In addition to class divisions, Pakistan in 1977 possessed marked regional, rural-urban and gender imbalances. Bhutto had again attempted to address some of these, but had not effected radical change, while simultaneously threatening established interests. With respect to gender, for example, Article 25 of the 1973 Constitution had outlawed discrimination on the basis of gender. Bhutto followed this up by opening professions such as the elite Foreign Services to women for the first time. On 31 January 1976 he had also established a 13-member Women's Rights Committee headed by the Attorney-General, Yahya Bakhtiar. Its recommendations included the reservation of posts for women in government services; the encouragement of female participation in sport, culture and the media; and most importantly that it be made mandatory 'for a woman to get her share of inheritable property including agricultural land'.[2] One explanation of Zia's discriminatory policy towards women was the need to appease traditionalists who wished to preserve threatened traditional gender relations under the slogan '*Chador aur char diwari*' ('The veil and the four walls'). Scholarly emphasis on the more notorious elements of Zia's politics of Islamic reform has ignored the fact that little progress was made where the implementation of Islamic precepts would have given women increased rights, as for example in the realm of landed property relations.[3]

The population growth by the 1980s at 3 per cent annual increase was one of the highest in the world. The 'youth bulge' with its attendant underemployment was a factor in the growing ethnic and religious extremism of the Zia era. Not only the rank and file but most of the leaders of the MQM in 1980s Karachi were in their 20s. The youthful population, with the exception of the interior of Sindh, was by the Zia era increasingly mobile. This was in part because of push factors arising from the mechanization of agriculture with the onset of the Green Revolution; it also resulted from the pull of new job opportunities. Migration was often two-staged, from villages to small towns, then on to major conurbations such as Lahore and Karachi. The latter had the highest population of both Baloch and Pakhtun in the world. Its political violence in the 1980s was a signal of a mushrooming population outstripping transport, housing and water supplies.

Small towns in the Punjab also saw rapid population increase. They emerged as hubs for growth with workshops sprawling along the main highways. Mosques were springing up across the towns and villages of the country, many of them funded from overseas. Karachi had emerged as a melting pot with large Pakhtun, Baloch as well as *mohajir* and Sindhi populations. Much of the country's transport networks were run by Pakhtuns. Zia was to exploit the politics of ethnic identity in Karachi to throw off balance Sindhi resistance to his regime. At the same time, he reflected the conservative values of an emerging urban middle class which both sought a sense of stability at time of rapid change in conservative religious outlooks and favourably contrasted its simplicity with the ostentation and decadence of the upper classes. The diplomat Iqbal Akhund wrote a series of anecdotes about Zia in which he recalls how Zia frequently stressed that he was 'a simple man'. On one occasion he broke off from an envoy's meeting to join junior office staff for midday prayers, while the ambassadors, federal secretaries and senior officials 'Kept walking back and forth and chatting on the terrace alongside the prayer tent'.[4]

Towards the end of the Bhutto era, internal migration had been accompanied by a rapid overseas migration. By 1980 it was estimated that nearly 1.5 million Pakistanis were working overseas. This number continued to climb. Indeed during the fifth economic plan (1978–83) over a third of the increase in the labour force was absorbed by overseas migration.[5] The vast majority of labour migrants were Punjabis and Pakhtuns. It was from these two ethnic groupings that Zia sought to co-opt support for his regime. While earlier labour migration had been to the West, the bulk of this population movement was to Qatar, UAE and Saudi Arabia. The movement had profound effects on both disposable income and cultural values. With respect to the former, Jonathan Addleton has declared, 'the Gulf migration broadened what had historically been a small middle class in Pakistan'.[6] The exposure of lower-class Pakistanis to the Islamic heartland further encouraged a mindset favourable to Islamization, although Zia was to find that its impact on sectarianism was to prove unpredictable and potentially destabilizing.

The urban Partition migrants from East Punjab also provided another important constituency for Zia's approach to politics. He came from a modest middle-class Arain family which had migrated from its ancestral home in Jullundur to Peshawar. He shared the views of the East Punjab Arain and Sheikh communities, which were marked by their anti-Indian outlooks and striving for a 'respectable' life after the trauma of uprooting. When addressing an International Islamic Conference in Islamabad, he declared: 'I will tell you what Islam and Pakistan means to me. It is a vision of my mother struggling on, tired, with all her worldly possessions in her hands, when she crossed the border into Pakistan'.[7] Some of Zia's closest military associates, such as his Vice-Chief of Army Staff, General Arif, and General Akhtar Abdur Rahman who headed ISI from 1984–8, came from East Punjab refugee backgrounds. A fellow Arain from Jullundur, Lieutenant-General Faiz Ali Chishti, played a leading role in the coup which brought Zia to power. To complete the roll call, acting Chief Justice Maulvi Mushtaq Hussein, the Presiding Judge of the Lahore High Court which sentenced Bhutto to death on 18 March 1978, was another Zia appointee from his native Jullundur district.

By the early 1980s, official figures revealed that overseas workers were annually sending remittances worth $2.2 billion to Pakistan.[8]

Informal transfers through the *hundi* system meant that in reality this figure was considerably higher. Along with the influx of foreign loans following Pakistan's 'frontline status' in the wake of the Soviet occupation of Afghanistan, the large remittances helped boost Pakistan's rate of economic growth[9] and may well have contributed to the longevity of Zia's rule. According to Shahid Javed Burki's figures, during the Zia years an average Pakistani's income increased by 41 per cent.[10] Punjabis experienced above average increases because the bulk of the remittances flowed into the province, further exaggerating regional inequalities. During the 1970s and 1980s around half of all Pakistan's labour migrants to the Gulf region came from Punjab. Such writers as Aijaz Ahmad and Omar Noman have understood Punjab's tranquillity during the Zia era in terms of this 'Gulf factor', as well as the region's traditional link with the army. The anti-Zia protests in Sindh arose not just from its political marginalization but from the fact that it sent few migrants to the Gulf so missed out on the prosperity stemming from a regular inflow of remittances.[11]

Within central Punjab, along the Punjab border with India and in the newly irrigated areas of Sindh, the old landowning class had been leavened with the emergence of military agriculturalists, many of whom had obtained land at knock-down prices following Ayub's 1959 land reforms. This development not only provided an additional constituency of rural support for the Zia regime but was a factor in encouraging Pakistanis with modest middle-class rural and urban backgrounds to see a military career as a means of advancement. Even before Zia assumed power, there was a shift in the composition of the officer ranks from the old feudal elites to the middle class. This provided Zia with an important support base in the army and has been linked by some writers with Islamization's appeal to the men in khaki.

The officer corps, as Steven Cohen has demonstrated, was increasingly in Zia's own image. While he had no intention to create an Islamic army, he believed that religious commitment could strengthen patriotism and professionalism. Zia personally attended the annual conference of *Tablighi Jamaat* at Raiwind, near Lahore, which could draw up to 2 million participants. He encouraged the *Tabligh*'s outreach to soldiers, with the result that many became committed to its activities. Indeed General Javed Nasir who headed ISI in 1992–3 was heavily involved with the *Tabligh*. The *Tabligh* was apolitical in its stance, but its Islamic activism carried a strong Deobandi commitment.

The *Jamaat* was to be later deployed in condemnation of the Pakhtun-based Taliban and its Punjabi sectarian allies when they tuned their firepower against the state.

Officers were also drawn to JI, although it was only on retirement that they openly participated in the organization. Cohen reveals, for example, that 19 retired generals attended the 1991 JI convention in Islamabad.[12] Field officers in Afghanistan, and especially those working for ISI, were increasingly exposed to more radical Islamic groupings. Such senior commanders as General Hameed Gul developed close ties with them. In many senses, the army's growing Islamic tinge reflected the change in composition of the officer corps and the fact that Pakistani society as a whole was becoming more religiously conservative.

Zia's rule must be understood in terms of not only the Pakistan context but also the changing regional and international context. The 1979 Iranian revolution both encouraged Islamic resurgence worldwide and also prompted competition between Saudi Arabia and Iran for Islamic leadership. Pakistan was to become a sectarian battlefield, as Zia sought to position the state as a major force for Sunni Islamic leadership. The Afghanistan conflict transformed Pakistan's relations with the US. The Carter administration's foreign policy outlook was strongly influenced by both human rights and nuclear non-proliferation concerns, and on both accounts Pakistan seemed unworthy of assistance. Economic and military aid was suspended in April 1979. US-Pakistan relations reached their lowest ebb later in the year when rumours that America was behind the anti-government assault on the Grand Mosque in Mecca prompted its embassy in Islamabad to be attacked by angry mobs on 21 November. Two US citizens and two Pakistani employees were killed in the clashes.

The situation was transformed dramatically by a change of administration in Washington and the Soviet occupation of Afghanistan on 28 December 1979. Following the Saur revolution in Afghanistan, a civil war developed between the Communist government and local *mujahadin*. It was however factional infighting in the Afghan government between Muhammad Taraki and Hafizullah Amin that finally prompted Soviet intervention. This move was seen in Washington in terms of the new Cold War contest with Moscow. Zia now became America's frontline ally in the fight against communism. Reagan stepped up Carter's earlier begrudging support following his election. Some $3.2 billion of funding flowed into Pakistan over a six-year period. It became the third largest recipient of US aid after Israel and Egypt.[13] As during the 1950s, American largesse bolstered the army to the detriment of democratic forces. A blind eye was turned both to human rights abuses and to the mounting 'scorecard' of Pakistan's violations of non-proliferation policy, despite the safeguards to this provided by the Pressler Amendment.[14] While for Washington the Afghan conflict was a new front in the global struggle with the Soviet Union, for Islamabad it presented an opportunity to acquire strategic depth against India. The carefully calibrated conflict succeeded in preventing full-scale Soviet retaliation against Pakistan. This successful strategy also encouraged military thinking in Pakistan that a proxy war could be directed against India in Kashmir.

There was, however, a 'blowback' from the Afghanistan conflict. This was seen in the leakage of weapons, the spread of drug addiction and the mounting Afghan refugee problem. Longer-term legacies included the ever closer ties between the army and the ISI with militant Islamic groups. According to a leading ISI officer, by 1987 at least 80,000 *mujahadin* had gone through training camps in Pakistan.[15] Militant groups had originated as armed offshoots of JI and JUI. The later movement of Islamic fighters between *jihadist* and sectarian groups was to increase sectarian violence drastically within Pakistan.

Zia's Authoritarianism

As Iqbal Akhund has noted, Zia stands in a long line of Pakistani rulers who have damaged institutions, acted arbitrarily and undermined respect for the law.[16] Their actions, designed to bolster their power, have stunted the prospects for democratization. Zia's rule, however, had an especially pernicious impact, because of both its longevity and its severity. Ayub, as we have seen, muzzled the press, but it would have been unthinkable during his rule to flog journalists before the gaze of world opinion. In May 1978, however, four journalists were flogged in Lahore because they had gone on hunger strike to protest against the closure of the leading PPP newspaper, *Musawat*.[17] The public flogging of political prisoners by bare-chested wrestlers remains one of the starkest images of the martial law regime. Martial Law Regulation no. 48 of October 1979 invoked a maximum penalty of 25 lashes for taking part in political activities, all of which had been banned. Editors of 'defamatory' publications could be punished by 10 lashes and 25 years of rigorous imprisonment. Early in September 1983, the Karachi branch of the Pakistan Medical Association called on the government not to involve doctors in the process of flogging and to 'stop such punishments on humanitarian and medical grounds'.[18]

Opponents of the regime were routinely tortured. This became so widespread at the time of the 1981 and 1983 military crackdowns that it attracted international condemnation. It also became immortalized in the creative writings of what became known as 'resistance literature'.[19]

While Zia took the brutal repression of dissent to new depths, he also indulged in the time-honoured techniques of censorship which throughout Pakistan's history had stunted healthy debate and the flowering of democratic values. Newspapers were subject to full pre-censorship from October 1979 onwards, whereby proofs had to be submitted for scrutiny and approval before publication. There were also 'advices' as to what should be included and how issues should be covered. The 1979 Motion Pictures Ordinance censored film productions on the grounds of both immorality and undermining religion or Pakistan's 'integrity or solidarity as an independent state'. The ordinance served only to suffocate creative talent within Pakistan, as videocassettes of pirated copies of Hollywood and Bollywood films remained readily available.

The state was however able to control educational curricula and textbook production. Pakistan Studies was introduced as a compulsory subject from secondary school to university level. Government-approved texts provided not only a one-sided version of history but, as K. K. Aziz has pointed out, encouraged xenophobia and the glorification of military struggle to an impressionable younger generation.[20] Like many despots, Zia sought to rewrite history. The official discourse swept to one side the ambiguities of the freedom movement and deemed the struggle for an Islamic state to be its main objective. Jinnah was portrayed as upholding Islam, while the *ulama* whose influence had been marginal to the creation of Pakistan were elevated to a vanguard role. Newspaper articles on the occasion of Jinnah's birth in December 1981 omitted his speech to the Constituent Assembly in which he called for religious freedom and the relegation of faith to the private sphere. The following year, the regime sought to use the film industry to present Jinnah as a proponent of an Islamic state. Production began on a film of Jinnah's life entitled *Stand Up From the Dust*. The Ministries of Information and Broadcasting and Culture were involved in the project along with the Pakistan Television Corporation and scholars and journalists sympathetic to the regime. The script was required:

> Not to be in conflict with the policies of the Martial Law regime.
>
> To portray Jinnah as a greater leader than Gandhi and show the creation of Pakistan was the outcome of the Quaid's supreme command over the Muslim League and his followers.
>
> To emphasize that Quaid-i-Azam's main motivation for founding Pakistan was to form an Islamic state as had been established by the Martial Law regime.[21]

The opening sequences of armed horsemen by the Arabian Sea reproduced the Two Nation Theory linkage of Pakistan's genesis with the emergence of Muhammad Bin Qasim, the first Muslim invader of India. A similar didacticism was present in the narrator's concluding comments: 'His achievement was Pakistan, an independent homeland for the Muslims of India, a sovereign state where Islam could flourish freely not merely in its religious rituals, but in culture, law, economics, in fact every aspect of life'.[22]

Zia's lukewarm response to the rushes ensured that the film was never publicly released, despite its considerable production costs. Nevertheless, as we shall see later in the chapter, the Islamization of Pakistan's society and economics formed the main legitimization of his regime. Zia also saw it as a solution to Pakistan's long-standing identity problem. Islam was however less effective in providing a national cohesive force than Zia anticipated.

The early Zia era was littered with promises to hold elections which were then postponed. This pattern was prompted by the anxiety that the PPP would triumph in any polls and take revenge on the coup's instigators. Such varied bystanders as Iqbal Akhand and Lieutenant-General Faiz Ali Chishti maintain that Zia's decision to solve the 'Bhutto problem' by his 'judicial murder' similarly resulted from Zia's sense of self-preservation.[23] Following a further postponement of elections in October 1979, Zia announced a ban on all parties and meetings. In the wake of the Movement for the Restoration of Democracy campaign in Sindh in 1983, Zia extended the ban on political activity by PPP members to ten years.

Like Ayub before him, however, Zia found that in order to increase the effectiveness of his government he needed to broaden its base. On the first anniversary of the coup, some civilians were taken into the Federal Cabinet which had previously been dominated by the bureaucracy and the military. The Sindhi Muslim League politician Muhammad Khan Junejo became the Railways Minister. At the end of 1981, Zia restored the colonial practice of setting up a consultative assembly of nominated members. In keeping with his commitment to Islamization, he gave it the title of *Majlis-i-Shura*. This ironically involved him in conflict with some of the *ulama* who maintained that a *shura* as prescribed in the Quran would have made decisions through mutual consultation and not just endorsed the decisions already taken by the government. JI increasingly distanced itself from the government because of the delays in introducing Islamization and began to call for elections which it hoped would enable it to oversee a fully-fledged Islamization process. Zia's reluctance to hold polls was another cause of the JI's drifting away, as was the banning early in 1984 of its powerful student wing *Islami Jamiat-i-Tulaba* (IJT) along with all other student organizations linked to political parties.

Zia adopted a two-pronged strategy with respect to elections. Firstly, he sought to bolster his own position as president by means of holding a national referendum; secondly, he determined that any polls should be held on a 'partyless' basis. The wording of the referendum which was hastily arranged for 19 December 1984 made it difficult to oppose Zia's continuation for five years as president without giving the appearance of voting against Islam.[24] In Karachi, 'everywhere it was the same desultory picture. Under marquees erected outside polling stations, one for men and another for women, yawning officials sat on plain tables handing out little chits to voters. Except that there were no voters to speak of. The officials beckoned like merchants in an oriental bazaar, to every passerby to please come in and vote'.[25] Such scenes were repeated across the country, although Pakistan Television broadcast pictures of large crowds at polling stations and the official turnout was recorded at just over 62 per cent. The performance concluded with Zia receiving a 97.71 per cent 'Yes' vote.

National Assembly elections were held on a non-party basis in February 1985. They paved the way for the lifting of martial law the following December. This was a civilianization of martial law rather than its democratization. The polls were popularly dubbed the 'deaf and dumb' elections because of the stringent ban on public meetings, processions and use of public address systems.[26] Even more than in Ayub's earlier partyless polls, the elections in the absence of party organization encouraged *biraderi* loyalties and patron-client ties to come to the fore. These were the very aspects of Pakistani electioneering which had traditionally stood in the way of modern-style politics. The partyless elections alongside developments in Sindh also contributed to an ethnicization of political identity. Zia made a further endeavour to ensure that he remained fully in control after the lifting of martial law, handpicking the Prime Minister, Muhammad Khan Junejo, and arming himself, through the 8th Amendment to the 1973 Constitution, with the discretionary power to dismiss the Prime Minister and dissolve the National Assembly. The President also retained the power to appoint provincial governors and the chief of the armed forces. This created an important legacy which was used by Zia's successors as President to fetter democracy. Zia was also careful to ensure that the Assembly indemnified all his acts after the 1977 coup.

Zia's aim was to crush the PPP, and this motive had lain behind his treatment of Zulfiqar Ali Bhutto. He never fully succeeded in this aim. Indeed, the deceased Prime Minister's daughter, Benazir Bhutto, who had spent a number of years in prison and in exile, emerged towards the close of his regime in a popular challenge to his power.[27] She returned to a tumultuous reception in April 1986. Zia did succeed, however, not only in constitutionally trammelling her power but in strengthening those groups which opposed the PPP. The ISI was to play a role in organizing them into a coherent grouping in advance of the 1988 elections which followed Zia's death. When Benazir returned the PPP to power, it was as she herself acknowledged with one hand tied behind her back.

Zia's grip on Pakistan was much stronger following the civilianization of martial law than Ayub's had been. In 1988, Junejo attempted to carve out an area of autonomy with respect to foreign policy and even, as we shall see later, sought to interfere with the military elite's perks. Zia did not hesitate to remove the Prime Minister in May. Junejo also paid the price for failing to capitalize on Pakistan's considerable strategic investment in Afghanistan. Shortly before his death, Zia appeared willing to scrap the whole basis of the civilianized martial law system. He was in a position to do this as, unlike both Ayub and Musharraf, he did not give up his post as Chief of Army Staff. He was also much more adept than Pakistan's other military rulers in wrongfooting opponents. Even detractors who regarded him as an intolerant and vindictive ruler admitted that he was in possession of considerable native cunning. His popularity with certain sections of the population was demonstrated by the huge crowds of mourners at his burial on 20 August 1988 at the Faisal Mosque in Islamabad.

Zia and Islamization

Islamization was the cornerstone of the Zia regime. It thrived within the regional context of the Afghan conflict and domestically drew strength from the rapid socio-economic changes of the later 1970s and the truncation of the state. Opinion remains divided as to whether it was a genuine product of Zia's Deobandi-influenced piety or a cynical ploy to acquire legitimization. In August 1983, the Advisory Council of Islamic Ideology conveniently pronounced that a presidential form of government was the 'nearest to Islam'. It was later to rule that political parties were non-Islamic. Whatever its motivation, it is clear that Zia saw Islamization as holding the key to Pakistan's decades-long search for stability and national unity. In one of his earliest pronouncements he declared that 'Pakistan, which was created in the name of Islam, will continue to survive only if it sticks to Islam. That is why I consider the introduction of an Islamic system as an essential prerequisite for the country'.[28] In May 1982, he maintained that the preservation of the country's ideological boundaries was as important for security as safeguarding its geographical boundaries.[29]

We have seen earlier that Pakistani Islam was not monochrome. The stark Deobandi approach contrasted with the colour and vitality of Sufi religious expression. Zia's Islamization increased tensions between these different expressions of faith. Significantly, Sufi shrines were at the forefront of the resistance to Zia in the 1983 revolt in Sindh. A crowd of 50,000 disciples of the Makhdum of Hala successfully blocked the national highway on one occasion. Even more damagingly, Zia's attempt to place Islam at the forefront of Pakistan's public life widened sectarian fissures. Contemporary Pakistan continues to suffer from the fruits of these divisions.

The *ulama* were no more united in their public pronouncements on Islam than at the time of the 1953 martial law in Lahore. They devoted much energy not only to sectarian disputes but to petty issues. Energies were expended in debates on whether blood transfusion and eye donation were against Islamic teachings. They also became preoccupied with attempts to impose dress codes on women and with unsuccessful appeals to the government to issue a martial law ordinance to make the wearing of beards compulsory.

Initially it was the lay activists of JI who were at the forefront of the Islamization process. The traditional *ulama* as represented in the JUI and JUP stood aloof from Zia's regime. The growing tensions between it and JI, however, encouraged Zia to co-opt the *ulama*. The Deobandi-influenced JUI for the first time began to adopt elements of Islamism to its increasingly 'neo-fundamentalist' world view. Farzana Shaikh has dubbed this process 'shariatization' and draws a sharp distinction between its attempt to establish the political hegemony of Islam and the desire to create an Islamic state.[30] While the former ideology is wedded to an Islamic universalism which could in given circumstances question the validity of the territorial state, the latter seeks to capture the state to Islamicize society, and in its more instrumentalist garbs sees Islamization as a useful tool to create a strong Pakistan state. The implications of these contrasting approaches were not fully evident in the Zia era. They are however exerting a profound influence in contemporary Pakistan where Taliban proponents of 'shariatization' are battling the state. As we shall see later, the radicalization of offshoots of JUI was intimately linked with Pakistan's ongoing involvement in Afghanistan and the army's attempt to use trans-national Islamic groups to achieve its strategic aims.

By 1983, a range of Islamization measures had been introduced covering the areas of judicial reform (the introduction of *shariat* courts); implementation of the Islamic Penal Code (Hudood Ordinances); economic activity (interest-free banking and Islamic taxes, *zakat* alms and *ushr* agricultural tax); and educational policy (emphasis on Urdu as the language of instruction, establishment of an Islamic University in Islamabad and state support for mosque schools). The latter was to possess the two far-reaching legacies of a politicized armed sectarian identity and a system of religious schools which has consistently evaded full state control. We shall turn first, however, to judicial reform.

(i) Judicial reform

It is important to note from the outset that the establishment of *shariat* courts not only alienated 'secular-minded' lawyers and generated confusing legal competing jurisdictions, but also ultimately disappointed the Islamist and *ulama* parties whom Zia had sought to co-opt in a '*mullah*-military' nexus. The *shariat* benches in the provincial High Courts were not only to apply new *shariat* laws, but to rule on whether existing laws were consistent with Islam or 'repugnant' to it. The great quantity of intricate petitions created a serious backlog. Some petitions were frivolous: the Shariat bench of the Sindh High

Court, for example, had to respond to a petition that women's hockey and cricket matches were repugnant to Islam because they allegedly violated *purdah* rules. The piecemeal construction of an Islamic judicial system created overlapping jurisdictions on the repugnancy issue between the Council for Islamic Ideology and the Federal Shariat Court which was established in 1980. In 1984 Qazi Courts, in which cases could be tried according to Islamic law, were added to a system which now encompassed federal and lower *shariat* courts, civil courts and summary military courts. The *ulama* complained because of the confused and tardy working of the courts, and the new system's limitations. The Council of Islamic Ideology had a strictly advisory role, while the Federal Shariat Court did not have the power to make a judicial review of Ayub's Muslim Family Laws Ordinance, which had been long condemned by them as un-Islamic in its character. The legal reforms also contributed to sectarian divisions, as the fact that no Shia judges were appointed to the Federal Shariat Court led the community to refuse to accept any of its judgements.

The greatest causes of Sunni-Shia conflict however arose from the economic reforms instituted by Zia which played out to a backdrop of increased Shia activism following the Iranian revolution.

(ii) Economic reform

The state's enforcement of Islamic taxes, which were previously offered as voluntary acts of piety, created bitter sectarian divisions. The Shias saw the Zakat Ordinance (designed to implement the obligatory Islamic alms tax) as part of an attempt to achieve the 'Sunnification' of Pakistan. The *Tehreek-i-Nifaz-i-Fiqh Jafria* (TNFJ, or Movement for the Implementation of Shia Law) was founded to oppose attempts to Islamicize Pakistan in keeping with Sunni jurisprudence. Shias did not object to *zakat* as a voluntary donation, but objected to the compulsory deduction of 2.5 per cent from all savings bank accounts and its distribution to Sunni charitable institutions. They staged a massive two-day protest in Islamabad in July 1980 which openly defied the martial law ban on public gatherings. Zia was forced to exempt them from paying the alms tax, but in response a number of Sunni extremists began to claim that Shias were non-Muslims. It was also from this time onwards that the Zia regime began to patronize Sunni *madaris* in order to contend with the Shia 'problem', both within the country and emanating from Iran. As one observer has noted, the growing numbers of state-funded *madaris* constructed in Balochistan and NWFP 'form a wall blocking Iran off from Pakistan'.[31]

The TNFJ was led from February 1984 onwards by Allama Arif Hussain, who had imbibed many of Khomeini's teachings while studying in seminaries in Iran and Iraq. Following his assassination in August 1988, a militant splinter group of TNFJ emerged. This group, *Sipah-i-Muhammad Pakistan* (SMP), became engaged in armed struggle with militant Sunni sectarian groups such as *Sipah-i-Sahaba Pakistan* (SSP) and the Sunni *Tehreek*. They received arms in the training camps set up in Pakistan for the *mujahadin* struggle against the Soviets in Afghanistan. In the aftermath of the Afghan War, they also had camps in the country in which to train and take sanctuary. There was a further splintering of militant Sunni sectarian forces with the emergence of the *Lashkar-e-Jhangvi* (LJ). Its activists were trained in Afghanistan by *Harkat-ul-Ansar* (HUA), a Deobandi anti-Shia group engaged in the Kashmir *jihad* and closely linked with Osama bin Laden. The interconnection between *jihadists* and Sunni extremists remains one of a number of doleful inheritances for contemporary Pakistan from the Zia years.

The introduction of the Zakat system not only created Sunni-Shia conflict over the legality and distribution of alms, but failed in the attempt to establish an Islamic welfare society. Only meagre amounts found their way to the 'deserving poor' and there were instances of corruption involving fake Zakat committees. Similarly the steps to encourage moral uplift through ordinances such as the Ramadan Ordinance which made eating, drinking and smoking in public a crime during the period of fasting, and the establishment of prayer wardens to persuade and inspire people to offer the five daily prayers, were not only open to abuse, but failed to achieve more than outward displays of piety.

(iii) Islamic Penal Code

Islamization failed to build a national consensus, because it enhanced sectarian divisions. It also sowed the seeds for 'an *ulama* wing of Islamism' which sought to influence the debate on national identity by redefining Pakistani nationalism primarily in terms of its relation to an imagined extra-territorial 'community of believers'.[32] Islamization also further deepened the divisions between the religious establishment and Pakistani liberals. Lawyers, human-rights activists and elite women were in the vanguard of the resistance to the punitive and discriminatory elements of Islamization. Non-Muslims, for example, were marginalized by the introduction of separate electorates and were increasingly vulnerable to charges of blasphemy. Amendment to the Pakistan Penal Code introduced by Presidential Ordinance made it a criminal offence for Ahmadis to 'pose' as Muslims and to use Islamic terminology or Muslim practices of worship. While separate electorates have been done away with, the latter legacy of Zia's Pakistan has encouraged militant Islamists to bring charges against Ahmadis for simply exercising their religious beliefs.

Elite women protested through the Women's Action Forum against the discrimination inherent in the Law of Evidence[33] and the Operation of the Hudood Ordinances.[34] The former not only undermined women's legal status, but denied them the equality of citizenship guaranteed by the Constitution. The latter made women who had been raped liable to Islamic punishment of whipping in a public place for adultery (*zina*). The Zina Ordinance was not only discriminatory, but was open to abuse in the form of nuisance suits against 'disobedient daughters' or 'estranged wives'. Women protesting outside the Lahore Court about the Law of Evidence were tear-gassed and *lathi*-charged by the police. The episode revealed the polarized views of religious conservatives and liberals. The *ulama* described the protest as an act of apostasy which challenged Quranic injunctions, while the Lahore High Court bar association condemned the 'barbarity' of the police. The Hudood Ordinances have not yet been repealed, a testament to the strengthened position of conservative attitudes as a result of the Zia era.

(iv) Educational reform

The most important educational legacy of the Zia era was the mushrooming of mosque schools. Many were financed out of *zakat* funds. They represented the only opportunity for schooling for poorer families in the wake of the failure of the state education system. The traditional prestige of studying in an Islamic institution was increased by Zia's decision to give degree-level status to their higher awards (*Darja-i-Alia*; *Darja-i-Alaimia*), not that the University Grants Commission had any control over their curriculum. By 1983–4 alone, over 12,000 were opened.[35] In 1947, there had been only around 250 mosque schools in the whole of Pakistan. As we have already noted, official support was given to the creation of some institutions to counter Shia activism. This encouraged the development of sectarianism, especially in the absence of an overarching curriculum. Many schools were loosely linked to the main Deobandi, Barelvi and *Ahl-e-hadith* Islamic traditions with which they were associated. Those funded from Saudi Arabia taught a mixture of Wahhabism and Deobandism. The proliferation of schools in areas of concentrated native Pushtun and Afghan refugee population encouraged a *jihadist* outlook to run strongly alongside sectarian attachments. Indeed Zia deliberately patronized some institutions in the context of advancing the Afghan *jihad*. The Taliban movement was to emerge later from this educational milieu with its radical 'neo-fundamentalist' outlook and trans-national commitments to *jihad*.

Most mosque schools did not of course provide military training in preparation for their students to go on *jihad*. A minority, attached to *Ahl-e-hadith* and JI, voluntarily provided elements of a modern curriculum alongside traditional Islamic teaching. Nevertheless, many of the students they turned out were ill-suited for careers other than within the burgeoning religious establishment. Cohen terms them as forming 'a class of religious lumpen proletariat'.[36]

While the mushrooming of the mosque schools was linked with the particular domestic and regional conditions of the Zia period, they have continued to grow in the intervening years. Western attention has been diverted to their functioning in the wake of 9/11. Some analysts are however coming to the view that videos, pamphlets and posters may be more important in encouraging radicalization than attendance at mosque schools. The latter's significance may lie more in their providing 'gathering places' where militants and potential recruits interact than in their educational indoctrination.

Western pressure on the Pakistan state to register *madaris* and control their curricula has met with a patchy response. Undoubtedly a small number are involved in the recruitment and training of militants. This connection was highlighted by the notorious Lal Masjid (Red Mosque) in Islamabad. This had to be seized by the army in Operation Silence in 2007 because the students of its two Islamic schools had sought through force to impose *shari'ah*. The mosque complex had been extended by Maulana Abdullah under Zia's patronage after he had agreed to recruit *mujahadin* for the Afghan *jihad*.

Zia also encouraged the development of the educational complex at Murdike near Gujranwala, run by the *Dawat-ul Irshad* (Centre for Preaching and Guidance). Its educational philosophy brought together the Islamic strands of *Tabligh* and *jihad* within the service of neo-fundamentalism.[37] This emphasized the requirement of a Muslim urge to a transformative power that rejected Western democracy while embracing science and technology. Perhaps unsurprisingly the *Dawat*'s key proponent of these ideas, Professor Hafiz Saeed, was a faculty member of the Engineering University, Lahore. Significantly he also came from an East Punjab refugee background which had seen 36 members of his extended family killed in the flight from India. The *Dawat-ul Irshad*, as we shall see in a later chapter, was to be linked in the decades after Zia's death with high-profile terrorist activities carried out in India by its militant offshoot, *Lashkar-e-Taiba* (LeT).

Zia also patronized the Deobandi Jamia-uloom-e-Islamia mosque at Binora in Karachi, which had been founded by a refugee from India, Maulana Yusuf Binori, shortly after independence. The red minareted mosque with its attached school now attracts students from all over the Islamic world and is the second largest Islamic educational establishment in Pakistan with around 8,000 pupils. Zia made its founder a member of the Council of Islamic Ideology and he chaired the organization in 1979. The mosque was at the forefront in mobilizing support for the Afghan *jihad*. Many of its former students were to become leading figures in *jihadist* organizations from the 1990s onwards. These included Maulana Masood Azhar, who was both a leading figure in *Harkat-ul-Ansar* and founder of *Jaish-e-Muhammad* (JeM), organizations which conducted terrorist activities in India and were closely associated with Osama bin Laden on his return to Afghanistan from Sudan at the beginning of 1996.

The Politics of Ethnicity in Zia's Pakistan

Zia's conception of Pakistan as an ideological state founded on Islam and culturally unified by Urdu exaggerated the longer-term homogenizing trends in state construction. Inevitably it was resisted by ethnic nationalists from the smaller provinces. Zia was however skilfully able to manage the situation in Balochistan and the North West Frontier Province, although Sindh proved irreconcilable.

Co-option in Balochistan involved the release of the 9,000 odd prisoners who had been incarcerated since the insurgency against Bhutto. While nationalist leaders such as Khair Bux Marri and Attaukllah Khan Mengel remained in exile, and continued to argue for independence and a Greater Balochistan, many *sardars* returned to their homes and re-entered the political mainstream through involvement with the Pakistan National Party. Zia also put the need for stability before dogma, by disassociating himself from the *ulama*-led *Tehreek Khatm-e Nabawat* (TKN, or Movement for the Finality of the Prophethood) which had been founded in 1978. It turned to the state to declare the minority Zikri population to be non-Muslims as well as seeking the implementation of *shariah* law in Balochistan.[38] Zia, unlike Bhutto with respect to the Ahmadi, stood firm against these demands, lending credence to some scholars' claims that he was not serious about the policy of Islamization, but merely wanted through it to secure legitimacy for his regime.

Co-option of the Pakhtun nationalists was vital to the ongoing Afghanistan conflict, but was also assisted by it. Pakhtuns were increasingly recruited into the army and the bureaucracy. By the end of the Zia era, Pakhtun representation in the army stood at around 20 per cent; even in the bureaucracy it was around 10 per cent. The elderly Pakhtun leader Abdul Ghaffar Khan was released and allowed to return to Afghanistan. His son Wali Khan was similarly released. The ANP stood aloof from the MRD agitation as it focused its energies on the struggle in Afghanistan. It was, however, to later protest that the NWFP had borne the brunt of the refugee costs and faced Soviet incursions and bombings, while Punjab had reaped Western economic and military aid. This sentiment was colourfully summed up when Wali Khan likened the 3 million Afghan refugees to a giant cow, with the Frontier holding its horns and the Punjab its teats.[39] Nonetheless, Pakhtun ethnicity was taking on an increasingly Islamic tinge, at the same time as Pakhtuns were securing increased representation in the Pakistan establishment. This was being accompanied at popular levels by economic engagement at a pan-Pakistan level, as Pakhtun labourers profited from the urban construction boom and the Paktun tightened their traditional grip on the transport sector of the economy. These developments help explain, along with the changing regional situation, the decline in irredentist attitudes. Ultimately the nationalist parties abandoned the demand for a separate 'Pakhtunistan' in favour 'of a province of "Pakhtunkhwa" to replace the North West Frontier Province'.[40]

Sindh, as we have seen earlier, did not send large numbers of labour migrants to the Gulf. It thus did not share in the remittance-fuelled prosperity. Army rule increased the traditional hostility to Punjabi domination, which was further intensified with the hanging of the first Sindhi Prime Minister of Pakistan in Rawalpindi jail. It was not surprising therefore that Sindh was at the forefront of the campaign against Zia launched by the disparate grouping of opposition parties which came together under the umbrella of the Movement for the Restoration of Democracy. The struggle intensified in 1983 with leadership being provided by the PPP and the peasant-based *Sindhi Awam Tehrik*. The insurrection secured the greatest support in the rural areas of Thatta, Dadu, Larkana and Sanghar. It was only quelled following the deployment of three army divisions backed up with helicopter gunships. Resistance continued, but was forced to take literary and cultural forms. Writers and poets like Rehmatullah Manjothi, Naseer Mirza, Tariq Alam, Niaz Hasmayooni[41] and Adal Soomro challenged Zia's ideological state. Atiya Dawood opposed the oppression of women in her writings. Mumtaz Bhutto raised the demand for a loose confederation in which Sindh would enjoy maximum autonomy. There were calls for complete independence.

The Zia era witnessed the emergence of a new *mohajir* ethnic political identity in Sindh. This was institutionalized in the MQM which was run from the outset by students who had been active from the late 1970s in APMSO. We have seen in earlier chapters how the *mohajirs* had become displaced from their dominant role in Pakistan by the Punjabi elites. We have also encountered the exacerbation of tensions between them and native Sindhis as a result of Bhutto's preferential politics. Despite this background, a number of writers have claimed that the ISI sponsored the MQM which emerged in March 1984 in order to weaken the PPP and MRD in Sindh.[42] Altaf Hussain, the dominant charismatic leader of MQM, has always vehemently denied these charges. Certainly, at its outset MQM allied itself with native Sindhis against Pushtun/Afghan, Baloch and Punjabi 'outsiders'. It is also clear that the 'partyless' elections of 1985 encouraged political mobilization along ethnic lines. In this context, it is understandable that MQM voiced the claim that *mohajirs* should be recognized as Pakistan's 'fifth nationality'.

The state's weak reach in a city which by the 1980s was awash with the drugs and weapons that had flooded Pakistan during the Afghan conflict is another factor in explaining the MQM's rise which owes nothing to the impact of the shadowy security services. The flows of drugs and arms were closely linked because the Afghan *mujahadin* financed weapon procurement through drug trafficking. Karachi was a vital hub for both flows. The MQM positioned itself as the *mohajirs*' protector in the wake of Pushtun/Afghan attacks on poorer *mohajir* localities in retaliation for the army and police raids on the Pushtun enclave of Sohrab Goth in December 1986. This north Karachi slum was an alleged haunt of the drug smuggling mafias. However, once MQM had gained hegemonic control over the *mohajir* communities and used this to run the local government in Karachi, the pattern of conflict shifted from a *mohajir*-Pushtun basis to a *mohajir*-Sindhi one. By the mid-1990s, *mohajir* gatherings were chanting, '*Sindh mein hoga kaise guzara, adha hamara adha tumhara*' ('How can we co-exist in Sindh? Half is ours, half is yours').[43] The mounting chaos in Pakistan's commercial heart may not have been the legacy of a Machiavellian divide and rule policy by Zia, but it was clearly the outcome of the politicization of ethnicity and socio-economic transformations which accompanied his rule.

Zia and the Army

Zia's political power was inevitably accompanied by the army's further expansion into the administrative and economic structures of Pakistan. The former reflected the perception that only the army possessed the capabilities to govern the country effectively. The latter was a corollary of state control as it freed both resources and any need for accountability.

It will be recalled that Ayub relied heavily on the bureaucracy to bolster his regime; Zia, however, ensured that it only played the role of a junior partner. He introduced a military preference in the federal quota recruitment system as well as providing senior officers with lucrative assignments in Pakistan's numerous corporations. General Fazle Raziq, for example, headed the Water and Power Development Authority. In the period 1980–5, 96 army officers were inducted into the Central Superior Services on a permanent basis, while another 115 were on temporary contracts.[44] Until Junejo was sworn in as Prime Minister, all the powerful provincial governors had been military men. This reflected both Zia's dismissive view of civilian competency and his need to provide a system of rewards to ensure the loyalty of his military powerbase. Senior appointments, not only in government departments and public services but in the welfare foundations, were at the discretion of the service chiefs. There were only isolated signs of disaffection, most notably at the time of an alleged plot to overthrow the government in 1985. Seven officers, all junior in rank, were convicted in July after their trial in camera before military courts.

Zia's survival instincts meant that, despite his personal piety, he did not make officers accountable for their financial dealings, but rather winked at corruption, by increasing their financial autonomy. Corps Commanders were, for example, allowed to operate secret regimental funds which had no auditing checks. The greatest potential for corruption however surrounded real estate development which the military moved into in a big way during the Zia era. Officers used the opportunity to acquire land cheaply for housing development and then sell it on at a profit.

The Milbus mushroomed as the welfare organizations of the army took on an increasing array of commercial activities. In 1977 and 1982 respectively, welfare organizations were founded for the Pakistan air force (Shaheen Foundation) and Pakistan navy (Bahria Foundation). They operated on a smaller scale than the Fauji Foundation and Army Welfare Trust but also developed a wide range of business activities. The Bahria Foundation ran everything from bakeries and travel agencies to its own university. The Shaheen Foundation in addition to its own airline was to move into the varied worlds of Pay TV, information technology and a knitwear factory.[45]

The senior welfare organization, the Fauji Foundation, moved into new areas of the economy such as fertilizer production, in which its first plant was set up in 1982; it also entered the oil and gas sectors of the economy, both in establishing companies and purchasing shareholdings in existing enterprises. Previously such businesses had been managed and directed by retired officers. Zia, however, introduced the practice of serving officers having extended employment in the welfare organizations and their subsidiaries. Major-General Rizvi, for example, was posted to head the Army Welfare Trust in 1984.[46] Neither serving nor retired officers possessed formal business training, but their expanded role was justified by the view that their military experience of personnel and logistical management was sufficient to equip them. Moreover, as Lieutenant-General (rtd) Mohammad Amjad claimed, 'If military officers can run the country, why can't they run business ventures? We are trained in management'.[47]

The army's entrenchment under Zia made the future consolidation of democracy much more difficult than it had even been in the Ayub era. For as the army's economic sphere expanded, it was increasingly less likely to tolerate civilian rule which might threaten this. Zia had ensured that the military's interests could be protected through the 8th Amendment to the 1973 Constitution, which gave the President the power to dissolve the National Assembly. He also toyed with the idea of institutionalizing the army's role at the heart of governance through the formation of a National Security Council. He eventually did not take up this option. This further consolidation of the military's influence was to await Pervez Musharraf's period of rule.

Zia and the Afghanistan Conflict

The Afghanistan conflict lies at the heart of many of the inheritances from the Zia regime. Indeed, without its existence it is debatable whether his rule would have been as prolonged. We have already noted the boost to his regime arising from US aid, and the favourable context the conflict created for his Islamization policies. This section aims to look in more depth at its strategic legacies and the weaponization of Pakistan which stemmed from the conflict

Like Ayub, Zia did not buy into the US Cold War approach to South Asia's geo-political situation. Rather he saw the US involvement in the region as a means to forward Pakistan's goals. India not the Soviet Union remained its main security threat. From June 1984 onwards there were bitter Indo-Pakistan military clashes in the remote Siachen glacier. Tensions were increased when India protested at the US sale of F-16 fighters to Islamabad as part of the Reagan aid package. They reached their height when the Indian army conducted a major military exercise codenamed Operation Brass Tacks on the Pakistan border during the winter of 1986–7.

Pakistan thus did not seek to defeat the 'Evil Empire' in Afghanistan, although it later took credit for the role it played in the demise of the Soviet Union. The primary goal in Afghanistan was to create a client state which would not only remove any lingering Indian influence and threat of Pakhtun irredentism, but secure 'strategic depth' in the event of a future war with India. In addition to providing a hypothetical bastion to which the Pakistan army could retreat, Afghanistan provided another potential training base, alongside those in Azad Kashmir, for preparing Islamic irregular forces for the covert war in Jammu and Kashmir. These goals persisted in the post-Zia decades. The Soviet collapse added the incentive of gaining economic access to the Central Asian Republics through Afghanistan. The Taliban regime in Afghanistan was to disappoint Islamabad's hopes of a compliant neighbour, while the aftermath of 9/11 presented the strategic nightmare of a resurgence of Indian influence in Afghanistan.

The US decision to use Islamic proxies against the Soviet occupying forces in Afghanistan put its strategic relationship with Pakistan at a premium. Pakistan was an important staging ground for the training of the *mujahadin*. The CIA worked closely with ISI, through the National Logistics Cell, in the supply of weapons.[48] The ISI greatly expanded its influence and capabilities[49] as a result of the Afghan conflict. Indeed some writers even speculated as to whether it developed capabilities for independent actions from the army in pursuit of strategic goals. This belief seemed to be justified by the fugitive Osama bin Laden's continued residence in Abbottabad. Another legacy of the US strategy which was to have long-term consequences not only for Pakistan but for the international community was the portrayal of the Afghan struggle as a *jihad*. This secured support from Egypt and Saudi Arabia. It also brought thousands of *mujahadin* from all parts of the world to join the conflict. One estimate puts the number of 'foreigners' involved in the Afghan fighting at 35,000, drawn from 40 countries.[50] They were of course outnumbered as fighters nearly 3:1 by Afghan and Pakistani *madrasa* students. But many remained in the region after the Soviet withdrawal and became involved in Islamist causes. Arabs predominated in the overseas contingents and wielded influence because of their wealth. Many leading figures in Al-Qaeda such as Sheikh Taseer Abdullah, Ayman al-Zawahiri, Sheikh Omar Abdur Rahman, Sheikh Abdullah Aziz and Osama bin Laden were involved in the Afghan *jihad*. Osama bin Laden also spent time in Pakistan raising recruits and support for the Afghan *jihad* from an office he ran in Peshawar from 1980. He forged links with militant groups which were later to join the 'International Islamic Front for Jihad Against US and Israel' which he founded in May 1998. Osama bin Laden's closest ties were with the Binora mosque and the *Dawat-ul Irshad* at Murdike, both of which were patronized by Zia. It is claimed that Osama bin Laden provided financial support for the building of a guest house at Murdike in which he stayed whenever he visited the complex. He also visited the Binora mosque at Karachi to recruit *mujahadin*. Its head, Mufti Nizamuddin Shamzai, arranged a meeting there between him and the future Taliban ruler of Afghanistan, Mullah Omar.

Zia sought to forward Pakistan's interests in Afghanistan in a number of ways. Weapons were supplied to the Afghan *mujahadin* in a carefully controlled manner, firstly to those groups which seemed most likely to be sympathetic to Pakistan's future interests in the country. This policy was to be repeated in the proxy war fought by Pakistan in Kashmir a decade later. Pakistan's most favoured *mujahadin* leader was Gulbuddin Hekmatyar, whose Hizb-e-Islami organization was closely allied with JI. The Pushtun JI leader Qazi Hussain Ahmed acted as a link between the Zia regime and Hekmatyar. It was only after Hekmatyar's failure to capture Kabul in the post-Soviet civil war that militant groups associated with Deobandi Islam found full favour with ISI, leading to the rise of the Taliban in Afghanistan. However, the army had never during the Afghan conflict confined itself to JI-affiliated Islamic protégés. Along with the CIA it had supported the Deobandi-linked *Harkat-ul Jihad al-Islami* (HUJI) and *Harkat-ul-Mujahadin* (HUM). HUJI had been founded by students from the influential Binora mosque in 1979; HUM splintered off six years later. As we shall see in a later chapter, the two groups were to come together in 1993 to form *Harkat-ul-Ansar* (HUA) which was not only closely associated with sectarian organizations such as SSP and LJ, but with Osama bin Laden.

The Zia regime's calibrated support to *mujahadin* groups was a factor in the leakage of weapons which gave birth to the Kalashnikov culture. Weapons were also sold to the highest bidders by ISI and some of the *mujahadin*. A possible explanation for the massive explosion at the Ohjri camp midway between Islamabad and Rawalpindi on 10 April 1988 is the ISI attempt to cover up the weapons leakage from US auditors.[51] A further weapons leakage which was to have long-term repercussions occurred following the Soviet withdrawal. As Yunas Samad has noted:

> Vast quantities of weapons including light weaponry as well as anti-tank guns and artillery pieces were stockpiled and put up for sale in the Federally Admin-

istered Tribal areas (FATA) particularly in those regions which were adjacent to territory controlled by the Mujahideen.[52]

Pakistan's Frontier region had always been a centre for weapons production and sale. But the availability of especially heavy weapons in its arms bazaars following the Afghan conflict was unprecedented. Islamic militants, drug mafias, ethnic groups and even the student wings of political parties were able to arm themselves as never before. The ready availability of arms helps explain the violence which marked life in such cities as Karachi in the decade following Zia's death.

Significantly, signs of the US desire to disengage rapidly from Afghanistan generated tensions between Zia and Junejo. Even before the latter signed the Geneva Accords in April 1988 which facilitated the Soviet withdrawal, the US was attempting to develop alternative channels of communication to the army. Junejo's role in the Geneva Accords precipitated his removal by Zia. He had also had the temerity to question the military elite's import of expensive cars, when they could use locally assembled Suzukis.[53] A longer-term consequence of the ending of the Afghan conflict was the civil war within the country itself and the existence of large numbers of battle-hardened Islamic veterans with no role to play. The Pakistan state's answers to these issues, in the creation of the Taliban and the switching of Islamic fighters from the Afghan to the Kashmir *jihad*, were to have unpredictable consequences.

Conclusion

Zia attempted to resolve Pakistan's long-standing quest for stability by means of Islamization and depoliticization. The result was mounting sectarian violence and increased ethnic conflict, both of which were to assume major proportions in the decade following his death. Zia's rule also further widened the divide between Western-educated elites and the mass of the population, with potentially destabilizing consequences. Military rule also exacerbated tensions between the smaller provinces and Punjab. Long-term ethnic opposition to the perceived Punjabi-dominated state in Balochistan and Sindh was not deflected by Islamization. In the Frontier, however, in the context of the Afghan War, the circumstances had been created for a Pakthun-Muslim communal identity to be gradually replaced by a Pakhtun-Islamic one.

Pakistan's praetorian state was undoubtedly enhanced by Zia's rule. The army entrenched itself still further into administration and business activities. The ISI greatly increased its capabilities and scope for autonomy. Zia established closer links than ever before between the army and Islamic parties, although disillusionment was to set in on behalf of JI. Civil society was exposed to the depredations of censorship, prayer wardens and public floggings. Where co-option failed, as in Sindh, brute force was deployed. Zia was never able, however, to crush completely the main focus of political dissent, the PPP; nor to entirely stifle civil society, as witnessed for example in the activities of the Women's Action Forum. This meant that future democratization was possible, albeit enfeebled.

The doleful inheritances of the Zia regime have long been acknowledged to include the flood of drugs and weapons into Pakistan and its impetus to bigotry and brutalising violence. With hindsight, it is becoming clearer that the most dangerous inheritance arose from the measures that Zia's regime took to counter India's regional hegemony. These included the stepping up of efforts begun in the Bhutto era to acquire nuclear weapons and the expansion of the even earlier Pakistan policy of utilizing Islamic extremists as 'strategic assets' in the enduring rivalry with India.

These developments were greatly assisted by the US need for the frontline Pakistan state's support in the struggle against the Soviet occupation of Afghanistan. Washington turned a blind eye to Pakistan's pursuit of its nuclear weapons programme. The CIA worked closely with ISI to organize, train and supply the Afghan *jihad*. Zia was more concerned about stealing a march over India in Afghanistan than in confronting the Soviet threat. The civil war which followed the Soviet withdrawal pointed to the fact that the Islamic irregulars might not be as easily manipulated for Pakistan's interests as the army had anticipated. The attempt to secure a protectorate in Afghanistan and to use *jihadists* in Kashmir nonetheless continued apace in the decade which followed Zia's death. Its cost was mounting tension with the US, rising sectarian violence in Pakistan and conflict between the subcontinent's two nuclear armed powers. The seeds were also being sown for Islamic extremists to turn their weapons on their erstwhile ISI and army patrons, although the bitter harvest would only be reaped following the dramatic developments of 9/11.

6

PAKISTAN'S DEMOCRATIC INTERLUDE 1988–99

The transition to democracy following Zia's death raised hopes that Pakistan would enter a new era with the beginnings of a modern party system, the addressing of long-standing social inequalities and the ending of the centre-state problems which had beset the country. The advent of Benazir Bhutto as Pakistan's youngest and first female Prime Minister also raised the possibility that gender inequalities would be addressed and Pakistan would move towards becoming a progressive and tolerant Muslim society. Such hopes were to be cruelly dashed. The alternation of Benazir Bhutto and Nawaz Sharif in office was marked by political infighting, financial scandals, limited legislative enactment and economic failure. Poverty increased as the result of sluggish growth, despite Nawaz Sharif's attempt to liberalize the economy. Democratic consolidation stalled. Where did it all go wrong? Why did civilian rule make no difference to the country's long-standing problems? Was the burden of history too great?

Looking back on this period, which he dubbed a 'sham democracy', Pervez Musharraf provided a deceptively easy answer. It was all the politicians' fault. They had plundered the country and brought it to its knees through a combination of corruption, maladministration and irresponsibility. There was nothing new here in a military ruler blaming the politicians for the chaos which required the corrective of army intervention. Such attitudes are embedded in the officer class. Major-General Rashid Qureshi, the first Director-General of Inter-Services

Public Relations for Musharraf, maintained that military officers were better qualified and more intelligent than the average civil servant and definitely more effective than a politician.[1]

Liberals argued to the contrary, that democracy had failed because of the burden of history. Pakistan's long-standing problems had been intensified by Zia. He had bequeathed a legacy of intolerance, bigotry and division which had proved difficult to remove. Supporters of the PPP went even further than this and maintained that the army through the ISI had deliberately consolidated anti-Bhutto forces in the *Islami Jumhoori Ittehad* (IJI or Islamic Democratic Alliance) alliance led by Nawaz Sharif in order effectively to block a transformatory political agenda.

This chapter will seek to uncover the workings of democracy from 1988. It will consider what differences it made to Pakistan's long-standing problems and the circumstances in which consolidation failed to occur. While accepting the truth in the burden of historical argument, it will also maintain that the leaders of this period made life more difficult for themselves, sometimes falling into the traps laid by the anti-democratic forces and even conniving with them to further personal agendas.[2] They also displayed an alarming readiness to stifle civil society if it suited and to challenge the independence of the legal system. We shall turn first to Benazir Bhutto's and Nawaz Sharif's failures to address the issue of party institutionalization, before examining the circumstances of the 'constitutional coups' which terminated their periods in office. The chapter will then consider the differences that democratic rule brought to centre-state relations, military entrenchment and relations with India. We will conclude with an assessment of the worsening tide of sectarian violence and the rise of militant challenges to the Pakistan state as the effects of using Islamic proxies could not be contained.

The Problem of Institutionalization

This text has argued that weak political institutionalization has been a major impediment to democratic consolidation in Pakistan. Leaders have preferred to rely on personal charisma and patronage networks to mobilize support. Mass political mobilizations have not been institutionalized; politics revolve around personalities and patronage, not ideas and institutions. This state of affairs continued in the 1990s.

Just like her father, Benazir undermined the PPP's development by regarding it as an extension of her own persona. After her triumphant return to Pakistan in April 1986 she had replaced old-guard members such as Mumtaz Ali Bhutto, Abdul Hafeez Pirzada and Ghulam Mustafa Jatoi with newcomers who were loyal to her rather than the party. Jatoi was so embittered that he formed his own National People's Party, which was a component member of the IJI which opposed the PPP in the 1988 elections. Asif Ali Zardari was to receive much blame for Benazir's estrangement from the PPP old-guard activists, but even before her marriage she displayed little interest in strengthening and democratizing the PPP as part of her wider crusade for democratization of Pakistan's politics.

The IJI never effectively transformed itself into a modern political organization. It had no central secretariat, or internal elections. Its main component, Nawaz Sharif's faction of the Muslim League, was similarly weakly institutionalized. Indeed, one advantage he possessed over Benazir was that he was more adept at the old-style factional politics. He took advantage of the 1988 election defeat defeat of the Pakistan Muslim League President, Muhammad Khan Junejo, increasingly to sideline the Junejo wing of the party and make his own faction dominant. This type of manoeuvring had been the hallmark of the Punjab's politics since independence and of the various Muslim League incarnations. While it is true that the Nawaz faction brought a greater urban and middle-class presence into the Muslim League than ever before, it was still precariously balanced around the personality and power of Nawaz himself. The pro-Junejo faction sided with Nawaz Sharif's opponents in the 1993 crisis and Manzoor Ahmad Wattoo, the Speaker of the Punjab Assembly, briefly unseated Nawaz's Chief Minister Ghulam Hyder Wyne. This was but a foretaste of the large-scale desertion of the PML(N) following Musharraf's October 1999 coup.

Both Benazir and Nawaz in the 1990s not only abjured the opportunity to strengthen party democracy, but detrimentally politicized state institutions. This was seen most clearly in their attempts to 'pack' the High Courts with party loyalists. When the Supreme Court in March 1996 sought to curtail this practice, Benazir Bhutto became embroiled in a dispute with President Farooq Leghari over its implementation. Eighteen months earlier, she had appointed 13 PPP activists to the Lahore High Court, some of whom had a dubious professional standing. In August 1997, Nawaz Sharif clashed with the Chief Justice,

Sajjad Ali Shah, over the filling of vacant positions in the Supreme Court. In its aftermath he was to become involved in contempt of court proceedings. The unedifying spectacle ensued of troops having to be deployed to ensure the security of the Supreme Court, which was stormed by the Prime Minister's supporters. When Leghari refused to install a new Chief Justice, Nawaz Sharif threatened him with impeachment. In 1993, the army had supported President Ghulam Ishaq Khan when he crossed swords with Nawaz Sharif, but on this occasion it remained aloof as it did not want further turmoil so soon after the 1997 elections. Leghari resigned on 2 December enabling Nawaz Sharif to install Muhammad Rafiq Tarar, who had close ties with his father, as President on the first day of 1998. Even before this, the acting President, Wasim Sajjad, had eased out Chief Justice Sajjad Ali Shah. While this was a victory in Nawaz Sharif's personal quest for power, it was a further blow to Pakistan's democratic development.

Democracy and Authoritarianism

Presidential power was used on three occasions during the 1990s to unseat elected Prime Ministers. Benazir Bhutto was twice unseated in this way (1990, 1997) and Nawaz Sharif on one occasion (1993). Executive action was justified in terms of the sitting Prime Minister's failure to discharge legal functions and to maintain law and order. The old standby of corruption charges was also levelled. Each dismissal was followed by a caretaker government in advance of elections which the deposed party claimed were rigged. In 1991, for example, the PPP published its own White Paper entitled 'How An Election Was Stolen'. The 1993 dismissal of Nawaz Sharif was different from the others in that it was accompanied by a full-blown constitutional crisis which saw both President and Prime Minister step down. While President Ghulam Ishaq Khan's close links with the military help to explain his actions in 1990 and 1993, Farooq Leghari's removal of Benazir Bhutto in 1997 was unexpected as he was her appointee and originally seen as a PPP loyalist. Prior to his success in the 1993 presidential election, Leghari had promised that he would be 'neutral and non-interventionist' and it seemed likely that Benazir Bhutto might become the first Prime Minister since 1985 to see through a full term in office. She was greatly shocked by her dismissal, which Leghari had undertaken secure in the knowledge that he had the army's approval.[3]

Nawaz Sharif drew the lesson from his painful experience in 1993 that presidential power should be clipped. He used his crushing victory in the 1997 elections to remove the Eighth Amendment to the Constitution. His attempt to accrue power was seen by opponents, however, as being motivated by the desire to establish an elective dictatorship, rather than to strengthen parliamentary sovereignty. Without the Eighth Amendment, the army's preferred option of a 'constitutional coup' was unavailable, so direct military intervention was required to unseat the Prime Minister in October 1999, who although a former protégé of Zia was now seen as dangerously seeking to interfere in the army's affairs.

In addition to the presidency, the army's political leverage could be exercised through the Council of Defence and National Security (CDNS). The idea that the army should formally share decision-making with politicians dated back to Zia's proposal for a National Security Council. The caretaker Prime Minister Meraj Khalid, following Benazir Bhutto's second dismissal in 1997, established the CDNS as an advisory body which could be disbanded by an incoming elected government. Significantly it was to be headed and convened by the President rather than the Prime Minister. The CDNS was opposed by JI as part of a wider 'Washington Plan' to impose the hegemony of the IMF and the World Bank and to cut Islamic movements down to size.[4] It undoubtedly institutionalized the arrangements known as the 'troika' in which power had been shared since 1988 between the President, Chief of Army Staff and Prime Minister, with the latter frequently in a junior role. Looked at in a longer-term perspective, the CDNS appeared as an updated version of Pakistan's viceregal tradition. Significantly, while all three service chiefs sat in its meetings, provincial prime ministers were excluded. When Nawaz Sharif resumed residence of the Prime Minister's house in February 1997, he expressed his distaste for the CDNS by failing to convene a formal meeting. This set the tone for growing tensions with the army's top brass, which culminated in his ouster less than 30 months later. His nemesis Pervez Musharraf resurrected the idea of providing a formal role for the military at the heart of political decision-making.

Accountability was another method by which the army sought to exert influence. We have seen in earlier chapters how, throughout Pakistan's history, discourses of corruption have been used by military rulers in a one-sided manner to control political opponents. They could be formally disqualified, or involved in lengthy legal cases which sapped their energies and discredited them with voters. Corruption regularly featured on the charge sheets when presidents dismissed Benazir Bhutto and Nawaz Sharif. They denied these allegations and maintained that they were politically motivated. But the image of corruption which surrounded in particular Benazir Bhutto's spouse Asif Ali Zardari caused long-term damage to his reputation. It is impossible to resolve the controversies surrounding corruption. Was it a case of the military allowing one set of corrupt politicians to replace another, so long as its basic interests were unchallenged, or did it manufacture the charges from the outset?

Certainly the way politics was conducted in Pakistan meant that its practitioners were open to charges of corruption. Neither Nawaz Sharif nor Benazir Bhutto, as we have seen, replaced the traditional patron-client approach to politics with strongly institutionalized party structures. Indeed just like the Muslim League before the vital 1946 elections, Benazir Bhutto had awarded tickets in 1988 to opportunist latecomers who had joined the party when it looked like the winning horse.[5] Nor did the PPP and Muslim League leaders discourage the view amongst parliamentarians that their purpose was to reward voters through acquiring development funds for their constituencies, rather than to scrutinize and pass legislation. The traditional recourse to rule by ordinance continued throughout this period. Even Benazir's sympathizers acknowledged that her 1988–90 ministry had failed to enact legislation. Most damaging of all was the continued use of credit facility from the nationalized banks to buy support in the assemblies. The scale of these financial irregularities was finally revealed in August 1993 when the caretaker government of Moeen Qureshi published a list of over 5,000 defaulters and beneficiaries of written-off loans. A total of some Rs 62 billion was involved, revealing the ease of access to bank loans for the well-connected. In another blow to the image of politics, Qureshi prepared a list, apparently with CIA help, which disclosed the names of prominent politicians who had been involved in drug dealing.[6]

Given the army's entrenchment in the Zia period, it would have been difficult even for 'clean' civilian governments to haul back its influence. Progress might have been made if there had been greater cooperation between governments and opposition. Mushahid Hussain, a former Nawaz loyalist who became prominent in the pro-Musharraf PML(Q), maintained for example that:

The politicians on both sides of the divide have again demonstrated their inability to rise beyond partisan considerations. Only when they are told to 'behave' by the men in 'khaki' do they 'fall in line' and it would have been better for their own image that such moves for reconciliation should have been initiated on their own accord rather than being pushed from above.[7]

When in power both leaders had used authoritarian measures to weaken opponents, while those out of office turned to the establishment as an equalizer. It seems as if no lessons had been learned from the democratic failures of the 1950s. Power was sought to reward supporters and to punish rivals, not to address Pakistan's long-standing structural problems. During Benazir Bhutto's first administration, Nawaz Sharif and other opposition figures were facing as many as 160 cases involving such issues as tax evasion and loan default. At one point, Pakistan railways also failed to deliver raw materials to the Ittefaq foundries in Lahore, on the pretext that they had insufficient wagons.[8] While enemies were inconvenienced, Benazir Bhutto during her first term in office sought to reward PPP supporters who had suffered during the bleak Zia years.[9] When Nawaz Sharif came to power in 1990, the boot was on the other foot. He studiously diverted developmental funds to his heartland of support in central Punjab. Benazir Bhutto faced charges relating to the misuse of secret service funds. The long run of cases against Asif Ali Zardari began shortly after the PPP was out of power. He was initially charged with fraudulently obtaining a bank loan; more seriously in May 1991 he was charged with the murder of political opponents.

Benazir could argue that such 'trumped up' charges made it impossible to act as a loyal opposition leader, especially as the Minister for Religious Affairs also termed her a '*kafir*' and Jam Sadiq Ali, the Prime Minister's principal Sindhi ally, called her a 'terrorist'. Nevertheless her action in 1993 in secretly meeting Ghulam Ishaq Khan and promising that if she was Prime Minister she would support his bid for a second term as President was inexcusable for a self-proclaimed democrat.

Each 'constitutional coup' was preceded by an elected leader's infringement of the army's interests. Opponents did not spring to their support, both because of the intense rivalries and because assertions of civilian authority were regarded as merely efforts at personal aggrandisement. Failure to address popular economic concerns also meant that there was no groundswell of support to restructure the civil-military relationship. Benazir Bhutto and Nawaz Sharif were partisan figures, rather than symbols of democratic struggle, although Bhutto had once held that role on her return to Pakistan. None of the elected governments that were dismissed by either constitutional coups or direct military action were loved throughout Pakistan. Their demise was taken as calmly as Zia's coup against Zulfiqar Ali Bhutto.

(i) Benazir Bhutto's fall from grace

Akhund Iqbal, who was Adviser on National Security and Foreign Affairs in Benazir's first ministry, has criticized her for taking office in 1988 in the knowledge that she would have to compromise with the establishment on key issues such as the defence budget, foreign policy and security matters. 'It resulted not in reconciliation', he maintains, 'but in giving the Establishment time to plot Benazir's downfall at its leisure and meanwhile to strew her path with thorns and brambles and lay around her booby-traps of all kinds'.[10] He rightly points out that from the outset her government was focused on survival, rather than on achieving its own programme of measures. The resulting drift was exacerbated by its lack of a clear vision, having jettisoned the populist outlook of the PPP's founding period. Even without a clear socio-economic agenda, progress might have been made with respect to strengthening institutions and respect for the rule of law which would have forwarded the progress of democracy. Instead of this, according to observers, Benazir became preoccupied in bickering with both the President and the IJI, her resistance to these opponents often taking on a 'rancorous' and petty character.[11] Her approach to the establishment of greater civilian control over the security agencies was 'equivocal'. She appointed a committee headed by retired Air Chief Marshal Zulfiqar Ali Khan to report on this matter, but shelved its report: 'She was of course well aware of what the "agencies" could do to her, but she may also have been tempted by the thought of what they might do *for* her'.[12]

According to Ayesha Siddiqa, Benazir's problems with the army began when she replaced Lieutenant-General Hameed Gul as head of ISI with her own appointee, retired Major-General Shamsul Rehman Kallu.[13] Gul had been responsible for directing the operations of the Afghan *mujahadin*. Iqbal Akhund, however, perhaps because he had recommended the change, maintains that when 'all was said and done, it was a routine matter, the transfer of an army officer from one important post to another' (Corps Commander Multan).[14] He does acknowledge, however, that the Army Chief Aslam Beg privately remarked that democracy was surviving 'thanks to the grace and favour' of the army.[15] Beg was to admit after his retirement that he had obtained 140 million rupees which were to be used by the ISI to support anti-PPP candidates in the 1990 elections. Akhund recalls that Benazir adopted a 'pragmatic' approach to the army. This was accompanied by an element of fatalism, along with attempts both to ingratiate herself and artfully to 'interfere' with its interests. She attempted, for example, to influence the army's selection board to extend the term of Lieutenant-General Alam Jan Mehsud, who was the Lahore Corps Commander. Significantly, following this endeavour to trespass on the army's professional domain, the Corps Commanders informed Ghulam Ishaq Khan of their dissatisfaction with the Bhutto government.[16] Benazir Bhutto was in a vulnerable position because of the mounting ethnic violence in Sindh. Within a month, she had been dismissed from office.

(ii) The removal of Nawaz Sharif's first ministry

It might have been expected, given his pro-establishment background and conservatism, that Nawaz Sharif would not have fallen foul of the army. He became estranged firstly because of differences of opinion with the Chief of Army Staff General Aslam Beg over the Gulf War, and secondly because of disagreements over the army's May 1992 intervention in Sindh which had been launched over his head. The caretaker administration of Ghulam Mustafa Jatoi following Benazir's ouster had linked Pakistan with the anti-Iraq coalition by despatching 11,000 troops to Saudi Arabia to guard the holy places of Islam. Beg however openly questioned the Foreign Office's pro-Western line to the backdrop of public sympathy for Saddam Hussein. The JI, the second largest component of the IJI coalition, along with JUP orchestrated these protests which took out Iraqi flags, photographs of Saddam Hussein and dummy scud missiles. American flags and effigies of President Bush were burned. Indicative of the growing support amongst some sections of the population for international *jihad* was the registration of thousands of volunteers to fight the Coalition forces by the *Anjuman-i-Tuleba-i-Islam*.[17] By the close of Nawaz Sharif's time in office, ties with Washington had reached an all-time low. In January 1993, Pakistan was placed on the watch-list of potential terrorist states for six months. The following August Pakistan faced US trade sanctions along with China for an alleged violation of the Missile Technology Control regime following the supply of M-11 missiles.[18]

The disagreement between the Prime Minister and his generals over Sindh was, however, even more damaging. The pretext for the army's launching of Operation Clean-Up in May 1992 was lawlessness in the interior of the province and factional violence in Karachi, following a split in the MQM. Nawaz Sharif was nonetheless unhappy about the army's intervention, which was directed against his MQM coalition partner. By this juncture Nawaz's grip on power was weakening following JI's departure from his government. His position was also undermined by continuous confrontation with the PPP-led PDA coalition and charges of financial mismanagement arising from the collapse of cooperative societies in Punjab.[19] As Stephen Cohen has astutely pointed out, Nawaz Sharif's rapid privatization programme may also have upset the military because it increased commercial competition to the detriment of the established interests of its powerful Foundations.[20] Nawaz ran into further difficulties when he differed with the President over the choice of army chief in January 1993. Ghulam Ishaq Khan had taken as a personal insult the Prime Minister's silence on the matter of his re-election. He removed Nawaz Sharif on charges of corruption, nepotism and maladministration. A former Muslim League loyalist, Balkh Sher Mazari, led a caretaker government which included Asif Ali Zardari, who had shortly before been released on bail after two years in prison.

Unlike Bhutto or Junejo before him, Nawaz Sharif challenged his dismissal by presidential fiat. This not only created a constitutional crisis, but raised his political stock from 'cowardly businessman' to 'fighter politician'. In an act of judicial independence which echoed the activism of the late Musharraf era, the Supreme Court supported Nawaz Sharif's petition against his government's dismissal. The struggle between President and Prime Minister now shifted to the Punjab Assembly. Ultimately, however, it was to be the army rather than democracy which emerged triumphant from this crisis. Following an emergency meeting of the powerful corps commanders, the pressure mounted on Nawaz Sharif. The army's formula at first appeared to be the calling of mid-term polls. On 18 July, however, the Chief of Army Staff brokered a deal in which both the warring President and Prime Minister stepped down. Moeen Qureshi became the caretaker Prime Minister, while the Senate Chairman Wasim Sajjad became acting President.

(iii) Benazir Bhutto's second dismissal

Benazir Bhutto appeared in a much stronger position when she took office in 1993 than had been the case five years earlier. The eclipse of the PML(N) in the National Assembly and Provincial Assembly polls which took place on 6 and 8 October meant that Punjab was no longer an alternative centre of power.[21] The new President was a PPP loyalist rather than a bureaucratic remnant of the Zia era. Indeed, Benazir's husband, Asif Ali Zardari, had lobbied hard for Farooq Leghari to take up residence in the Aiwan-e-Sadr presidential house in Islamabad. Benazir's standing in Washington also served her well as it earned her kudos with the generals who wanted a resumption of military aid. Nawaz Sharif was to jeopardize these hopes when he publicly stated on 23 August 1994 that Pakistan possessed nuclear weapons. Effective lobbying in Washington in 1995 ensured however that the Pressler Amendment of August 1990 was waived. This had cut off aid and halted arms sales until Pakistan agreed to a verifiable capping of its nuclear programme. Nonetheless, Bhutto soon found herself under familiar pressures.

Patronage politics remained the order of the day. This opened up charges of corruption which were soon swirling around Benazir's spouse who had been inducted into the government. He earned the nickname 'Mr 10 per cent' for his alleged liking for 'kick-backs' in awarding commercial contracts. The government continued to rely on ordinances, rather than legislation, to put through its programme. Those who had suffered during the Zia era were disquieted to see Benazir's elevation of his associates. In June 1995, for example, she appointed Lieutenant-General (retd) Raja Muhammad Saroop Khan as Governor of the Punjab. Old-style PPP activists increasingly turned to Benazir's brother, Mir Murtaza Bhutto, as an alternative leader. Murtaza had returned from exile in Damascus in November 1993 and was seen as a radical-style figure more in tune with the PPP's early days. The struggle between siblings to appropriate Zulfiqar Ali Bhutto's charisma caused a painful split between Benazir and her mother Nusrat, who was dislodged from her long-standing role as co-chair of the PPP early in December 1993. Murtaza's death in a police encounter outside the new Clifton Gardens in Karachi on the evening of 20 September 1996 sent the rumour mill into overdrive.[22] Zardari was claimed by some to be behind the episode. An emotional Benazir claimed that

Murtaza was murdered in a conspiracy aimed at eliminating the Bhutto family, and widened the breach between herself and Leghari by appearing to implicate him.

By 1996 the PPP faced growing economic problems. Debt had accumulated in Zia's last years in office, while GDP rates slumped. Taxation continued to fall on the middle classes, whilst large landowners like the Bhuttos themselves paid virtually nothing in agricultural taxes. These structural problems had been hidden during the years of US aid to Pakistan as a 'front-line state'. In simple terms the country was living beyond its means. Benazir's government found it impossible to meet the financial targets to ensure a second tranche of IMF funding. Following the IMF withdrawal, the government announced a one-year moratorium on further economic reforms. But by the close of Benazir's rule it had to go back to the IMF cap in hand for assistance. The result was even more stringent conditionalities. The government's political constraints hindered its ability both to raise taxes and to meet the expectations of its poorer supporters. While public budgets generally were cut, defence expenditure remained inviolate and opaque.

In one respect, Benazir vigorously pursued the establishment's agenda: that of utilizing Islamic proxies to secure strategic goals in Afghanistan. Indeed, it was during her time in office that the Taliban were formed and instructed by the army and ISI. Benazir used her father's expert on Afghan affairs, Naseerullah Babar, to pursue this policy. It was also useful that the JUI(F) formed part of her coalition and that she had close ties with its leader, Maulana Fazlur Rahman, as this gave access to the network of Deobandi mosques in NWFP and Balochistan from which the Taliban could be recruited. The ISI's role in training and organizing Taliban recruits was invariably denied to Western audiences, where Benazir presented herself as the face of a secular and moderate Pakistan.

Despite her pursuit of the army's regional security interests, memories of her father meant that Benazir was at best tolerated by the military establishment and always remained an outsider. Some writers argue that when it became clear that her 'charm offensive' with Washington had failed to secure the requisite military replenishment, she was quickly deemed expendable.[23] In addition to the corruption claims and the country's faltering economic situation, Benazir Bhutto was also vulnerable because of the deteriorating law and order situation. In Karachi, the commercial heartbeat of the country, a virtual mini-insurgency was underway. There was also growing sectarian violence in the city which was a 'blowback' of the state's continued cultivation of Sunni militants to pursue its strategic goals. The mounting list of government 'misdemeanours' provided a ready-made justification for a further 'constitutional coup'. It was only the timing that was in question. Benazir was in fact dismissed on the eve of the US presidential elections, probably to ensure that her diminishing supporters in Washington were suitably distracted. The Daughter of the East once more fell from grace as an unlamented figure. In addition to the usual charges of corruption, Benazir was dismissed because of the prospect of 'imminent economic collapse', for attempting to destroy the independence of the judiciary and for the responsibility of 'extra-judicial' killings in Sindh. The self-proclaimed public face of Pakistan's drive for democracy had again failed to advance its cause. It was Nawaz Sharif's turn to hold office once more. His removal of the Eighth Amendment to the Constitution meant, however, that the days of 'constitutional coups' were over.

Civilian Rule and Milbus

All the elected governments from 1988 onwards singularly failed to address the military's entrenched economic position, or defence budgetary allocations. Indeed Benazir Bhutto resisted strong pressure from both the IMF and World Bank with respect to the latter. Just as in her father's time, democratic rule did not mean a reversal of the priority status for defence expenditures. These fell by just 0.3 per cent of GDP during her second government. At its close, defence expenditure stood at 5.6 per cent of GDP. The equivalent figures for health and education were 0.8 and 2.4 per cent respectively.[24]

The only token effort to curtail the army's business empire came in 1999 when Nawaz Sharif suggested the restructuring of the Army Welfare Trust. He had earlier bailed it out of economic difficulties, just as Benazir Bhutto had done in 1995–6. The army-run businesses faced greater economic competition than in previous decades, but privatization provided new opportunities, often on favourable terms. This was not unexpected given the fact that the large-scale privatization programme, which commenced during Nawaz Sharif's first government, was noted for its lack of accountability, along with private entrepreneurs' absence of concern with social obligations.[25] At a time in the early 1990s when private investment in radio and television had not been opened up, the Shaheen Foundation was enabled to open an FM radio channel and Pay TV station. Towards the end of the decade, the Fauji Foundation's sugar mills received heavy government subsidies of the sale of sugar to India. The military's Frontier Works Organisation and National Logistical Cell also benefited from the business opportunities provided by the Sharif brothers' national and provincial road construction programme. The military-run companies virtually marginalized the Highways Department and destroyed commercial competitors. Shahbaz Sharif enabled the National Logistical Cell to move into toll collection, once construction work had been completed.

Milbus thus continued its expansion during the decade of civilian rule. The Foundations moved into new commercial areas, such as the finance sector (Askari Bank), private security companies, oil and gas (Fauji Oil Terminal and Distribution Company Ltd) and IT (Fauji Soft and Askari Information Services). The military-run schools and universities commercialized their activities by opening them up to civilians. They were attractive to the elite because of their discipline and facilities, despite the differential rates of fees for students from military and civilian backgrounds.

Why did the civilian governments acquiesce in the military's economic activities? The main explanation is summed up by the comment from Nawaz Sharif's Finance Minister, Sirtaj Aziz: 'Had we begun to curb their financial interests ... it would have had an immediate reaction from the armed forces'.[26] President Ishaq Khan expressed a similar sentiment to Elahi Buksh Soomro, Speaker of the National Assembly, likening the issue to a 'beehive' that should not be touched.[27] Along with this realistic awareness of the asymmetrical power relations between the military and the politicians, civilian leaders may have profited from Milbus. Benazir Bhutto, for example, was alleged to have interests in the Shaheen Foundation's radio and television projects; while Nawaz Sharif's sugar factories benefited, along with the Fauji Foundation's, from the excise duty exemptions which assisted their exports to India during 1997–9.[28]

The Politics of Ethnicity and Centre-Province Relations 1988–99

The restoration of democracy provided opportunities for the co-option of ethnic leaders, although the Zulfiqar Ali Bhutto era warned that civilians could be as centralizing and authoritarian as generals. The different trajectories of Baloch and *mohajir* politics during 1988–99 reveal the limitations of the integrative capacity of parliamentary democracy and how it could be undermined by ethnic mobilization.

Baloch politics were marked by democratic engagement and increased factionalism during the period. The opportunity to secure power and influence at the centre encouraged the Baloch nationalist leaders to seek coalitions with the mainstream parties. Sardar Akhtar Mengal formed the Balochistan National Movement and worked with the PPP from 1988 onwards. His factional rival Nawab Akbar Bugti launched a new party, the Jamhoori Watan Party (JWP), which allied with Nawaz Sharif. It fought the 1997 elections on a platform of provincial autonomy and called for the redrawing of provinces within Pakistan. Following the polls it formed a coalition government with the PPP and the Balochistan National Party. The latter was founded in December 1996 by Mengal and Bijenzo; it supported Nawaz Sharif in the National Assembly. These shifting alliances and scaling down of separatist demands to calls for provincial autonomy were clear signs of the domestication of Baloch separatism, as had happened earlier in NWFP and for example in Tamil Nadu in India. Two events towards the end of Nawaz Sharif's second ministry were, however, to reveal the fragility of this process: firstly, the decisions of the National Finance Commission with respect to gas royalties reopened the grievances of Balochistan's exploitation; and secondly, the nuclear tests in Balochistan in May 1998 had been conducted without consulting the provincial government. Mengal resigned in protest at this slight to Baloch honour. Musharraf's coup intensified the sense of marginality and resulted in another round of armed conflict between nationalists and the state.

In Sindh, the PPP continued to limit the scope of both old-style Sindhi nationalism, as represented by G. M. Syed, and its more radical variants, organized in the Sindhi *Shagird Tehreek* and the *Awami Tehreek*. The veteran G. M. Syed crossed swords with Benazir Bhutto in 1988 over her initial coalition with MQM and the agreement to build more cantonments in the province. He explained to *Dawn* late in September the following year that the concept of Sindhu Desh meant 'an independent and sovereign state' which would be a member of the United Nations.[29] Shortly afterwards he was arrested following an incident in which his Jiye Sindh supporters burned the Pakistan flag during a demonstration at Sukkur airport. Mumtaz Ali Bhutto, who had formed the Sindh National Front the previous March, talked of 'Sindh for the Sindhis' in a 15-point manifesto.[30] The fact that the Sindh National Alliance failed to win any seats in the 1988, 1990 and 1993 elections indicated, however, that democracy could exert an integrative capacity.

The opposite lesson could be drawn, however, from the *mohajir* experience, where separatist tendencies strengthened with the restoration of democracy. Indeed, by the mid-1990s Pakistan was faced by almost a mini-insurgency in Karachi. Its exact causes remain a matter of controversy. Some authors see this as yet another example of the state's radicalization of ethnic movements through its heavy-handed response. Other accounts see the situation as being deliberately manipulated by ISI to provide a running sore for the elected governments.

The conflict in urban Sindh had its roots in the legacies from the Zia era. The MQM increasingly became involved in fratricidal conflict and in an insurgency against the state. The *mohajir* population at large were held captive by this. Their representatives proclaimed a sense of 'betrayal' that those who had made the greatest sacrifices to achieve Pakistan were now forced into conflict against it.

The violence in Karachi and Hyderabad from 1988 onwards has been well documented.[31] What is important here are the following issues: firstly the ways in which democratization opened the way for MQM to project its local power onto the national political scene; secondly to assess the impact of the violence on civil-military relations; thirdly to assess its relative importance to the failure to consolidate democracy.

The MQM's command of a block of seats in the National and Sindh Provincial Assemblies acted more as a source of political instability than stability. Its support was sought in an atmosphere of horse-trading and political infighting as much to unsettle governments as to provide stability. Despite its proclaimed ideology, which at times had separatist undertones, the MQM like other ethnic parties was eager to seek access to the corridors of power to secure its interests. The painful lesson of letting its rivals a free rein by boycotting the 1993 national polls was not repeated. The MQM displayed a remarkable degree of expediency in its coalition-making activities. It was prepared to work with the PPP in 1988, although the latter was associated with rural Sindhi interests. In 1997 it joined up with Nawaz Sharif's PML(N) government, despite the fact that the first military crackdown had been launched against it during his 1990–93 government. The army and ISI were similarly expedient in dealings with the MQM: the suspicion that the organization was receiving support from India did not, for example, prevent it from being seen as a useful tool in the destabilization of Benazir Bhutto's first ministry.

The MQM, in return for support to the PPP at federal level, not only secured a share of provincial power in 1988–90, but paved the way for the December 1988 agreement between Benazir Bhutto and Altaf Hussain. Its most contentious element involved the repatriation of 'stateless' Biharis from Bangladesh to Sindh. This intensified the fears of native Sindhis that they would be reduced to a minority status in their own province. Important backers of the PPP such as the Pirs of Hala pressured Benazir to break off ties with MQM. It was the breakdown of the December Karachi Declaration which intensified ethnic conflict and led to an abortive attempt to unseat Bhutto in a no-confidence motion, following secret talks between the MQM and Nawaz Sharif. Democracy was badly bruised by the episode, although Benazir managed to secure a majority of 12 to defeat the motion. Following her later dismissal from power, she was charged with having used Rs 20 million of secret service funds to buy votes.

During the months which followed, the MQM was at the forefront of what became known as the Combined Opposition Parties movement. A peaceful strike in Karachi at the beginning of February 1990 degenerated into violence which left 57 people dead, a number of whom were innocent victims caught in the crossfire between the police and 'unknown persons'.[32] Ishaq Khan reportedly 'summoned' Aitaz Ahsan to explain the mayhem in the country's commercial capital.

Differences between the government and the army over handling of the deteriorating security situation in Sindh came to a head when the police fired on an unarmed MQM procession in the Pucca Qila locality of Hyderabad on 27 May 1990. The local *mohajir* population greeted the army with flowers as it moved in to replace the Sindhi police. When General Aslam Beg, returning from a visit to Bangladesh, went straight to visit the area, *mohajir* leaders called on him to impose martial law.[33] It was not just the episode which undermined civil-military relations, but its aftermath. The army asked for extensive powers to maintain law and order in Sindh, including the permission to establish military courts. Benazir's refusal was cited by President Ghulam Ishaq Khan among the reasons to dismiss her some six weeks later.[34]

While the army's reservations about the handling of the law and order situation in Sindh were genuine, the generals were more perturbed about the declining economy, Benazir Bhutto's 'unreliability' in handling India and her attempt to interfere with internal promotion matters. Her recourse to patronage politics to sustain an increasingly embattled government provided a better justification in terms of 'corruption' than the law and order failure. From Benazir Bhutto's perspective the situation in Sindh was a drain on her power, but nowhere near as debilitating as the bitter conflict with the IJI Punjab government.

Similarly, the law and order situation in Sindh played a role in Nawaz Sharif's mounting difficulties with the army, towards the end of his first ministry. As with the Bhutto case, however, it was not the key factor in his dismissal. The extension of Operation Clean-Up launched in May 1992 from rural Sindh to Karachi created difficulties between Nawaz Sharif and his MQM coalition partners. The army utilized the breakaway Haqqiqi faction of the MQM to come down hard on the MQM, most of whose leading figures were either in exile or had gone underground. A number of Nawaz Sharif's close Punjabi political allies embarrassed him by criticizing the army's security operation. As we have seen, however, it was the open confrontation with the president, amidst a gloomy economic foreign affairs situation, which most concerned the army. Significantly, it was not the elected leaders but the military itself that eventually made the decision to withdraw its security operations in Karachi. This action in December 1994 was in fact to spark the most violent round of violence in Karachi, marked by sectarian clashes, MQM faction fighting, ethnic violence and then a full-scale insurgency against the security forces.

Punjab had always been the cornerstone of Pakistan, to the extent that smaller provinces chafed at what they saw as the state's Punjabization. During Benazir Bhutto's first ministry, however, Punjab was unusually pitched against the federal government. While Nawaz Sharif occasionally turned to cultural symbolism to bolster his conflict with Benazir Bhutto, the hopes of language activists of a Punjabi cultural renaissance were to be dashed. Once the circumstances had passed, the Muslim League in the Punjab returned to its traditional pro-establishment tracks that had brought economic benefits for those sections of the province's population attached to the army, the bureaucracy and their local political allies.

The 1988 election results had delivered the Punjab to Nawaz Sharif, who headed the nine-party IJI coalition. The IJI had captured 108 seats to the PPP's 97, but had secured its position by winning over 32 independent candidates. It was clear to everyone that the establishment had ensured that Benazir would be kept in check by encouraging a rival government in the country's major province. The by-elections for 20 seats in the National Assembly and Provincial Assembly on 28 January 1989 were fought bitterly, with the PPP and IJI using rival government institutions to garner support. In the months which followed, the struggle became increasingly personalized. For seven months the federally controlled Pakistan Railways claimed that the non-availability of wagons prevented it from delivering scrap iron to the Sharif family Ittefaq foundries. At an IJI rally at Lahore's historic Mochi gate on 11 September 1989, Nawaz Sharif and other speakers such as Sheikh Rasheed launched blistering attacks on Benazir Bhutto. She was declared to be an enemy of Pakistan seeking to 'establish Indian hegemony' and the claim was made that 'We will hold (them) accountable and dump the Bhuttos' remains in the Arabian Sea'.[35] Such anti-Sindhi and anti-Indian sentiments became a common IJI refrain. This propaganda revealed the constraints on a permanent improvement in Indo-Pakistan relations following the cordiality between Benazir Bhutto and Rajiv Gandhi at the December 1988 Islamabad SAARC summit.

Nawaz Sharif also posed as the protector of Punjab's interests and the upholder of provincial autonomy. On 15 November 1989 he inaugurated the Bank of Punjab with its own paid-up capital of Rs 100 million. The PPP called this act unconstitutional and a 'treason against the Federation'. In reality the Punjab Prime Minister was operating legally, but the symbolism of the bank's logo, the rising sun royal insignia of Maharaja Ranjit Singh, the last ruler of an independent Punjab, was not lost on his opponents. Within a fortnight the Punjab Revenue Minister, Arshan Khan Lodhi, also announced plans for setting up a provincial television station, because 'Pakistan Television, under instruction from the Federal Government, was not projecting Punjab's point of view on various issues'.[36]

Given his previous political record, Nawaz Sharif's attempt to wear the turban of Punjab appeared implausible. As the PPP Federal Interior Minister, Aitaz Ahsan, astutely summed it up: 'Had Nawaz Sharif been in the Centre, he would have been the greatest opponent of provincial autonomy'.[37] Within Punjab itself, the Sharifs were seen as the upholders of the central regions and of the East Punjab migrant constituency. His attempts to project a monolithic Punjabi identity were countered by the formation of the Seraiki Qaumi Movement. It called for a new province comprising Bahawalpur, Multan, Dera Ghazi Khan, Dera Ismail Khan and the Jhang divisions. Feudal power relations in southern Punjab restricted Seraiki activists from securing seats, but the presence of pluralism within Punjab could not be gainsaid.[38]

Significantly, when Nawaz Sharif came to power at the centre all talk of provincial autonomy was forgotten and it was business as usual. Punjabi businessmen were for example favoured by the Privatisation Commission of General Saeed Qadir. Political connections outweighed commercial considerations in the denationalization process. The Gujarati Memon Adamjee family failed to gain control of the privatized Muslim Commercial Bank, although it outbid the Chinoti-Punjabi Manaha-Sapphire group.[39] The Punjabization of Pakistan appeared to have been resumed. In Sharif's second government this reached new heights with 85 per cent of his federal ministers hailing from Punjab. At one time all the key posts of President (Rafiq Tarar), Prime Minister and Chief of Army Staff (Jahangir Karamat) were held by Punjabis. The ANP took the lead in establishing a new anti-Punjabi movement called the Pakistan Oppressed Nationalities Movement (PONM), which called for population quotas in the army and bureaucracy, a truly federal political system and the creation of a Seraiki province.

Sectarian Militancy and Violence

We have seen how Zia's domestic politics, together with such regional developments as the Iranian revolution and the Afghanistan war impacted on sectarian militancy in Pakistan. Conflicts became bloodier as a result of the spread of the Kalashnikov culture. Relations developed between sectarian organizations, *jihadists* and criminal gangs involved in drug smuggling. Veterans of the Afghan War became involved later in the Kashmir *jihad* or with militant sectarian groups. The regional dimension continued to exert an influence during the 1988–99 period as the rise of the Taliban provided new sanctuaries and training opportunities for Sunni militants. LeJ activists involved in the attempt to assassinate Nawaz Sharif on 3 January 1999 were, for example, trained at the HUA-run Khalid bin Waleed camp in Afghanistan, as were the perpetrators of the Mominpura massacre of 25 Shias in Lahore in January 1998.[40]

Democratic governments did not always want to crack down on sectarian militants because of their political usefulness. Moreover, when violence got out of hand and there was a pressing need to do so, it was not always possible to square this with continued support for their transnational Islamic allies. Naseerullah Babar's crackdown on sectarian violence in 1994–6, as part of his Operation Save Punjab, coincided with the organization of the Taliban and support for HUA activities in Kashmir.[41] SSP developed especially close ties with the Taliban and saw its growing power in Afghanistan as a victory for Sunni Islam. Its leader, Azam Tariq, made increasingly virulent statements against the Shia.[42]

Many of contemporary Pakistan's leading militant organizations emerged in the Punjab in the post-Zia decade. They included *Sunni Tehrik* (1993), LeJ (1990), LeT (1997) and *Sipah-i-Muhammad* (1991). The latter was a Shia group whose heavily armed headquarters at Tokar Niaz Beg, a small town outside Lahore, became a virtual no-go area for the police. Significantly a number of the new generation of militant leaders came from Partition refugee families. They included Hafiz Muhammad Saeed, the future *amir* of LeT, and Maulana Masood Azhar, the founder of *Jaish-e-Muhammad* in 2000, whose audacious attack on the Indian parliament building in New Delhi the following year was to bring India and Pakistan to the brink of nuclear war. Azhar had been brought up in the southern Punjab city of Bahawalpur, which became notorious for its links with militancy.

It was not of course only in Punjab that militant organizations emerged at this time. Militant Pakhtun groups dedicated to the forcible implementation of the *shari'ah* took their cue from the Taliban. They included the *Tehreek-e-Nifaz-e-Shariat-e-Muhammadi* (TNSM) of Maulana Sufi Muhammad, which was based in the Malakand region of the NWFP. Its mini-insurgency in 1994–5 was a dress rehearsal for the much more serious challenge it mounted to the state in 2009. The *Tehreek-e-Tulaba* also emerged in the Orakzai Agency and *Tehreek-e-Taliban-e-Zargari* in Hangu. The stage was being set for FATA and the adjoining areas to become a major hub of militancy. The future ties between Punjab-based sectarian organizations and the Pakhtun Taliban, which led in 2009 to Western-fevered concern about the creation of a 'Punjabi Taliban', were presaged when a contingent of SSP militants fought alongside the Taliban as it captured the Northern Alliance stronghold of Mazar-i-Sharif in August 1998.

The growth of militant sectarian organizations resulted from the splintering of movements such as SSP as a result of factional divisions, assassinations of leaders, conflicts over resources and the formation of newly named movements in response to police activity. This last development was to continue apace in the Musharraf era. The proliferation of sectarian organizations was accompanied by a rising tide of violence, which took the form of targeted killings, bomb and machine-gun attacks on mosques and *imambaras*. While the casualty figures were not as high as during the first decade of the twentieth century and did not result from suicide attacks, the violence at the time was unprecedented. Between 1990 and 1997 there were 581 deaths and 1,600 injuries. A week-long orgy of violence in the remote Kurram valley alone resulted in 100 deaths and scores of injuries. The local Sunni and Shia tribes had lived peacefully until the arrival of Sunni Afghan refugees.[43] The SMP and SSP fought gun battles in the increasingly anarchic city of Karachi. The Karachi head of the SSP was killed in a gun battle at the Masjid-e-Akbar on 7 December 1994.[44] The Jhang district of the Punjab, the birthplace of the SSP, was particularly disturbed. The SSP represented the bid for power of an increasingly mobile middle-class urban community made up in large part of Sunni migrants from East Punjab. Power had been traditionally wielded both in Jhang city and in the district by the local Shia landowning elite.[45]

Sectarian violence and the rise of Islamic militancy were symptomatic of the declining reach of the state. The total elimination of government authority in the tribal agencies was already being presaged. Even in the settled districts of the Frontier and parts of southern Punjab, there were the signs of emerging sectarian and militant challenges to local government authority. Sectarian and Islamist mobilization had been encouraged by the sidelining of the mainstream parties by Zia. The restoration of democracy established an environment in which at different times both the national parties protected sectarian activists from prosecution and sought to appeal to Islamist constituencies. This restricted the state's responses to violence.

The PPP's traditional secular image and the Bhutto family's Shia orientation had ensured Shia support in the 1988 elections. Nawaz Sharif's IJI alliance included Sunni *ulama* parties along with JI. As part of his ongoing struggle with the PPP, he was prepared to turn a blind eye to the activities of Sunni sectarian organizations in the Punjab. What was more surprising however was the accommodation with these groups displayed during Benazir Bhutto's second government. She had sought to increase her Islamic legitimacy by an alliance with the JUI(F).

This also enabled her to pursue a regional agenda in Afghanistan which pleased the army. The downside was that the JUI(F) utilized government patronage in support not only of *jihadist* but also sectarian groups. Benazir further alienated the Shia landholding elite by attempting to shore up the PPP position in Punjab by making an SSP leader, Sheikh Hakim Ali, a provincial cabinet member, despite the fact that he had eight murder cases registered against him.[46] The PPP government failed to charge the SSP leaders Azam Tariq and Zia-ul-Rahman, who were implicated in the murder of Shahnawaz Pirzada, a prominent Shia from the Bahawalnagar district, whose son Riaz Pirzada was a PPP MLA. It was small wonder that Shia landlords began to switch their traditional PPP allegiance to the PML(N).

Nawaz Sharif emerged from the 1997 elections in so strong a position that he did not need to placate the SSP and its offshoots. His determination to crack down on sectarian forces led him to introduce an Anti-Terrorist Law in August 1997. This established special terrorist courts and gave the security services the right to 'shoot to kill' and indemnity for acts done in 'good faith'. Sectarian violence abated for a while, only to resume in 1998. The further government repression prompted LJ to attempt to assassinate the Prime Minister by means of a roadside bomb. A spate of targeted assassinations of Shia leaders led the TJP to call for martial law. Ironically, a factor in the resurgence of sectarian violence was the increased ties between the army and HUA as it sought in the ill-fated Kargil adventure to use force to wrench Kashmir from India.

Indo-Pakistan Relations During the Democratic Era

The hopes that a restored democratic order might end the enduring rivalry with India and secure a peace dividend for the subcontinent did not seem initially misplaced. Benazir Bhutto established good relations with Rajiv Gandhi. Indeed they were so cordial that some in the military establishment thought that she threatened national security. Following the fourth annual session of the SAARC heads of state and government meeting in Islamabad in December 1988, agreements were struck between India and Pakistan not to attack each other's nuclear facilities. This was the highpoint of Benazir's rapprochement with India. She was constrained not only by the anti-Indian sentiment in Punjab, but by the fact that the military controlled key security areas relating to nuclear policy and Afghanistan. The public admission of this state of affairs was provided by the retention of Zia's Foreign Minister, Yakub Ali Khan, in her cabinet.

There is evidence that Pakistan scaled down its support for Sikh separatists during Benazir's first government.[47] This was not the result of democratization as such, but in response to the threat of India retaliating to such actions as it had done in 1965 in Kashmir. This intention was in fact signalled by the Operation Brass Tacks exercise. India may well have backed off from a conventional war because Pakistan signalled its possession of a nuclear deterrent. The police crackdown in Punjab led by K. P. S. Gill, better border security and the cutting off of the flow of supplies and training for Sikh militants enabled India to break the back of the Khalistan movement in the early 1990s. The spontaneous uprising in Kashmir however, in 1989, provided new opportunities for Pakistani covert action. Islamic proxies were readily available and battle hardened from Afghanistan. The topography of Kashmir also offered better prospects for insurgents than did the Punjab. Throughout the democratic era, Pakistan fished in Kashmir's troubled waters.

By 1990, Pakistan had begun to direct its support away from the Jammu and Kashmir Liberation Front (JKLF), the largest insurgent force to those organizations, which it more closely controlled. Training initially took place in Azad Kashmir, with the JI-affiliated *Hizb-ul-Mujahideen* receiving support. Within five years, training camps had been established in Afghanistan and groups such as HUA and LT moved to the forefront of the *jihad*. The radicalization of the struggle increased both its brutality and expanded its aims. The goals of independence (JKLF's) or accession to Pakistan (*Hizb-ul-Mujahideen*'s) were widened so that the struggle in Kashmir was part of a worldwide struggle between the true faith and unbelievers. This was summed up in the HUM leader Fazl-ur-Rahman's comment that 'Delhi, Calcutta, Mumbai and Washington are the real targets of Militants. Muslims should cooperate with militants for dominance of Islam in the world'.[48] Commitment to the universal *jihad* led militant organizations into close ties with Osama bin Laden with portentous consequences for the South Asian region and the wider world.

Benazir Bhutto and Nawaz Sharif did not attempt to haul in support for the *jihad* in Kashmir during their democratic watch. They may not have been fully appraised of the strategy, as Nawaz Sharif was to claim with respect to the 1999 Kargil operation masterminded by his nemesis Pervez Musharraf. Patriotism could have encouraged them to cooperate with it. Benazir Bhutto returned to the theme of a 'thousand years' war with India' in a speech in March 1990 as relations deteriorated.[49] Yet both in 1988 with Rajiv Gandhi and again in 1996 with I. K. Gujral, Benazir displayed willingness to improve ties with India. Similarly, Nawaz Sharif was prepared to engage in his celebrated bus diplomacy with Atal Behari Vajpayee. This resulted in the Lahore Declaration which committed India and Pakistan to nuclear confidence-building measures and to a willingness to solve the Kashmir dispute through peaceful means.

Whatever the explanation, the failure of Pakistan's elected leaders to oppose the adoption of covert military strategies undermined democratization. The disagreements between Nawaz Sharif and Pervez Musharraf in the wake of Kargil were a factor in the October 1999 coup. More widely, the period from 1988 can be seen as a 'missed opportunity' to achieve a peace dividend. Increased trade resulting from a normalization of Indo-Pakistan relations along with the reduction of military expenditure could have freed resources for the funding of socio-economic development. The reduction of social and regional inequalities would have increased political stability. Instead the cultivation of Islamic militants for *jihad* increased the appeal and scope for militancy within Pakistan itself. The Murdike headquarters of LeT, for example, held a conference in November 1997 which proclaimed that democracy in Pakistan should be ended as 'the notion of the sovereignty of the people is anti-Islamic'.

> Pakistani newspapers noted that the venue was festooned with signboards proclaiming that the appropriate response to democracy was through grenade and bomb explosions ('*jamhooriyat ka jawaab*, grenade *aur* blast').[50]

This was mere rhetoric at the time, but just over a decade later took on a terrifying reality as the Taliban battled with the Pakistan state.

7

THE JANUS STATE

PAKISTAN UNDER MUSHARRAF

Pervez Musharraf came to power on 13 October 1999 in dramatic circumstances which could almost have been scripted in Bollywood. Nawaz Sharif's attempt to sack him in a national television broadcast and 'hijack' his plane en route from Colombo to Karachi enabled the Chief of Army Staff to pose as a reluctant coup maker. In reality, tensions had been growing between the army and the Pakistan Prime Minister since the Kargil conflict in July in which Musharraf was a leading strategist. The former company commander of a commando battalion and member of the elite Special Service Group had been promoted to Chief of Army Staff in October 1998 because, like Zia before him, he was seen as an apolitical figure without a power base in the army. Both coup makers were from partition migrant families in a Punjabi- and Pashtun-dominated institution. It was there, however, that the similarities ceased. Musharraf lacked Zia's Deobandi-influenced piety and was more of the old-style Pakistani army officer, not averse to Scotch and soda and as at home on the golf course as the parade ground. He was thus far more like Ayub than Zia. His liberalism had been nurtured by family background. His father, Syed Musharrafuddin, was educated at Aligarh. His mother, who held a degree in English literature from Delhi's Indraprastha College, was equally liberally educated. Musharraf, because of his father's posting to the Pakistan Embassy in Ankara, had spent seven years of his childhood (1949–56) in Turkey.

This chapter argues that, despite Musharraf's liberalism, he shared the army's traditional disdain for politicians. He possessed public relations skills, but lacked the political skills to overcome the lack of legitimacy accorded to a coup-maker.[1] While Musharraf possessed a liberal tinge, he was schooled in the instinctive authoritarianism of the Pakistan army. He thus became increasingly ruffled and impatient when his policies were questioned. He surrounded himself with loyalists who gave the advice he wished to hear. He eventually blundered into the situation in which he needed to declare an emergency following his suspension of a popular and independent-minded Chief Justice. Musharraf, who had declared himself the saviour of Pakistan's democracy, was badly caught out. This action in November 2007 dealt a final blow to his international standing. Washington had grown weary of his 'Janus-faced' approach to militancy, after initially enthusiastically embracing him as an ally in the 'War on Terror'. The Pakistan public also increasingly opposed his calibrated approach to 'good' and 'bad' militants. A liberalized media exposed Pakistan's President to claims that he was a Western 'stooge'.

The atmosphere had been very different at the outset of his regime. This is captured, for example, in the subheading to the chapter in Hassan Abbas's work, *Pakistan's Drift to Extremism*, which is entitled 'The Season of Hope'.[2] Musharraf, both in terms of his personal liberalism, being photographed with pet dogs, and in his taking the title of Chief Executive rather than Chief Martial Law Administrator, had sought to differentiate himself from Zia. Musharraf's role model in early speeches, in keeping with his childhood and mid-career training in Turkey, was Kemal Ataturk. Enthusiasts for his regime continued to view him as the 'second Jinnah', committed to the founding father's vision of a 'moderate, progressive Muslim society'.[3] Islamic moderation remained a watchword throughout the Musharraf era, although much less was heard about the 'good governance' agenda which he had vowed would replace the 'sham democracy' of the 1990s.

Despite the rhetoric, Musharraf did not modernize the taxation system, or roll back the Islamization legacies of the Zia era. Administrative reform shook up local government, but did not free rural society from the thraldom of patrimonial politics. There was little headway in tackling misogynist practices arising either from tribal custom or from the Hudood Ordinances. Musharraf's attachment to a 'good governance' agenda, Islamic moderation and composite dialogue with India thus failed not only because of external economic and political buffetings, but because of the internal weaknesses and contradictions at the heart of the Pakistan state.

Reports which focus on his personality traits to account for the failings miss the vital point[4] that Musharraf, like earlier Pakistan military rulers, needed to co-opt political allies. In doing so he lost the ability to introduce wide-ranging change and was as much in thrall to the vested interests of the religious establishment and the feudal class as were elected leaders. Military-backed rule thus once again proved unable to modernize Pakistan, even with a liberal and progressive-minded figure at its helm. Even the surging rate of economic growth proved to be an unsustainable bubble because of the failure to tackle long-term structural problems.[5]

This chapter thus argues that the Musharraf era exemplifies three long-running themes in Pakistan's post-independence history: firstly, that military governments are ultimately unable to modernise society, governance and the economy because of their lack of legitimacy; secondly, that Pakistan's utilization of Islamic proxies has derailed relations with its neighbours and come at an increasing domestic cost; thirdly, that military rule is likely to increase ethnic tensions within the smaller provinces of Pakistan. The Musharraf era also however reveals the complexities in Pakistan's development which can puzzle if not elude headline writers and analysts alike. For here was a state in which a military 'dictator' could pursue more liberal media policies than his elected predecessor; one in which Baloch tribal chieftains with the absolute power of life and death over their dependants could represent national struggle from state 'exploitation'; a state which is simultaneously remarkably resilient and 'soft' in terms of its ability to implement basic economic and administrative functions.

9/11 and its Aftermath

9/11 and the US' and its allies' subsequent 'War on Terror' exerted as profound an impact on Musharraf's Pakistan as had the Soviet invasion of Afghanistan on Zia's regime a generation earlier. In both instances, Pakistan found itself a front-line state in a struggle whose ramifications reached far beyond the region. While 9/11 restored Musharraf's international standing and brought a massive influx of resources, it also threatened the state's established security policies.

Reversal of support for the Afghan Taliban and a toning down of support for the Kashmir *jihad* would have in themselves alienated sections of Pakistani opinion. The accompanying military action from 2004 onwards in the Tribal Areas set the regime not only against its former protégés, but firmly against the tide of public opinion. This would not have mattered in former times, but Musharraf had made a point of liberalizing the media to provide 'democratic' credentials for his regime.

There are a number of colourful and contrasting depictions of the circumstances in which Musharraf brought the powerful army corps commanders round to the policy of opposing their former Taliban protégés in Afghanistan.[6] Economic weaknesses, with debts of $38 billion, along with strategic threats possibly from both the US and India, lay behind this decision. It was subsequently referred to as the 'turnaround' in official circles. Superficially this was accurate, as Pakistan had been one of just three countries which had formally recognized the Taliban regime in Kabul. We have seen earlier that the Taliban were regarded as a means of securing Pakistan's strategic interests and at least in part owed their rise to power to military and security assistance from Islamabad. However, the Taliban had not proved compliant neighbours for Pakistan. A goodwill visit by a Pakistani football team to Kandahar ended in the humiliation of public head-shaving after the visitors had violated the Taliban dress code by wearing shorts. Despite Islamabad's appeals over the fate of the Baniyan Buddha statues, the 2,000-year-old sculptures were blasted from their cliff face in February 2001. Ultimately, however, the Taliban lost their value as a 'strategic asset' to Pakistan because of the growing influence of Osama bin Laden and Al-Qaeda in Afghanistan, after they were forced to abandon Sudan.

Pakistan supported the Operation Enduring Freedom in November 2001 by granting over-flight and landing rights to the US, by sharing intelligence and facilitating the logistical supply of forces engaged in Afghanistan. In return it gained leverage and acceptance from the international community when its standing was low not just because of the military seizure of power, but also the issue of nuclear proliferation. The US was well aware that the egotistical Dr A. Q. Khan, whom Musharraf had removed from his position as head of the nuclear programme in March 2001 and later placed under house arrest, was not simply a lone 'rogue' element in his secret dealings with Libya, Iran and North Korea.[7] The inflow of foreign military and economic aid boosted

Pakistan's flagging economy. In 2000, Pakistan's fiscal debt was 5.3 per cent of GDP and its total debt stood at 92 per cent of GDP. It is true that Pakistan had been granted an IMF standby credit of US$ 596 million before 9/11.[8] But it was the country's post 9/11 international standing which led to the inflow of foreign aid, higher remittances from overseas Pakistanis[9] and the rescheduling of debt by the Paris Club of donors to help the accelerating growth rates. President Bush's removal of economic sanctions, which had been in place since the nuclear tests and the Musharraf coup, paved the way for over $600 million in economic support funds to be received in 2002. The improving economic outlook saw annual rates of economic growth rise from an average of 3 per cent at the beginning of the Musharraf era to a peak of over 6 per cent. The parlous foreign exchange reserves, which were only sufficient to cover one month's imports at US$ 908 million in 2000, rose to around 11 billion by 2004.[10] One striking piece of evidence of the increased prosperity was the expansion of mobile-phone use in the six-year period 2001–7: from 600,000 to around 50 million.

Musharraf was unable, however, to make rapid economic growth sustainable, by tackling structural weaknesses in the economy. These included not just low taxation rates and poor physical infrastructure, but low human capital. Pakistan lagged behind most of South Asia with respect to Human Development Indicators such as infant mortality, primary school enrolment and expenditure on education. As the Human Development Report for 2007 summed up, 'Economic growth in Pakistan is yet to be adequately linked with human development by deliberate redistributive public policy. Indeed the predicament of Pakistan lies in the utter divorce of income distribution policies from growth policies'.[11] With a third of the population living below the poverty line and over half having no access to education, basic health services or sanitation, growth remained captive to exogenous favourable events and to the continued provision of credit for wealthier consumers.[12] Critics of the Musharraf economic reforms were justified in their stance that macro-economic improvements with respect to indebtedness and foreign reserves were primarily the result of a one-off windfall arising from Pakistan's stance post 9/11.[13]

Musharraf, like Zia, had been given political as well as economic breathing space by the turn of international developments. He won kudos by opening up licences for private TV and radio broadcasting and allowed newspaper editors free rein. This policy provided a veneer of liberalism to his regime. It may also have been prompted by notions that the state-run TV system had lost Pakistan the media war with India over Kargil, and that local private channels could usefully compete with foreign satellite providers who were increasingly threatening old-style policing of television. The new media however gave discursive space not only to liberal voices, but to spokesmen of militant groups. It also reported on the 'collateral damage' arising from military action in Waziristan. It is unlikely that Musharraf would have become so universally unpopular because of his 'pro-American' stance if the old restricted media had survived. Ultimately private TV companies such as GEO fell foul of the government in 2007 when they sided with the Chief Justice, Iftikhar Muhammad Chaudhry, in his struggle with Musharraf. The introduction of the emergency which curbed both the media and political opponents did immense harm to Musharraf's international standing. It coincided with both Washington and London's increasing frustration with the ambiguities surrounding Pakistan's response to the threat of trans-national terrorist activity in the region.[14] During his final period as President, Musharraf came under increasing pressure to replace his system of military-backed rule with a fully-fledged democratic system. This was seen by both Western analysts and liberals in Pakistan as holding the key to tackling not only the country's chronic instability, but the terrorist threat which was seen as emanating from its porous border regions with Afghanistan. This sentiment was summed up by Zahid Hussain when he wrote, 'The war against militancy and Islamic extremism can be best fought and won in a liberal democracy'.[15]

Post 9/11 the Pakistan state engaged in increasingly complex and fraught responses to the militant groups which had either traditionally operated out of sanctuaries in its territory, or had crossed into Pakistan in the wake of the US toppling the Taliban government in Afghanistan and the capture of Al-Qaeda's Tora Bora redoubt in December 2001. While security and later military operations were undertaken against 'foreign fighters' and leadership cadres of Al-Qaeda, the Pakistan state did not pursue the Afghan Taliban or Kashmir *jihadists*. Some ISI operatives and military commanders undoubtedly sympathized with the Afghan Taliban whom they had nurtured. The policy of providing sanctuary however primarily reflected Musharraf's pragmatism and commitment to the long-term Indo-centric security strategy. The US overthrow of the Taliban regime represented a major setback as it brought non-Pakhtuns to the corridors of power in Kabul who had traditionally looked to India for support. Increasing Indian influence in Afghanistan raised fears of encirclement in some security analysts' minds. This was not a totally irrational response, as Pakistani intelligence claimed Indian involvement in the growing insurgency in Balochistan. Pakistan also sought to counteract India by continuing to provide sanctuary to Kashmir *jihadist* organizations, more to keep up pressure on New Delhi than in a post-Kargil anticipation that Kashmir could be wrenched from India through a military victory.

Afghan Taliban from bases in Waziristan increasingly infiltrated into Afghanistan as the West diverted its attention from that country to Iraq. For a number of years Afghan Taliban leaders freely operated from headquarters in Quetta (the so-called Quetta Shura). Cross-border infiltration into Kashmir also continued during 2001. The bold move by Pakistan-based LeT and JeM to expand their *jihad* from Jammu and Kashmir to the Indian heartland by attacking the parliament in New Delhi on 13 December 2002 forced the Musharraf regime to readjust its policy. Both LeT and JeM had received logistical and financial support from the military and ISI in their past development. This had not gone unnoticed either in New Delhi or Washington.

The high-profile attack on the Indian parliament brought India and Pakistan to the brink of war. It resulted in Musharraf's banning not only LeT and JeM but the militant sectarian SSP and TNFJ organizations. The security operations against them were largely ineffective and in some instances desultory. According to one report, while the head of LeT, Hafiz Saeed, was under arrest following the attack on the Indian parliament, he still had access to an international telephone and was in touch with supporters and sympathizers in the US.[16] Banned organizations were able to reform under new titles and by adopting legitimate business covers as charitable organizations. The SSP for example operated as *Ahle Sunnat-wal-Jamaat*; JeM as *Tehreek-e-Khuddam-ul-Islam*; and LeT as *Jamaat-ud-Dawa*. They provided jobs for militants returned from the *jihad* front and assistance for the families of those martyred. JuD was to provide humanitarian assistance to the wider population in the wake of the 2005 earthquake in Azad Kashmir and following the 2010 flood disaster.

In a striking departure, the army and the Frontier Corps began military campaigns in the Tribal Areas in 2004. The aim in the face of mounting pressure on Western forces in Afghanistan was to root out

Afghan Taliban who had close ties with Al-Qaeda and 'foreign forces' (mostly Arabs, Chechens and Uzbeks) who had found sanctuary in South Waziristan. The operations were marked by military setbacks, and growing resistance from local tribesmen who not only sympathized with the Afghan *jihad* cause, but tenaciously upheld long-term commitments to independence from outside intrusion and Pakhtunwali codes of revenge for deaths to kinsmen caught in the crossfire and protection of 'guests'. A combination of increased resistance and hostile public opinion led to a series of peace deals in South Waziristan. The first was the so-called Shakai Agreement in April 2004. Later in February 2005 another peace deal was signed in South Waziristan with Baitullah Mehsud (Sra Rogah Deal).

Local pro-Taliban militant support was eventually institutionalized in 2007 with the formation of the *Tehreek-e-Taliban Pakistan* (TTP) by Baitullah Mehsud. The move was a direct response to the Pakistan army's seizure of the Lal Masjid (Red Mosque) in Islamabad on 10 July 2007 in a bloody battle which claimed over 150 lives. The circumstances of this episode and the controversies surrounding it will be explored later in the chapter. The TTP brought together local militant commanders from the various Tribal Agencies, some of whom were committed to the local Islamization of society, others who were much more closely committed to Al-Qaeda and the international *jihad*. The extent to which Deobandi mosques and schools alone provided the ideological motive for militant recruitment will be explored later. In addition, the TTP's generous financial inducements, charitable support for militants' dependants which has echoes in the army's formal Fauji Foundation and the veneration in which martyrs are held, seen in the pilgrimages to the tombs of Shahids, all played a part. The TTP helped fund its activities through local taxes, which had more overtones of a protection racket than Islamic charitable giving. Despite its decentralization, the TTP was capable of unified and sustained operations. Outside the Tribal Areas, the long-established *Tehreek-e-Nifaz-e-Shariat-e-Muhammadi* (TNSM) operated under its umbrella in Swat. JeM, SSP and LeJ formed what became known as the Punjab Taliban. In all as many as 40 militant groups were brought under the TTP umbrella. While it remained committed to the Afghan *jihad*, it was increasingly drawn into conflict with the Pakistan state and sought to usher in an Islamist revolution. The Afghan Taliban focused its efforts across the Durand Line, and its sanctuaries in Pakistan were not engaged by the security forces.

The fighting was bloodiest in South Waziristan, reaching a peak in the winter of 2007–8. There was also conflict in North Waziristan in October 2007, which led 80,000 people to flee their homes. Over the course of 2008, government forces also fought militants in the Bajaur and Mohmand agencies. Military activity in FATA was to increase greatly in the post-Musharraf period, after a lull following the ANP's assumption of office in the Frontier which saw further abortive peace agreements. The launching of operations in Waziristan was accompanied by growing terrorist blasts in Peshawar, which were eventually to spread to Punjab. Some Western analysts once again raised fears that Pakistan was a 'failed' state. Despite their immense human toll, such outrages did not presage an Islamist takeover of the state, which continued to rest on the twin bulwarks of the army and the economic, cultural and political commitment of the Punjabi population to the Pakistan state project.

Washington also had its long-term strategic interest in the stability of Pakistan, now a nuclear power as well as an ally in the 'War on Terror'. As we have seen, it poured huge resources into the country post 9/11. The Bush presidency for a number of years feted Musharraf, thereby strengthening his own position. This policy was not universally supported by such prominent US critics as the veteran South Asia specialist, Selig Harrison.[17] The US also exerted influence to pull back India and Pakistan from the brink of war in 2002 and encouraged the reopening of diplomatic dialogue. In the later years of the Musharraf presidency, however, relations with Washington became strained over the extent of Pakistan's commitment to the 'War on Terror'. The activities of the Quetta Shura were noted, as was the fact that the arrest of known militants frequently followed Western pressure;[18] and although such leading figures as Khalid Sheikh Mohammad (Al-Qaeda number 3 figure) and Mullah Obeidullah (the Taliban regime's Defence Minister) were netted, and militants like Abu Hamza Rabia and Mushin Musa Marwalli Arwah were killed, many others remained at large. Leading militants such as Fazlur Rehman Khalil (HuM) and Maulana Masood Azhar (JeM) were released during 2002–4. It was especially irksome for Washington that Osama bin Laden remained at large.

The Musharraf regime responded to US criticisms by reporting that by May 2006 over 600 Al-Qaeda members had been arrested in Pakistan and perhaps as many as 1,000 had been killed. The effect that this had on organizational capacity can be gauged by the fact that Ayman al-Zawahiri repeatedly called for an uprising against Musharraf and for his assassination as an enemy against Islam. There were a number of attempts on his life. Worryingly, information began to emerge of some servicemen being implicated in the two bomb attacks in the space of less than a fortnight in December 2003 and the 6 July 2007 attack at Rawalpindi airport.

The US response to what it saw as Islamabad's half-hearted commitment to halting the flow of militants into Afghanistan was to use remote control missiles (drones) to attack militant bases in Pakistan and even to threaten 'hot pursuit' of militants onto Pakistan soil. This stance further enflamed anti-American sentiment in Pakistan which was running at a high level despite US economic largesse. The drones did not always hit their military targets but caused civilian casualties in the Tribal Areas. The hatred of America was deeply corrosive of Musharraf's standing. It was probably in an attempt to shore this up that Islamabad complained in public about the drone attacks, while privately supplying intelligence information which enabled the successful targeting of Al-Qaeda commanders and such notable Pakistan Taliban figures as Baitullah Mehsud. While only rhetoric was deployed against drone attacks, the 'hot pursuit' policy raised the real danger that there might be engagement between Pakistani and US ground forces. It was not until the post-Musharraf period, as a result of Taliban excesses in Swat and terrorist attacks on 'soft' civilian targets, that public opinion began to shift away from the notion that Pakistan was being asked to fight America's war and was suffering as a consequence. Washington's unilateral action in the killing of Osama bin Laden in Abbottabad reversed this trend.

Relations with India

Pakistan's relations with India veered from the edge of war to the brink of a major breakthrough on Kashmir. The highpoints were the Agra summit of July 2001 and the meeting between Musharraf and the Indian Prime Minister Vajpayee during the Islamabad SAARC summit in January 2004. The low point was the military stand-off following the terrorist attack on the Indian parliament. In the event the Musharraf era closed with no decisive change to the decades-long enduring rivalry. The prospect of a 'peace dividend' for the region remained as tantalizing as ever. Throughout this period, Islamabad's foreign policy remained fixed on the Indian 'threat', despite the pressure to reverse its strategy in Afghanistan. The overthrow of the Taliban represented a major strategic setback. The US-backed interim government of President Karzai brought members of the anti-Pakistan Northern Alliance who had previously been supported by India, Russia and Iran to the heart of government in Kabul. Rather than Afghanistan providing strategic depth, there was now the possibility of a two-front threat from India emanating from the country. Islamabad claimed that the new Indian consulates opened in Kandahar and Jalalabad were part of a growing Indian presence which had security threats attached to it. Similarly, there were allegations that India was fishing in the troubled waters of Balochistan through its consulate at Zahedan close to the Pakistan-Iran border. Undoubtedly India, through its humanitarian assistance and involvement in reconstruction projects, established a growing influence in post-war Afghanistan. Pakistan's tolerance of Jalaluddin Haqqani's network, which launched operations against ISAF/NATO troops from its base near Miranshah in North Waziristan, was a response to the Afghan Indian threat, as Islamabad wanted leverage with a future Pakhtun moderate Taliban grouping.[19] While requiring a stake in any post-Karzai Afghanistan, Pakistan's earlier experiences with the Taliban rule made it aware that a client state was an unrealistic aim.

The US worked hard to get Islamabad and New Delhi to improve their relations so that Al-Qaeda could not provoke war between the nuclear-armed South Asian powers. The US also had a vested interest in ensuring that tensions with India did not result in the reduction of Pakistan forces on the border with Afghanistan. In addition to US pressure, the lessening of cross-border infiltration from Pakistan into Kashmir from 2002 onwards paved the way for India to agree to a resumption of the composite dialogue process which had been abandoned following Kargil.

Musharraf was an unlikely partner for dialogue, as he was seen in New Delhi as the architect of the Kargil war which had claimed over a thousand lives. However, he displayed far greater flexibility than previous civilian leaders in his suggestions for unlocking the logjam of the Kashmir dispute. He not only declared that the UN Security Council Resolutions which had been the centre point of Pakistan diplomacy over six decades could be 'set aside', but in December 2005 raised a series of proposals which included soft borders, demilitarization, self-governance and joint mechanisms of supervision for the Kashmir region. Alongside these public pronouncements, the Musharraf regime engaged in back-channel diplomacy which by April 2007 had made progress in the settlement of the Kashmir dispute. India as the status quo power was more inclined to put Kashmir on the back burner, while encouraging a range of confidence-building measures. They included the opening of a bus service with much fanfare between the two sides of Kashmir in April 2005. In reality, the Pakistan military still regarded India as the main strategic threat, despite the improvement of diplomatic relations from the nadir of 2001–2.

Political Developments

Pervez Musharraf termed the post-Zia era a period of 'sham democracy'. It was, he maintained, marred by corruption, economic incompetence and disunity. He identified this litany of failure with the personalities of Benazir Bhutto and Nawaz Sharif, thereby having a ready-made excuse for their political exclusion. Benazir remained in political exile in London and Dubai. Nawaz Sharif was found guilty in July 2000 of charges of corruption, kidnapping and hijacking. He was allowed to leave Attock jail in December and go with family members to exile in Saudi Arabia. Although Musharraf was initially adept at speaking the language of an internationally acceptable 'good governance' agenda, with its vocabulary of transparency, accountability and empowerment, the attempt to build a 'real' democracy boiled down to the tried and trusted approaches of the country's previous military rulers: namely, a process of accountability to discipline political opponents, rather than root out across-the-board corruption; the curtailing of political activity; and the attempt to build direct links with the populace by means of local government reforms which bypassed the influence of the political opposition. While these measures temporarily weakened opponents, they were unable to secure legitimacy for a regime which faced mounting criticism at home and abroad. It thus had to restart a quasi-democratic political process. This involved alliances with the more opportunistic elements of the religious and feudal elites. From the attempt to bypass patrimonial politics, Musharraf was back to square one, relying for example on the manipulations of kinship networks and patronage by the Chaudhrys of Gujrat to underpin his power in Punjab.

Musharraf transformed Nawaz Sharif's Ehtesab commission into the National Accountability Bureau (NAB).[20] This was tasked under the Chairmanship of Lieutenant-General Syed Mohammad Amjad to investigate corrupt politicians, bureaucrats and businessmen. Its closed courts and snaring of opposition politicians in a string of cases led to charges of its being a partisan body. Significantly, politicians who were known for corruption, but who had switched allegiance to pro-establishment parties, were not investigated. This led to some accusations that the Musharraf loyalist PML(Q) was created by NAB.[21] Undoubtedly the fear of being involved in court cases led to defection from the PPP with some 20 members forming the Pakistan People's Party Parliamentarian Patriot group. Its post-2002 election alliance with the PML(Q) was crucial in ensuring the Musaharraf loyalists a majority in the National Assembly. While the NAB set about its political witch-hunt, significantly only 8 of the 522 people who were prosecuted in its first four years of activity came from the armed forces.[22]

Political activity was curbed not just by the NAB, but by sedition laws and the Maintenance of Public Order Ordinance. Freedom of association was curtailed from 15 March 2000, when an order was introduced banning public rallies, demonstrations and strikes. It was only shortly before the October 2002 polls that the ban on political activities was lifted. Even then rallies and processions were forbidden. The mounting problems besetting the Musharraf regime in 2007 led to a further period of curbs. On 3 November a state of emergency was introduced through a Provisional Constitutional Order. This was ended on 15 December, just one day before the campaigning for national elections was due to begin. In the event the polls were delayed until February 2008, following Benazir Bhutto's assassination.

Local government reform was overseen by a new National Reconciliation Bureau headed by Lieutenant-General (retd) S. Tanwir Naqvi. The new district administration system gave considerable power to the elected district Nazims at the expense both of the bureaucracy and the provincial-level politicians. Significantly, the old Ziaist ploy was adopted of holding the local elections on a non-party basis. Nazims were unconstrained as to how they spent government block grant funding allocated to their district, which bypassed both the bureaucrats and the provincial legislators. In the long run, the Nazims were as unable to provide a bulwark for the Musharraf regime as were the Basic Democrats for Ayub. Some Nazims cashed in their new-found opportunities for wealth and rose to become provincial-level politicians. The reforms further encouraged patronage rather than issue-based politics.

The reforms did not increase administrative efficiency. On the contrary, the weakening of bureaucracy and the failure to follow through the promised police reform promulgated in the ordinance of 2002 contributed to a further decline in governance. This was marked by both inefficiency in the delivery of services and waning confidence in the state's ability to sustain the rule of law. Transparency International's 2007 report maintained that the 350,000-strong police force was the most corrupt public sector agency in Pakistan.[23] Such scholars as Alan Krueger and Jita Maleckova maintain that the resulting sense of marginality and frustration is even more significant than poverty itself in providing a breeding ground for terrorism.[24]

Administrative reforms localized politics and further politicized local administration. Depoliticization at the provincial level boosted the politics of identity and patronage-based politics, as had happened in the Zia era. The *kutchery* style of politics was extended upwards from the local bodies. Simultaneously, local administration was politicized to an even greater degree than previously. This undermined government efficiency. Rather than addressing the issue of weak institutions which had beset the state since its foundation, Musharraf contributed to what has been termed the 'graveyard of institutions' in Pakistan.[25] Alarmingly, by the close of the Musharraf era, there was a decline in the reach of the state, not only in the traditionally lightly controlled FATA region, but in parts of the North West Frontier Province abutting the Tribal Areas and in South Punjab. This encouraged the activities of militant groups who had been initially patronized by the state, but increasingly pitted themselves against it.

Musharraf, like Ayub and Zia before him, found it impossible to engineer legitimacy for his regime. His power base lay with the army not through the ballot box. Attempts to secure some degree of popular legitimization brought further problems. The June 2002 referendum designed to legitimize his presidency had many of the hallmarks of Zia's 1984 rigged referendum. Indeed, Musharraf was led to apologize for the patent interference which had delivered 98 per cent of the votes in his favour. The opposition parties maintained that the turnout was a mere 5 per cent of the electorate. The official government figure was 70 per cent. The *New York Times* neatly summed it up when it declared that 'the balloting had actually diminished Musharraf's stature'.[26] The irregularities certainly dispelled the favourable impression created by the political reforms which increased the number of seats for women, reduced the voting age to eighteen, and stipulated that only those who held degrees were eligible for election to the National Assembly. The most far-reaching reform, however, ended separate electorates, thus enabling the return of minorities to the political mainstream for the forthcoming parliamentary elections.

The national and provincial elections in October 2002 were in fact stage-managed similarly to the referendum. The Political Parties Amendment Act of 28 June, which set eligibility requirements for parties, turned the clock back to the Zia period. Another Presidential Ordinance issued the following month limited Prime Ministers to two terms of office, thereby ruling out Benazir Bhutto and Nawaz Sharif. In the event neither of the two most important opposition leaders returned to Pakistan to campaign. Musharraf further armed himself against possible opposition by issuing the Legal Framework Order which established a National Security Council and restored the President's power to dismiss the Prime Minister.

At the same time as restricting opponents, Musharraf cultivated ties with the Islamic parties and the more opportunistic elements of the Punjab's rural elite. The religious parties' unprecedented electoral success, which saw them gain 45 per cent of the votes and 29 National Assembly seats in NWFP, arose in part from the inflaming of Pashtun sentiment following the US military intervention in Afghanistan. It will be recalled that no Islamic party had previously obtained more than 5 per cent of the national vote. The six-party MMA coalition was also greatly assisted by the neutralization of the mainstream parties and support from the military establishment. This was seen most visibly in the lifting of legal cases against religious leaders. The other major beneficiary of official support was the so-called 'King's party', the PML(Q), which emerged with 77 National Assembly seats and formed the largest party. It mainly comprised pro-establishment former members of the PML(N).

After a period of horse-trading following the election, the PML(Q) took office under the leadership of the Baloch politician Mir Zafarullah Khan Jamali. He was as much a puppet of the President as Mohammed Khan Junejo had initially been under Zia. Jamali was to be replaced, after a brief transitional period under Chaudhry Shujaat Hussain, by Shaukat Aziz, a former Citibank executive. Aziz had even less political standing, but was the technocratic type of public figure preferred by military leaders from Ayub onwards. Following his swearing in as Prime Minister, he promised to seek 'guidance' from the President in order to provide 'good governance' for the people.[27]

Musharraf maintained a tight control over the PML(Q), although he did not join it as Ayub had done with the Convention Muslim League. The President arbitrated in its internal disputes and eased tensions with allies such as MQM when they arose. As Ayesha Siddiqa has perceptively remarked, this approach 'Instead of strengthening democratic institutions, as Musharraf claimed...encouraged clientelism'.[28] Factionalism within the ranks of the PML(Q) was an inevitable result. The most powerful group comprised the followers of Chaudhry Shujaat Hussain and Pervaiz Elahi, which was cemented around landed and *biraderi* ties. The generally weak political position of the PML(Q) was revealed in the 2008 elections. In the absence of rigging and with Musharraf's star on the wane, the PML(Q) saw its support eroded by a resurgent PML(N) and PPP.

The MMA proved more difficult partners than the PML(Q). Its JI component was especially critical of Musharraf's failure to stand down as Chief of Army Staff while holding the dual office of President. The JI was also hostile to the government's pro-American policy. It finally parted ways with its JUI(F) coalition partner and with Musharraf over the military action against the Red Mosque. The MMA's limited action in implementing Islamic measures made it open to being outflanked by radical Islamists. At the same time it did little to meet the Frontier population's aspirations for improved economic conditions. The main consequence of the MMA government was however its inactivity in the face of the growing influence of the TNSM in Swat. The provincial government in Peshawar had responsibility for the region but did nothing to quell the increasing vigilante actions within it.

We have noted earlier that military rule has not only undermined Pakistan's political institutionalization, but has also weakened the ability of civil society to underpin democratization. Musharraf differed from both Ayub and Zia in that, apart from the short-term emergency in November 2007, he did not crack down either on the media, or on civil society institutions.[29] Ironically, perhaps the greatest testament to Musharraf's liberalism was the scope it allowed for civil society organizations led by lawyers to push him out of office.

Centre-State Relations

Military-backed government raised again the old claims of Punjabization. Musharraf adhered to centralization as much as any previous military ruler, despite his talk of devolution. Indeed the practical effect of the 'localization of politics' arising from his local government reforms was as Mohammad Waseem has pointed out, to 'enhance unbridled centralism'.[30] Yet the Musharraf era revealed the extreme limitations facing a centralizing administration committed to top-down modernization if it lacked political legitimacy. Attempts to develop Balochistan on behalf of the national interest ran into increasing particularist opposition. Similarly, Musharraf was unable like Zia before him to address Pakistan's mounting water management and electricity supply problems by forcing through the Kalabagh Dam project.

As early as the mid 1980s, plans were drawn up for a major dam to be constructed at Kalabagh on the Indus. Its proponents argued that the hydro-electricity produced by it (over 2,000 MW generation capacity) would meet the growing energy 'gap', while it would also address the increasing water shortage. Despite promises of international support and the expenditure of vast sums of money on the project plans, provincial opposition to the federal government's proposals prevented the scheme going ahead. The greatest opposition came from Sindh, with fears that the dam would reduce the Indus flow with resulting desertification in the interior and increased flooding by sea water of the coastal delta, destroying the mangrove swamps. There was also resistance to the scheme in NWFP where it was claimed that, in addition to flooding parts of the Nowshera district, the dam's construction would lead to increased water logging and salinity. While expert opinion attempted to address these anxieties through such proposals as reducing the dam's height, the root of the problem was the long-term lack of trust of Punjab in these provinces. Punjab was seen to be the main beneficiary of the project at its neighbour's cost. Calls to put the national interest before provincial anxieties fell on deaf ears.

Musharraf sought to cut through this stalemate by announcing in December 2005 that the Kalabagh Dam would go ahead. He could not, however, command the country as easily as he could the army. Within less than six months, the mounting campaigns in Sindh and NWFP forced him to abandon the proposal. This was democracy of a kind in operation, but the problems of water supply and electricity generation would not be so easily wished away. Unsurprisingly the post-2008 PPP-led government of President Zardari did not reopen what would have been a can of worms for its Sindhi supporters. The 2010 flood disaster, however, pointed to the fact that Pakistan faced more immediate problems of water management arising from climate change than it had previously anticipated. The Prime Minister, Yousaf Raza Gilani, went on record that the flood disaster in Sindh would have been mitigated if the Kalabagh Dam had been constructed. Lack of trust, however, continues to threaten timely measures such as smaller dam projects, let alone the politically charged Kalabagh scheme whose construction in any case would take around six years.

Insurgency in Balochistan

The Musharraf era did see the completion of one major construction project: Gwadar port. This too, however, generated centre-province tensions. Indeed it was a contributory factor in the third round of insurgency in Balochistan since independence. The return of a military-guided government committed to the development of Balochistan in the national interest provoked long-standing antipathy towards the province's 'colonial status'. The establishment of cantonments in Balochistan in the wake of 9/11 made it appear that a Punjabi-led occupying force was taking over. Musharraf's encouragement for Pushtun Islamist parties further created a sense of Baloch marginalization in provincial as well as national politics. The circumstances were thus created for a new phase in militancy.[31] Musharraf appears to have had little respect for the Baloch Sardars, believing that they objected to any development of the region which might weaken their autocratic power. From this perspective their claims to be upholding Baloch rights and interests are merely hypocritical. Security concerns that New Delhi was assisting a low-intensity insurgency may further have encouraged a high-handed attitude which failed to consult Baloch interests when drawing up the development projects in the province.

The Pakistan government attached great strategic and economic importance to the Gwadar development. The deep sea port at the entrance of the Arabian Sea is designed to provide naval strategic depth for Pakistan (it is 450 km further from the Indian border than Karachi). It came into operation in 2008 and is being managed by the Port of Singapore Authority. The economic aim is to make Pakistan a transit hub for trade, especially in oil for Central Asia and the rapidly developing Xinjiang region of China. Baloch nationalists fear that trade profits will be siphoned off to other provinces. They are also concerned about the influx of non-Baloch labourers in search of employment opportunities. Another grievance is the fact that local land has been acquired by real-estate agencies at low prices, subsequently sold on at vast profit to non-Baloch. On 3 May 2004, three Chinese engineers were killed by a remote-controlled car bomb as they made their way to work at Gwadar. Security was immediately stepped up and protection provided to the 450 Chinese technicians. Responsibility for this outrage was claimed by a shadowy organization known as the Balochistan Liberation Army.[32] It had been engaged in a low-intensity insurgency since 2000. Its roots can be traced back to the 1973–7 insurgency when it was funded by the Soviet Union. Some analysts have claimed that its re-emergence was facilitated by Indian support, alarmed at the Chinese strategic interests at Gwadar.[33]

By 2005, violence had escalated and shifted from Gwadar to the Bugti tribal area, a locality so rich in natural gas that it provides around a third of Pakistan's energy needs. The Bugtis were not involved in the 1973–7 Balochistan insurgency. The tribal *sardar* Nawab Akbar Khan Bugti had traditionally been regarded as loyal to Islamabad. He had for example become Chief Minister of Balochistan in 1988. He founded his own political party which drew mainly on Bugti support: the Jamhoori Watan Party. The rape of Dr Shazia Khalid was the catalyst for the conflict between the Bugtis and the Pakistan state. She was assaulted on 2 January 2005 by an army officer. The incident occurred at the Pakistan Petroleum Plant at Sui. It was seen by Nawab Bugti as an attack on his tribe's 'honour' as Shazia was a 'protected guest'. Bugti's attempt to prevent an official cover-up led to mounting conflict and attacks on gas pipelines by tribesmen. Bugti fled his residence at Dera Bugti shortly before it came under attack. From a cave in the Bhamboor Hills he directed what became an insurgency against the authorities. He died a martyr for the Baloch cause on 26 August 2006, when an intercepted satellite phone-call revealed the cave at Tarnai, near Kohlu, in which he was hiding. F-16s and helicopter gunships bombed the area killing the veteran Baloch leader and 38 of his followers. The insurgency had by this time spread from the Bugtis to their traditional Marri tribal rivals. The Marri tribal area became the centre of military activity following a rocket attack on 14 December 2005 on a Pakistan Frontier Corps camp outside the town of Kohlu, which was being visited at the time by President Musharraf. There was also firing on the helicopter which was carrying the Frontier Corps' Inspector-General Shujaat Zamir. Three days later, Kohlu town was bombed along with its surrounding areas. The Marri in these circumstances finally settled differences with the Bugtis, so that there could be a common front in the Baloch struggle.

The Marri tribe provided the main personnel for the Balochistan Liberation Army (BLA),[34] which commenced a campaign directed against security personnel, gas pipes, electricity pylons and railway tracks. On 1 May 2006, the BLA claimed responsibility for blowing up a railway bridge on the main Quetta railway line in the Kohlu district. In the same month, President Musharraf banned it as a terrorist organization. At least 450 persons, including 226 civilians, 82 soldiers and 147 insurgents, were killed in 772 incidents in Balochistan in 2006.[35] The attacks continued into 2007: in May a series of railway line explosions severely disrupted communications between Balochistan and the rest of Pakistan. Punjabi 'settlers' became the victims of target killings. The insurgency in Balochistan, because it was not linked with the 'War on Terror', attracted far less international attention than that in the Tribal Areas. However, the region is of immense strategic and economic significance for Pakistan's future development.

The State and Islam

Musharraf portrayed Pakistan as a moderate Islamic state which would act as a source of stability in a volatile West Asia region. He launched the concept of Enlightened Moderation at the 2002 OIC conference in Malaya. He also emphasized Sufi teachings as a counter to extremism. In November 2006, he launched a National Sufi Council amidst great fanfare in Lahore. Education sector reforms sought to modernize the curriculum of religious schools, with $50 million allocated to pay the salaries of teachers of non-religious subjects. Mounting sectarian violence, claims by both India and Afghanistan of continuing cross-border terrorism, the involvement of members of the Pakistani diaspora in acts of international terrorism and a rising tide of suicide bombings and *fiyadeen* attacks[36] within Pakistan belied this image.

Suicide bombings were introduced to Pakistan via the Iraq conflict. The first major attack claimed the lives of a busload of French naval construction workers outside the Sheraton Hotel, Karachi on 8 May

2002. By the end of the Musharraf era such episodes were a weekly occurrence. For an international audience, Pakistan became synonymous with terrorism. According to the *South Asia Terrorism Portal*, the number of violence-related deaths rocketed from 183 in 2003 to 3,599 in 2007.[37] The Musharraf regime's attempts to secure legitimacy subsequently shifted, as it presented itself as a bulwark against the destabilization of a nuclear-armed state.

Government efforts ensured that a number of religious scholars, headed by the Chairman of the Barelvi education board, *Tanzimul Madaris Pakistan*, issued a *fatwa* on 19 May 2005 which forbade suicide attacks on Muslims and places of worship and public congregations. Deobandi *ulama* steadfastly refused to provide a blanket condemnation of suicide attacks. Even more damaging was the government's inability to clamp down on mushrooming 'hate literature'. The banning of 90 books by the Interior Ministry in 2006 which contained such literature was the tip of the iceberg. Monthly copies of *Mujalla Al-Dawa* and *Ghazwa*, the mouthpieces of LeT, continued to circulate in the Musharraf era. These included *jihadist* articles and the glorification of militant actions.[38] Even more extremist materials than newspapers and magazines were the CDs in circulation which included footage of the beheadings of US 'spies'. These could be obtained quite readily on newsstands outside militant mosques. Extremist messages were also broadcast by radio stations. The most famous of these were run by Mullah Fazlullah in Swat, but there were dozens if not hundreds of other FM stations operating in FATA.

Was the government unable to curb such material, or did it choose not to do so? At the heart of Musharraf's stance was a pragmatic view of Islam's usefulness for state policy. He could not break with the religious parties in the MMA, as he needed their support. This set up contradictions with his policy of Enlightened Moderation. Ultimately he would only go so far in risking the opposition of religious groups, which in any case became increasingly disaffected by his pro-US stance. He thus adopted on the whole a cautious approach, whether this was curbing militants, attempting to roll back state-sponsored Islamization, or responding to Western pressures to reform the curriculum of the *madaris*. Musharraf never abandoned the policy of utilizing ties with Islamic proxies to secure strategic interests in both Afghanistan and Kashmir. He of course had to tread more carefully after 9/11. This involved, as we have seen earlier, distinguishing between militant organizations which had links with Al-Qaeda or were acting independently of the establishment's control and those which might yet prove useful for the pursuit of national strategic goals.

A combination of Musharraf's own liberal attitudes, mounting sectarian conflict and the need to secure a favourable international image for his regime led him initially to attempt to roll back some of the Islamization measures which had been introduced from the Zia era onwards. In May 2000, Musharraf attempted to introduce a limited reform to take away the power of local police officials to respond to blasphemy charges. There had been a number of cases directed against the Christian minority which revealed that the blasphemy ordinance was being used maliciously. Strikes organized by the religious parties led him however to back down. Four years later, he returned to the issue calling for both the Hudood Ordinance and the Blasphemy Ordinance to be 'studied afresh' so that they were not misused. This pronouncement was accompanied by the creation of an independent National Commission for Human Rights.[39]

It was not until 2006 that President Musharraf moved to reform the Hudood Ordinance, following mounting pressure from human rights groups and women's organizations that women who were the victims of rape were being punished while their male assailants were not being prosecuted. Rather than annul the Hudood Ordinance, thereby risking the hostility of Islamist groups, the government introduced the Women's Protection Bill which, when it became law on 1 December, allowed rape to be prosecuted under civil law.[40] Opponents called this measure mere 'eyewash'. It failed to protect women, but was useful in burnishing Musharraf's moderate image in the West.

The Musharraf regime also moved cautiously on the issue of *madrasa* reform, again seeking to balance the need for international approval against the risk of stirring up domestic opposition. While the government had ridden out the October 2001 street protests against US intervention in Afghanistan, orchestrated by the religious parties, Musharraf subsequently trod warily. The role of *madaris* in encouraging extremism had come under considerable international scrutiny since 9/11. The initial Western understanding, although this was later challenged, saw the *madaris* as being the last educational resource for the poor who had been abandoned by the state. Education in these institutions exposed individuals to abuse and to an atmosphere which increased intolerance and militancy. While not all *madaris* trained militants, they provided an ideological justification for violence.[41] The growing tide of sectarian violence provided Musharraf with his own motivation for exerting a tighter grip. After an initial lull in sectarian killings in 2000, they threatened to get out of hand, as they had done in the closing months of Nawaz Sharif's rule. It was not until 2002 that he introduced an ordinance making the imparting of sectarian hatred and militancy in *madaris* a crime punishable by two years' rigorous imprisonment. The ordinance also drew up a three-year project to provide government funds and technical assistance for the widening of the curriculum to include 'modern' general subjects including English and Science. Nevertheless the implementation of reform was slow and large numbers of *madaris* remained unregistered. Of the 13,000 or so that were registered, the vast majority did not participate in the reform programme, which was seen as being American-driven.

Strategic concerns, as we have noted, lay behind the calibrated response to militancy in FATA. Undoubtedly, however, Musharraf's need of MMA support impacted on his response to the growing activities of militant groups who sought to impose *shari'ah* both in the Malakand division and in the federal territory of Islamabad. We will turn first to the situation in Malakand before examining the Lal Masjid (Red Mosque) affair in Islamabad, which marked a key turning point.

The spill-over of the Swat insurgency in April 2009 was to herald a major military offensive not only in Swat but later in South Waziristan (see Chapter 8). Earlier events in Swat were often seen in the West as heralding the spread of Talibanization from the peripheral border areas to Pakistan's heartland. What Swat demonstrates is the longer-term roots of contemporary Talibanization in some of the Pashtun areas. The TTP operations in Swat were in reality those of the TNSM writ large. The latter organization had emerged under the leadership of Maulana Sufi Muhammad, a former JI leader, in response to the legal vacuum created by the merger of the Swat Princely State with the rest of Pakistan in 1969. It had developed in response to the local population's sense that the old-style *riwaj* system of law, which allowed disputants to be tried by customary law or *shari'ah*, had worked, but the new provincially administered Tribal Area criminal and civil codes were inadequate. The implementation of *shari'ah* was sought not only as an Islamization measure but to secure speedy and fair justice for the local population.[42]

Swat's merger with Pakistan had also been accompanied by increased corruption and tensions between the dominant Yusufzai elite and the

Gujjar lower classes. As early as 1995 the TNSM had become engaged in armed struggle with the Pakistan state, so what was to happen in Swat in the following decade was by no means unprecedented. The TNSM not only espoused the cause of legal reform but appealed to the poorer sections of Swat society, most notably the Gujjars and Kammis who had acquired land at the ending of princely rule but were vulnerable to harassment from the local leading Yusufzai Khans. Sufi Mohammad had encouraged his followers in 2001 to fight the US invasion of Afghanistan, during which many had perished. When Musharraf cracked down on militant groups following the attack on the Indian parliament, the TNSM was banned and Sufi Muhammad was arrested. His son-in-law, Maulvi Fazlullah, who was to become the Taliban commander in the region, stepped up the campaign to enforce *shari'ah*. The black turbaned movement grew in strength under his leadership and forged links with other militant groups in the Tribal Areas. This was evidenced when his brother was killed in a US drone attack on an Al-Qaeda compound at Damadola in Bajaur. The MMA government, which had responsibility for Swat and the rest of the Malakand division, did not check the expansion of TNSM power, even though this was at the expense of the state functionaries. Fazlullah announced that the TNSM was a component of the TTP following its creation in 2007. It was this step, along with the burning of girls' schools and the continuing use of illegal FM stations to broadcast calls for Islamic revolution, that led to the military operations in Swat late in the Musharraf era. The military operation Rah-e-Haq, in which more than 200 policemen and soldiers were killed in fighting with the supporters of TNSM, drove Fazlullah to take refuge in the hills. The new ANP government in Peshawar was no more committed to defeating the TNSM than the MMA had been. As we shall see in Chapter 8, the peace treaty of May 2008 enabled Fazlullah to regroup before temporarily seizing power in Swat from the Pakistan state.

Some Western critics maintained that the July 2007 Lal Masjid (Red Mosque) affair in Islamabad, if not stage-managed by Musharraf, was the outcome of his deliberately allowing militancy to fester. He could then present himself as the only barrier to a 'Talibanized' Pakistan. The reality is more likely that a combination of the need for MMA assistance, knowledge that the liberated media would sensationalize any action and the fear that there would be a backlash in the Tribal Areas led to a policy of inactivity. Moreover, the prayer leader of the Red

Mosque, Maulana Abdul Rashid Ghazi, had continued links with ISI. These may have afforded him protection as part of the post 9/11 carefully calibrated response to militancy.[43] They may also have been his undoing, leading him to overstep the limits in his campaign to enforce *shari'ah* and to refuse incentives to surrender as the stand-off developed. Respected Pakistani commentators maintain that it was impossible, given the mosque's proximity to the ISI headquarters, that the agency was unaware of the stockpiling of weapons and the presence of militants from such banned organizations as JeM within its compound.[44]

The Red Mosque in Islamabad had been constructed in 1965 with the Deobandi scholar Maulana Muhammad Abdullah as its *imam*. Its close links with the military dated from the Zia era (see Chapter 5) when it had been important in raising recruits for the Afghanistan *jihad*. The mosque was also associated with hardline Sunni sectarianism. Maulana Abdullah had ties with SSP and was assassinated by Shia militants in 1998. The mosque's running was taken over by his sons Abdul Aziz and Abdul Rashid Ghazi. The latter, who was a History graduate from Quaid-e-Azam University, had until that point been following a secular path. Despite its former establishment links, the mosque became a focus of opposition to the Musharraf regime when it reversed its security policies post 9/11. Abdul Rashid Gazi went underground in 2004 after being accused of involvement in a plot to blow up government buildings in Islamabad. He reportedly had close links with such leading Al-Qaeda figures as Ayman Al-Zawahari. Every Friday demonstrations were raised at the mosque in support of Osama bin Laden.[45]

The provocation for eventual military action against the mosque however came as a result of the activities of Maulana Abdul Aziz's wife Ume-Hassan, who headed the girls' *madrasa* (Jamia Hafsa) which was attached to it. Baton-wielding *burqa*-clad students took over a nearby children's library and abducted women who they claimed were running a neighbouring brothel. Their initial protests in January 2007 had been prompted by the government's demolition of illegally constructed mosques in Islamabad. For many years the Capital Development Authority had turned a blind eye to their expansion. The vigilante actions of the Jamia Hafsa students formed the backdrop to clashes with the male Lal Masjid students, who sought to impose *shari'ah* by unlawfully destroying CDs and cassettes of local shopkeepers. They also kidnapped a number of policemen.[46] After months of inaction, troops stormed the mosque on 10 July 2007 and 50 militants were killed, including Abdul Rashid Ghazi. He was soon to be extolled in posters, conference gatherings and on web pages as a 'gallant warrior' and martyr.

While the military operation was successful, it resulted in an intensification of the insurgencies in the Tribal Areas under the umbrella of a newly formed TTP. When Ghazi's brother was released, while he disavowed suicide attacks and bombings, he publicly thanked Allah for bestowing upon people like Fazlullah and Sufi Muhammad the power to enforce *shari'ah*. Punjab-based sectarian militants not only joined the TTP, but for the first time targeted the state, initially in the Pashtun areas, but ultimately in the Punjab itself. As we shall see in Chapter 8, these attacks became increasingly daring and were directed at the army and ISI, which had in the past helped to nurture and protect organizations such as LeJ and SSP. The immediate aftermath of the Lal Masjid operation saw an average of one suicide attack a day during July. Suicide bombers targeted security forces, government buildings and symbols of Western presence in Pakistan, such as the Marriott Hotel in Islamabad which was hit in September 2008.[47] Musharraf survived a further assassination attempt, but Benazir Bhutto was to fall victim to the mounting tide of violence which in 2008 saw over 2,000 terrorist attacks, killing or injuring around 7,000 people.[48]

Civil-Military Relations and Milbus Under Musharraf

The military's penetration of Pakistan's state, economy and society has been a constant theme throughout this text. Its emergence as a key interest group which intervened to safeguard institutional interests in the name of the nation's stability and security dates back, as we have seen, to the early post-independence era. Under Ayub and Zia, the military role in the running of the state grew apace, although its power was never hegemonic, both because military regimes failed to acquire political legitimacy and because they had to rely to a degree on civilian allies drawn from the rural elite, the Islamic establishment and the bureaucracy. Under Musharraf, military control increased at the expense of the bureaucracy, although the Islamic parties remained restive allies in comparison with the more supine landowners. Before turning to the intensified role of the army in both Pakistan's administration and economy, it is important to note that Musharraf institutionalized its role at the heart of politics.

This was achieved firstly by restoring the powers of the President to dismiss the Prime Minister and assemblies which had been a feature of Zia's legacy, but had been removed during Nawaz Sharif's second stint in office. This measure was important as Musharraf once again restored a direct linkage between the presidency and the military by virtue of his dual office holding as COAS and President. In the early 1990s, civilian presidents had worked closely with the army, but always at one step removed. The Legal Framework Order which was incorporated into the constitution early in 2004 ensured presidential power in Pakistan. Secondly, Musharraf gave the military a permanent role in governance through the passage of the National Security Council Act in 2004. The idea that the military should have a permanent presence in deliberation of national policy-making drew inspiration from the Turkish model of civil-military relations. The notion of a Pakistani version was mooted during the Zia era. Musharraf's introduction of the National Security Council revealed both the long-term suspicion of the army that the state's functioning could not be left to elected politicians and an established pattern of intervention to safeguard its interests. Despite the misgivings of some of the Islamic parties,[49] the 2002 elections had delivered a National Assembly that was sufficiently pro-establishment to ease through the legislation. Supporters of the measure stressed that the NSC was merely consultative and that by bringing the army into the heart of governance it would strengthen democracy by encouraging responsibility and removing the need for future coups. This ignored the fact that the NSC not only reduced still further the possibility of the army being held accountable to civilians, but also was reflective of the weakness of democracy rather than a step towards its consolidation.

At the same time as institutionalizing the imbalance in civil-military relations, the Musharraf regime increased both the size of the military's internal economy and the penetration of serving and retired military personnel in all major institutions. This included not only businesses and commercial undertakings where they may have acquired military based technical skills, but also as heads of universities and think tanks. Within government itself, around 4–5,000 posts were held by military officers.

Long-established military enterprises, such as the Frontier Works Organisation, further extended their activities by seeking private sector partnerships, as for example in the project along with the Habib

Rafique Group and Sacchal Construction to build a Lahore-Sheikhupura-Faisalabad motorway.[50] The military's interest in real-estate development was another marked feature of this period. In 2002, for example, a presidential order enabled the Defence Housing Authority in Lahore to come into existence by taking over the Lahore Cantonment Cooperative Housing Society which had been in existence since 1925. The army was not alone in speculating in real estate which, according to Ayesha Siddiqa, 'can be considered as one of the primary sources of economic activity in the country, especially after 9/11';[51] but it remains a 'major stakeholder' and most importantly there is clear evidence here of its political power being used to forward economic interests. Property prices escalate in army-run housing schemes because they are seen as more 'secure' and have a better infrastructure than civilian-run schemes.[52]

The direct military association with power opened it up to corruption, which reduced its standing in the public's eyes. This declined further as Musharraf's own popularity slumped whilst he continued to hold the dual offices of President and Chief of Army Staff. The army regained its high standing as a result of its tackling militancy and the disastrous floods in July-August 2010. Nonetheless it is important not to see the army's burgeoning economic interests in a totally negative light. Most military enterprises were run reasonably efficiently. The Fauji Foundation's support for ex-servicemen and their dependants not only provided the conditions for the steady supply of recruits, but through, for example, its educational facilities enabled the army to act as the only meritocratic institution in Pakistan. This was evidenced most clearly when General Ashfaq Kayani replaced Musharraf as Army Chief in November 2007. Kayani's father had been a non-commissioned officer.

Musharraf's Decline and Fall

Musharraf, like his military predecessors, lacked legitimacy and cast about for ways to secure a popular mandate. He was more adept at political manipulation than Ayub, but lacked Zia's native cunning. By 2007, the year in which he needed to secure re-election and parliamentary elections were scheduled, he faced mounting unpopularity because of his perceived pro-American stance. At the same time his Western allies were urging him to come to terms with Benazir Bhutto to shore up democratic and liberal forces in Pakistan against a growing tide of militancy. Musharraf not only shared the army's mistrust of the PPP, but personally disliked Bhutto and her husband Asif Ali Zardari. His initial preference was to secure his position as President before allowing her to return to Pakistan on his terms. He attempted this manoeuvre by securing re-election as President from the loyalist parliament dominated by the PML(Q). The questionable legitimacy of this action encouraged the mainstream opposition parties to boycott the indirect electoral college comprising the National Assembly, Provincial Assemblies and the Senate. This duly re-elected Musharraf as President for five years on 6 October. This did not shore up Musharraf's position, however, which had already been severely weakened as a result of his suspension in March 2007 of the Chief Justice of the Supreme Court, Iftikhar Muhammad Chaudhry, on allegations of misconduct and nepotism. The Chief Justice had displayed increasing independence. Musharraf feared that he might pose a legal threat to his re-election process. His action however seriously backfired as Pakistan's lawyers came out onto the streets in mass protest which widened from its concern with the independence of the judiciary into an anti-Musharraf movement. This was the beginning of what was to become the 'Go Musharraf, Go' campaign which eventually culminated in his resignation.

Musharraf was unable to prevent Benazir Bhutto's and Nawaz Sharif's return to Pakistan shortly after his re-election. Benazir Bhutto had returned on 18 October after an amnesty had been granted and all corruption charges against her were lifted. Her triumphant return was marred by an assassination attempt in Karachi in which a suicide bomber killed 136 people and injured at least 450. Nawaz Sharif returned from his Saudi exile in less dramatic circumstances on 25 November. It was increasingly clear that Musharraf would only be able to preserve his position by working with the leaders of the two parties which would come out on top in the impending elections. In another ill-considered step, however, he painted himself further into a corner by taking the drastic step of declaring a state of emergency on 3 November. This was prompted not by fear of Bhutto and Sharif so much as concern that the Supreme Court would invalidate his recent re-election. The new restrictions on the mainstream media which had been given freedom to grow earlier in his regime were epitomized by the Pakistan Electronic Media Regulatory Ordinance. The state of emergency was lifted on 15 December in time for parliamentary elections after new appointees to the Supreme Court ratified Musharraf's election. Earlier on 28 November he had stepped down as Chief of Army Staff, handing control of the army over to General Ashfaq Kayani. This decision, which had been long demanded by opponents, did nothing however to restore his credibility and merely further exposed him to opposition without the army's 'cover'. The emergency had done irreparable damage to both his domestic and international standing. The Commonwealth had suspended Pakistan from membership on 22 November. Musharraf may have won the battle for the presidency but had lost the wider war of political acceptability. This was amply demonstrated by the concerted attempts to secure his impeachment in the wake of national elections.

These had been delayed from January to February 2008 following Benazir Bhutto's assassination in Rawalpindi on 27 December 2007. Political opponents claimed that Musharraf was behind her murder. Subsequent reports have pointed out lapses of security for which he must bear responsibility.[53] In the wake of the revulsion and shock which followed her death, some writers feared for the unity of the Pakistan federation. These anxieties were to be proved exaggerated. The main consequences were to prevent any establishment rigging of the polls. The PPP undoubtedly benefited from a sympathy vote, while the PML(N) returned to power in its Punjab heartland at the expense of the discredited pro-Musharraf PML(Q).[54] The pattern of pre-2002 elections was restored in which the religious-based parties were reduced to the margins. The ANP was the main beneficiary of this process in the NWFP. In a striking reversal of fortune, the widower of Benazir Bhutto and new co-chair of the PPP, Asif Ali Zardari, emerged as the key figure in Pakistan politics.[55]

Musharraf's fate was sealed when Nawaz Sharif agreed to join Zardari's coalition government. While the cooperation between them was short-lived, they were able to demand the President's impeachment with a reasonable expectation that they could muster the necessary two-thirds majority in the National Assembly and Senate to pass an impeachment resolution. Musharraf pre-empted this process by announcing his resignation on 18 August. He maintained that the charges against him were false and that his decision was prompted by the need for national unity. Pakistan's long journey to democratic consolidation was set to enter a new phase.

Conclusion

The mixed legacy of Musharraf's nearly nine years in office was reflected by the jubilant celebration of political opponents and civil society groups, while the responses of the business classes and of many ordinary citizens were more muted. It may have been this along with an undoubted patriotism which later raised his ambition for a possible return to the political stage through the vehicle of a new party, the All-Pakistan Muslim League (APML). By the time of its launch at the beginning of October 2010, the Musharraf era appeared an oasis of relative stability and efficient governance following the chaos and insecurity of the Zardari years. Memories are short in politics so Musharraf's moves were not greeted with the condemnation which had accompanied his departure from the political scene.

In 2008, however, Musharraf, if not exactly a busted flush, appeared to have few tricks left up his sleeve. He had promised to improve Pakistan's governance and economy but had bequeathed a deteriorating situation to his successors. Rather than being the self-proclaimed saviour of the country, he had not begun to address the problems which had bedevilled it since 1947. Political institutions had been further weakened and the issue of provincial autonomy versus centralization still awaited a resolution. Half-hearted attempts had been made to roll back the Islamization measures introduced by Zia. At the same time, the challenge of *shariatization* had increased, in part because of the ambiguous attitude of the Musharraf regime to Islamic parties and Islamic proxies. The initial hopes for improvement in relations with India had stalled, along with the composite dialogue process. Similarly the proclaimed empowerment of the masses through political reform had proved a chimera. Perhaps, in these circumstances, the best summary of the Musharraf regime would run along the lines that much was promised but little was delivered. Pakistan still had to resolve the issues which had blocked off its economic and political development since independence. If Pakistan was not a failed state under Musharraf's stewardship, it remained immobilized. Yet there had never been greater need for structural reform.

8

SURVIVING THE STORM

ZARDARI'S PAKISTAN

Pakistan's 2008 elections were the fairest since those of 1971. They unexpectedly led Benazir Bhutto's controversial widower, Asif Ali Zardari, to a position of political leadership in Pakistan.[1] Like Benazir's victory in 1988, the expectations that elections would usher in a new era failed to materialize. Once again a lengthy period of military-backed rule gave way only to a fragile democracy. Claims of corruption were reminiscent of the 1990s, although this time it seemed that judicial activism, rather than executive action, could signal the end of a democratically elected government. The post-2008 period also shared with the 1990s the spectre of economic crisis and a continuing decline in governance. Both were exacerbated by the 'War on Terror' which according to government figures had cost Pakistan $31.4 billion by 2008–9.[2] It would be wrong, however, to see the Zardari era as merely a repetition of the failed democratization of the late twentieth century. Some political lessons had been learned in that the zero-sum game between the PPP and PML(N) of the 1990s was avoided. Despite periods of tension and outright confrontation, the official opposition was critical of the military, rather than seeking to connive with it to remove the government. President Zardari's public commitment to a politics of reconciliation was not merely rhetoric. He attempted to roll back presidential power, and to address long-standing grievances arising from centre-provincial relations. At the time of writing it is unclear, however, whether this will result in a reinvigorated federalism, or will accelerate centripetal forces.

The constitutional achievements were overshadowed by the ongoing security crisis. The writ of the state in such parts of the country as North and South Waziristan and Swat was dramatically challenged. Public attitudes shifted in 2008–9 so that America's 'War on Terror' in the region was also seen as Pakistan's own conflict. Decades-long strategies of using Islamic proxies in the struggle with India came home with a vengeance. The military found that it could not even secure its own facilities, whether this was the attack on the army headquarters in Rawalpindi in October 2009, or on the Mehran naval base near Shahrah-e-Faisal in Karachi on 22 May 2011. The latter attack held commandos at bay for 17 hours and resulted in the destruction of two P-3c Orion maritime surveillance aircraft. The mounting human toll and a reaction against Washington's unilateral action in killing Osama bin Laden provoked another shift in opinion, as support for military action against militancy waned in June 2011.

The security crisis accompanied a wider crisis in governance. This resulted in part from a lack of competence and coherence in the federal government. The President's skills lay in fixing deals, rather than in enunciating a strategic vision. The lack of coordination was exposed to a media spotlight which was a product of the 24/7 news coverage of politics. No other popularly elected government in Pakistan's history had been under such scrutiny. The media frenzy resulted from the proliferation of cable networks during the first decade of the twenty-first century. Well-known TV hosts and anchor men, such as Geo TV's provocative Kamran Khan, have come to exert far more influence in shaping popular attitudes than would have been conceivable even a decade earlier. Media coverage of government incompetence and President Zardari's absence from the country at the height of the July/August 2010 floods were defining moments. The dramatic rise of judicial activism, which was another legacy of the Musharraf era, heightened the sense of a beleaguered government. In the 1990s, 'constitutional coups' had been overseen by the President. In post-Musharraf Pakistan it seemed that the Supreme Court could at any moment bring down the elected government and possibly usher the return of the army. While the 'troika' of the President, Prime Minister and Chief of Army Staff had wielded power in the 'democratic' 1990s, it seemed at times at the beginning of the second decade of the twenty-first century that a new pantheon of power-holders had emerged, including the President, the Chief Justice and the Chief of Army Staff.

The challenges of democratic consolidation were thus different and even more acute than in the 1990s. However, there were also continuities arising from Pakistan's 'burden of history' alongside the new developments. Any balanced assessment of the government's post-2008 performance must first take note of the economic and security inheritances from the Musharraf regime.

Economic Inheritances

The PPP-led government had inherited a declining economic situation in 2008. Debt rescheduling and relief together with a massive influx of foreign investment and remittances from overseas Pakistani workers had fuelled an unsustainable consumption-led boom in the post 9/11 period. Pakistan's GDP grew at an annual average rate of 6.1 per cent in the five years to 2005–6.[3] President Musharraf and his technocratic Prime Minister Shaukat Aziz had taken the credit for the rapid economic growth. While they encouraged external capital flows, they did not address long-term problems such as low taxation rates, an export sector highly dependent on textiles and low levels of human development. Warning signs of increasing budgetary debt and pressure on foreign exchange reserves were ignored by the Musharraf regime, which faced mounting political opposition and a deteriorating security situation from 2006–7 onwards. The external impact of rising commodity prices increased indebtedness as the state continued to provide fuel and food subsidies. By the time of the February 2008 polls, the economic growth of the earlier Musharraf era was over.[4] Pakistan's security and economic crises were also becoming more closely interlinked. Direct foreign investment was declining, while the rising tide of suicide bombings was not only taking a toll on human life, but on infrastructure and employment opportunities. As the militant writ extended in north-western Pakistan, both boys and girls saw their education disrupted.

The new PPP government remained preoccupied with the post-election political struggle involving the PML(N) and the role of the President. It thus underestimated the growing economic crisis. By the autumn of 2008, rising oil prices had created a spike in inflation which peaked at over 25 per cent; foreign investment declined as the international banking crisis hit; the depreciation of the rupee and the collapse of exports at a time of increasingly costly food and energy imports raised the prospect of Pakistan defaulting on its external debt.[5] Foreign exchange reserves had fallen by November 2008 to only around $3.4 billion, just one month's worth of imports.[6] President Zardari had to reverse his earlier public stance and seek support from the International Monetary Fund, when it became clear after his October visit to Beijing that China would not bail out Pakistan. Stabilization occurred with the current account deficit narrowing from 8.5 per cent of GDP for fiscal year 2007–8 to a projected 2–3 per cent for 2009–10. The budget deficit also narrowed and inflation dropped from its 25 per cent peak in November 2008 to 13 per cent. The improved economy saw an upturn in portfolio investment.

Nonetheless, even before the major setback of the 2010 flood disaster, the security situation acted as a drag on the economy, which did not match the bounce-back of other Asian economies from the world recession. The slowing pace of growth, along with persistent inflation, has resulted in increasing poverty and inequality. This situation resembles that of the last democratic interlude of the 1990s.[7] The IMF mission in mid-July 2010, led by the Assistant Director for Middle East and Central Asia, Adnan Mazeri, expressed concern over uncontrolled expenditure, rising inflation, slow revenue reforms and poor performance in the power sector.[8]

The July/August 2010 floods covered a fifth of Pakistan's land mass. As they made their way southwards, they affected 20 million people, destroyed around 875,000 homes and caused around $1 billion dollars' worth of damage to crops.[9] The cause of the flooding was the unprecedented 72 hours of rain over the Khyber Pakhtunwaha province and Azad Kashmir at the end of July. Khyber Pakhtunkhwa was to receive four times its average monsoon rainfall in a ten-day period beginning 28 July (3,462 mm rain). This created flash floods from the Rivers Kabul and Swat and the inundation of the Swat valley. It meant that if the system of barrages and barriers did not hold, there would be widespread flooding of the Indus and Jhelum Rivers downstream. The overwhelming of the Taunsa Barrage followed by breaches in the Muzaffargarh and TP link canals were key factors in the disaster in the Muzaffargarh district, the worst affected Punjab district with over 2.5 million people displaced and hundreds of villages destroyed. This devastation sparked off debate about engineering faults, the desirability for more dams and barrages, the criminality of the Irrigation Department in their failure to keep up embankments and the fact that some flood protection schemes existed only on paper.[10] Much of the debate was about blame displacement and apportionment. It was clear, however, that the silting of canals and river beds thus raising their height was a factor in the disaster. There was also the usual round of flood-time complaints that officials had deliberately breached canals and embankments to save urban centres by directing the waters towards rural localities in Upper Sindh. When the floods encroached further in Sindh, the claim was made that some feudal landowners had directed flood flows away from their own properties, even if this meant inundating the fields and homes of poorer populations.[11] Inter-provincial tensions were provoked between Balochistan and Sindh following the flooding of Dera Allah Yar and the surrounding Jaffarabad district, with Baloch authorities claiming that their Sindhi counterparts had breached canals and embankments so that the waters were diverted in their direction.[12]

The floods not only necessitated a huge rescue and relief operation but, according to economic commentators, threatened to undermine Pakistan's halting recovery from the 2009 recession. Some estimates were that up to 2 percentage points could be taken off the projected growth rate in GDP of 4.5 per cent. In addition to the damage to an already weak infrastructure and the worsening of the power supply situation, standing crops of rice and cotton were destroyed in Punjab and Sindh. In Punjab alone over 1.6 million acres of crops had been inundated.[13] It was reported that in the major cotton growing district of Rahim Yar Khan the crop could be 20 per cent less for the year 2010–11 than its predecessor.[14] This impacted unfavourably on the textile industry, which is crucial to Pakistan's exports. The slowing down in growth of GDP has occurred at the time of a youth bulge in the population which has generated additional labour demands, with an annual increase at around 2.4 per cent in the working-age population.[15] It seems clear that without a return to high rates of growth in the years ahead, Pakistan will face a growing crisis not just of poverty and unemployment, but of radicalization of its youth.[16]

Security Inheritances

As with the economy, so with the security situation, the newly elected government inherited a sharply deteriorating position. From 2007 onwards, militant groups linked with Al-Qaeda had increasingly turned their firepower on Pakistan's 'apostate' rulers. The state had created the conditions in which *jihadist* organizations could both acquire financial autonomy and embed themselves in local society. Moreover, as the long-term presence of Osama bin Laden in Pakistan was to disclose, small cells within the security apparatus had developed an ability to pursue their own agendas, beyond the control of their commanders. The state was to pay the price for its long-term strategy of utilizing Islamic proxies.

Sectarian and ethnic violence and insurgencies have occurred throughout Pakistan's post-independence history. Two new developments in the Musharraf era were the rising tide of suicide bombings after 2006 and the engagement of the Pakistan army in the Tribal Areas for the first time. The Pakistan military increasingly had to fight erstwhile militant proxies. The conflict intensified, as we saw in Chapter 7, following the commitment of Pakistan troops against the militant-dominated Lal Masjid (Red Mosque) in central Islamabad in July 2007.

The 2008 elections, although delayed by the shocking assassination of Benazir Bhutto, were accompanied by a lull in the suicide attacks and passed off peacefully. The resurgence of the ethnic Pakhtun ANP raised hopes that more sustained dialogue could bring peace to the Tribal Areas. There had been short-lived peace agreements in the Musharraf era. These broke down as the state became drawn into increasing conflict in the Tribal Areas. The military intervention from 2009 onwards, however, was on a far greater scale than that of the Musharraf era. The militants responded with increased suicide attacks in Pakistan cities.

The decision to launch a large-scale military offensive was prompted by the deteriorating situation in the Malakand division. Politicians and public alike began to see that the writ of the state was being undermined and that militancy was not just an external problem, the result of US intervention in Afghanistan, but posed a threat to Pakistan's existence. One should not, however, overplay the new national unity of purpose in security matters trumpeted by the PPP government. For as later surveys have revealed, while there is widespread hostility to the TTP, sectarian groups and militants which have for a long time been associated with the Kashmir *jihad* continue to enjoy support.[17]

The TTP had been formed in December 2007 and brought together several groups under the leadership of Baitullah Mehsud, who based his power in South Waziristan. Mehsud was claimed by the state to be the instigator of numerous suicide attacks, including the assassination of Benazir Bhutto. The TTP was not a monolithic organization, but rather coordinated the activities of existing radical Sunni groups. After the post-election lull, a new upsurge in activity began from the end of 2008. It was focused in Swat, which had seen the rise of the TNSM since the late 1980s. Its support was greatest amongst the Gujars and Ajar population, which clustered along the west bank of the Swat River.

The Malakand insurgency included both TTP and TNSM participation. The Swat Taliban was in fact led by Maulana Fazlullah, the son-in-law of Maulana Sufi Muhammad. He made use of a controversial FM radio station to propagate his demands, which included the introduction of *shari'ah*. The organizational headquarters of his movement was based in his Inam Dheri seminary. The contemporary insurgency was more ruthless than that of the 1990s, but similarly sought to challenge the writ of the state by targeted attacks on government installations. Suicide bombings formed a new element, leading to scores of deaths, as for example in the attack on a police station at Charbagh on 23 August 2008. The revived insurgency began late in 2006 and was initially based in the Sebujini area of Swat. The Pakistan army was first deployed against the local militants in October of the following year.

An agreement was signed between the NWFP government and militants led by Maulana Fazlullah on 21 May 2008. It was hailed as bringing permanent peace, but was seen by the militants as a sign of state weakness. Within six months, sporadic fighting broke out again. Pir Samiullah, a Barelvi leader, was killed in the course of this and his body was later exhumed and hung in Mingora Square. This public space became notorious for the dumping of corpses, including that of Bakht Zeba, a Swat district councillor who on Global Children's Day had criticized the Taliban for its destruction of girls' schools.[18] Well over 1,500 schools were in total destroyed by the Taliban. It also turned its attention to the curbing of 'vice'. A prominent dancer from the Banr bazaar district of Mingora was killed in the square on 2 January 2009 and militants threw money and CDs of her recordings on her body.[19] Despite these abuses, a fresh peace deal was concluded the following month in which Sufi Muhammad acted as a mediator. It was accompanied by the promulgation of the Nizam-e-Adl Regulation which introduced *shari'ah* in Malakand. When the Nizam-e-Adl Resolution was voted in the National Assembly, only MQM abstained from what many observers regarded as a surrender to militancy.[20] The Taliban's violation of the agreement and the movement of militants into the neighbouring districts of Buner and Lower Dir in April formed the backdrop to the military operation known as *Rah-e-Rast* (the Virtuous Path). About 20,000 troops were deployed to suppress the Taliban; hundreds of thousands of civilians were displaced in fighting, which according to government figures claimed over 400 military casualties and 4,000 militants.[21]

Military operations were extended into the South Waziristan base of the TTP in October 2009.[22] Unlike the earlier half-hearted operations of 2004 which led to the first of a number of peace accords, none of which succeeded, the army made unexpectedly rapid progress in its operation codenamed *Rah-e-Nijat* (Path to Deliverance) which commenced on 17 October. Success was dependent on isolating the pro-Baitullah group from other militant organizations in the region led by Maulvi Nazir Ahmad and Hafiz Gul Bahadur.[23] The TTP had also been disrupted by Baitullah's death in a US missile attack in August. Within twenty days, the army had seized all the major towns and villages. Militants chose not to stand and fight, and disappeared into neighbouring North Waziristan. At the same time they opened up a new front with a wave of suicide bombings in Peshawar, which by December 2009 had also spread to Rawalpindi and Lahore. These attacks continued into 2010.

According to the National Crisis Management Cell of the Interior Ministry, 1,835 people lost their lives and 5,194 suffered injuries in the 1,906 terror attacks which occurred in 2009–10.[24] The continuing security crisis led a US index published in *Foreign Policy* magazine in June 2010 to rank Pakistan as the 10th most failed state in the world, just three places below Afghanistan in a list headed by Somalia.[25] Earlier in the month, the US State Department's Global Peace Index placed Pakistan as the world's 5th most unstable country after Iraq, Somalia, Afghanistan and Sudan, recording a second year's successive fall in scoring and rank.[26] The Pakistan government increasingly considered an extension of security operations to North Waziristan. This was the base of a number of militant groups including the Haqqanis, who according to the US had links with Al-Qaeda and were at the forefront of the insurgency in eastern Afghanistan. It had already undertaken operations in the Bajaur Tribal Agency. More controversially, it also raised the possibility of the army conducting operations in south Punjab as evidence mounted that bombings were being undertaken not just by militant organizations based in the Tribal Areas, but by members of banned sectarian organizations operating from the latter region.

The PML(N) government of Punjab denied the existence of a Punjabi Taliban, but growing terrorist attacks in such cities as Islamabad, Rawalpindi and Lahore led Western and Pakistani journalists to talk of a Punjabi Taliban[27] at the end of 2009. This was linked for example to the suicide attack on the Marriott Hotel in Islamabad in September 2008, which claimed over 50 lives, and the audacious 10/10 attack on the army's headquarters in Rawalpindi.[28] The Punjab Taliban was analyzed as a loose network comprising primarily the banned *Sipah-i-Sahaba Pakistan* (SSP), *Lashkar-e-Jhangvi* (LeJ) and *Jaish-e-Muhammad* (JeM) organizations which had previously focused their activities on Kashmir and domestic sectarian violence.[29]

While the attacks of the 'Punjabi Taliban' intensified with the commencing of military operations in South Waziristan in October 2009, the new orientation of SSP, LeJ and JeM again must be understood in a longer-term historical context. These groups did not attack the state's security apparatus before the 2007 army assault on the Red Mosque in Islamabad.[30] The Punjab-based *Lashkar-e-Taiba* stood aloof from the network and refrained from attacking the Pakistan security forces. While its headquarters was in central Punjab, SSP, LeJ and JeM traditionally gathered support in the south Punjab region.[31] Like LeT they had benefited from the support of the country's intelligence services in the context of the 1990s Kashmir insurgency and the Zia regime's earlier sponsorship of Sunni Islam in the wake of the Iranian revolution.

The five 'core' south Punjab districts of Dera Ghazi Khan, Rajanpur, Bahawalnagar, Bahawalpur and Rahim Yar Khan have all figured prominently in journalistic accounts of the 'Punjabi Taliban'. Dera Ghazi Khan was the scene of a major sectarian bomb blast early in February 2009, after which investigations revealed links between local supporters of SSP and the then TTP leader Baitullah Mehsud. Its strategic situation abutting troubled South Waziristan and Balochistan and the presence of nuclear production facilities raised Western concerns about the region's 'Talibanization'. According to a WikiLeaks cable sent from the US Consulate in Lahore in November 2008, a couple of '*jihadi*' camps were operating in Bahawalpur and another on the outskirts of Dera Ghazi Khan. The same cable claimed that an estimated \$100 million had been sent from Arab countries to extremists in southern Punjab districts.[32]

How can we account for the impact of militancy in south Punjab? This region is undoubtedly poorer than other parts of Punjab. The Dera Ghazi Khan and Rajanpur districts are 3rd and 1st respectively for caloric poverty in rural Punjab.[33] Nonetheless, their position is relatively good with respect to most of Balochistan, Sindh and the NWFP. If poverty alone were the determinant of militancy this should be focused on the interior of Sindh, yet it has no purchase there.

Taking a cue from the connections between Pakistan's religious schools (*madaris*) and militancy, some analysts pointed to the proliferation of Deobandi *madaris* from the 1980s onwards in such districts as Dera Ghazi Khan, Rahim Yar Khan, Bahawalpur and Bahawalnagar.[34] According to 2008 Intelligence Bureau estimates, the Rahim Yar Khan district has 559 *madaris* followed by Bahawalpur (481) and Bahawalnagar (310).[35] Bahawalpur has the greatest concentration of mosques of any Punjabi city apart from Lahore. One factor in the mushrooming of these mosques and religious schools in south Punjab is the traditional influence of Sufi Islam in the region. This shrine cult is regarded as un-Islamic by Deobandis, who have focused their efforts in the region to counter it. In April 2009, there were press reports of JeM activists attempting to take over Barelvi mosques associated with Sufi Islam in the Bahawalnagar, Bahawalpur and Rahim Yar Khan districts. Sufi shrines have been targeted elsewhere in Pakistan. They have been blown up in the Frontier and the famous Sufi shrine of Hazrat Datta Ganj Baksh in Lahore was the scene of a deadly suicide attack at the beginning of July 2010.

While recent attention has focused on the spill-over of militants from South Waziristan into Dera Ghazi Khan, the early 1947 Partition-related migration offers a fascinating although as yet unexplored insight into militancy. It is clear that in such localities as Bahawalpur it is not the indigenous population but Indian migrants who provide the main support for Deobandi institutions. Work on the SSP in Jhang has shown that in this region of central Punjab the radical Sunni cause is supported by migrant populations who are excluded from power by the Shia feudal landholding elites.[36] Undoubtedly sectarianism and support for the Kashmir *jihad*, popular amongst migrants from India, provide the basis for radicalization. This is in all probability the case in south Punjab, although Sunni radical sectarianism is directed not just against Shias but also Barelvis. Militant recruiters have a large pool to work with, as migrants from India make up around 50 per cent of the population of Dera Ghazi Khan city. Much work is required on this, but what we do know at present is that the founder of JeM in 2000, Maulana Masood Azhar,[37] was born in the old city of Bahawalpur; like Hafiz Muhammad Saeed, the leader of LeT, his family were Partition migrants from India in 1947. Although JeM has been banned since 2001, it maintains a strong presence in the city where it has its *Dar al Jihad* headquarters.

Commentators feared that the flood disaster would exacerbate the security situation, just as it had done with respect to the weak economy. The floods hit particularly hard the south Punjab and Swat regions which had been centres of militancy. This not only piled further misery onto their long-suffering populations, but further demonstrated the lack of the state's reach in their aftermath. In the absence of an adequate government response, there was evidence that charities associated with militant organizations were very active in relief efforts. A number of press reports noted the activities of the *Falah-e-Insaniyat* foundation, which is the charity wing of the militant group *Jamaat-ud-Dawa*. While such activities were not designed specifically to recruit fresh *jihadis*, they point to the failure of the state to compete for the 'hearts and the minds' of the local populace.[38] A similar state of affairs with respect to relief had existed in Azad Kashmir in the wake of the 2005 earthquake. A number of leading political figures from both the PPP and PML(N), including the Punjab Chief Minister Shahbaz Sharif, warned that in the absence of an adequate response to relief and rehabilitation extremist groups would gain a grip on the population.[39] The desperation of people in the Muzaffargarh district was brought home by reports of attacks on a convoy carrying relief goods near Jadeywala which forced the Pakistan Poverty Alleviation Fund and International Organisation for Migration temporarily to suspend their work.[40]

Militant groups, like the population at large, were affected by the communications collapse in the flood-hit areas. Nonetheless, the suicide bomb attack in the heart of the Peshawar cantonment which killed Safwat Ghayyur, the commandant of the Frontier Constabulary, on 4 August revealed not only that the TTP's operational network remained intact, but that it had no compunction in continuing its attack on the security forces at the height of a national emergency.

After the bin Laden episode, there was evidence not only of the long-established split between Al-Qaeda and LeT, but of increasing distance between the latter and the TTP. LeT had earlier stood aloof from the

'Punjabi Taliban'. It not only continued to receive support from the Pakistan authorities because of its potential value as a strategic asset against India, but was seen as increasingly useful to the Saudis' efforts to restrict protests in Pakistan against the kingdom's suppression of pro-democracy protests in Bahrain. As we have seen earlier, WikiLeaks cables have revealed US awareness of Saudi funding for LeT and other Punjab-based *jihadist* groups. TTP because of its links with Al-Qaeda was anti-Saudi Arabia and was as likely as extremist Shias to attack Saudi interests in Pakistan. Significantly it expressed its 'full support' for the shooting of a Saudi diplomat in Karachi on 16 May 2011.[41]

Political and Constitutional Developments

The 2008 polls had generated optimism that Pakistan could break out of its post-independence cycle of poor governance, authoritarianism, regional tensions and instability, not only because of the defeat of the Musharraf loyalists by the mainstream parties, but because of the hope that there would be sustained cooperation between the PPP and the PML(N). It was widely acknowledged that the prospects for democratic consolidation in the 1990s had been undermined by their infighting.

Benazir Bhutto's assassination brought the party leaderships closer together than ever before. The post-election PPP-PML(N) government however proved short-lived, although it had functioned long enough to force President Musharraf to step down under the threat of impeachment. Asif Zardari was elected as his successor. The PML(N) withdrew from the government led by Prime Minister Yousuf Reza Gilani because of Zardari's delay in reinstating the judges along with the Chief Justice of the Supreme Court, Iftikhar Muhammad Chaudhry, who had been dismissed by Musharraf during the emergency of November 2007. Their reinstatement had formed an integral part of the March 2008 Bhurban agreement under which the PML(N) had joined the governing coalition. The disagreements between Nawaz Sharif and Asif Zardari over the judiciary at the national level impacted on Punjab politics where the PPP was a junior partner in the government headed by Shahbaz Sharif. Months of rising tensions saw President Zardari blunder in imposing governor's rule in Punjab on 25 February 2009, following the Supreme Court's disqualification of the Sharif brothers from holding office.

The PML(N) threw itself behind the gathering popular protest movement for the restoration of the judges. In the wake of a widespread breakdown in law and order, the army chief General Kayani met with Prime Minister Gilani. The tenor of their conversation is unknown, but the PPP government, despite public claims not to give into 'blackmail', reinstated Chief Justice Iftikhar Chaudhury and the other judges on 21 March. This ended the running sore between the PPP and PML(N). The lifting of governor's rule and the return of Shahbaz Sharif to the office of Punjab Chief Minister marked the next stage in the normalization of relations. Nevertheless, the long-term effects of the PPP's attempt to override the Punjab government were seen at the end of September 2009, when Shahbaz Sharif held a clandestine meeting in Rawalpindi with General Kayani.[42] When news leaked out, it was seen as an attempt by the PML(N) to get onside with the army in anticipation of Zardari's fall from power. During the 1990s, both Benazir Bhutto and Nawaz Sharif had undermined democracy, by cultivating the military in this way.

It would be wrong nonetheless to say that the 1990s were being totally replicated. Some progress in the way of replacing a politics of confrontation with one of accommodation was admittedly made with the implementation of key elements in the charter for democracy which had been agreed in May 2006 between Benazir Bhutto and Nawaz Sharif with the passage of the 18th Amendment in April 2010. The removal of the President's power to dismiss the Prime Minister and dissolve the Assembly represented a major triumph for parliamentary democracy; although the accompanying renaming of NWFP as Khyber Pakhtunkhwa generated controversy and violence in the Abbottabad and Mansehra districts of Hazara division.

President Zardari's watchword, despite his blunder in intervening in Punjab politics in February 2009, has been 'reconciliation'. Relations with coalition allies at the centre and in the provinces had not always run smoothly, let alone with the PML(N). Conflicts, especially with MQM, led to dropping the tabling of the controversial National Reconciliation Order in parliament. This left the fate of the indemnity bill promulgated during the Musharraf era to the Supreme Court which nullified it. The MQM also opposed the Sharia Regulation for the Malakand division, which unsuccessfully attempted to secure peace in the Swat valley. The unreliability of the MQM and its eventual departure from the national coalition led the PPP to fall back on an alliance with the PML(Q). This appeared an expedient for staying in office and shoring up support in the Punjab in the face of the PML(N) resurgence there, rather than as part of a wider politics of reconciliation.

Democracy in the 1990s had been undermined by the party's weak institutionalization as well as by the zero-sum game approach to politics. Since the February 2008 elections, little has changed with respect to the former. Pakistan political parties continue to be undemocratic institutions with power flowing top-down from their leaderships. The Sharif brothers' firm grip on the PML(N) is mirrored by Asif Zardari's control of the PPP. He has surrounded himself with loyal supporters and in the process has replaced many of Benazir Bhutto's allies.

Parliamentary life has also remained as unchanged. MLAs prioritize patronage for allies and supporters over the scrutiny of legislation. Most members of the national and provincial assemblies possess a rent-seeking rather than public service attitude. The continuing dominance of landholders in the assemblies has prevented meaningful taxation and land reforms. A state of affairs persists in which 10 per cent of the population possesses over 25 per cent of the national income. The PPP will continue to disillusion its supporters, if it does not tackle these issues by matching rhetoric with action. What is required is not just populist measures such as the Benazir Income Support Scheme, but reforms which tackle the long-term causes of poverty. The party under Asif Ali Zardari's leadership is, however, even more conservative and managerial than it was under his late wife.

The continuing economic imbalances feed contemporary ethnic and Islamic militancy.[43] Democratic rule since 2008 has seen an increase in military expenditure rather than its reining in. The defence budget for 2010–11 has been set at an astronomical Rs 442.2 billion. Rising defence costs have been incurred in the military operations in Malakand and the Tribal Areas. According to official estimates, Pakistan has faced increased expenditure amounting to $43 billion in combating militancy and terrorism in the period 2001–2010.[44]

Today as throughout Pakistan's history, the requirements of military expenditure alongside those of debt servicing leave little available for social expenditure in a constrained tax environment. Public expenditure on education as a percentage of GDP stands at just 2 per cent according to the Pakistan Economic Survey 2009–10. This compares unfavourably with such neighbouring countries as India (3.3 per cent) and Bangladesh (2.6 per cent).[45] In the wake of Osama bin Laden's killing, there was unprecedented criticism of the military from the opposition PML(N) during the defence budget debate on 18 June. There were calls not only for greater transparency, but for a curb on salaries and perks so that they should be on a par with those of senior officers in India.[46] In reality such measures would not enable Pakistan to match India's social expenditure. This could only be achieved through greater taxation, primarily on agricultural income.

While low educational expenditure undermines Pakistan's long-term democratic and development prospects, in the short term these are damaged by inflation which is persistently high. Everyday existence for millions of Pakistanis is also made miserable by the increasing shortages of power and water. The continuing interruptions in power supply have brought people onto the streets. Energy shortages limit the economic growth required to raise people out of poverty.[47]

The PPP's debacle during the floods emergency further undermined its popular base. The trust deficit was seen in the low take-up of the President's Flood Relief Fund and the channelling of international aid through NGOs and UN agencies rather than the Pakistan government. Moreover, the army's role in meeting the disaster once again revealed it as the strongest and most effective state institution. Even before the floods, the army had recovered the prestige it had lost during the end of the Musharraf era: a US survey (Pew) revealed growing approval ratings for the army, with 84 per cent of those surveyed expressing positive views, compared with 68 per cent in 2007.[48] The recovery in the army's popularity reflected not just the 'professional stance' taken by its Commander-in-Chief Ashfaq Pervez Kayani, but also the army's effectiveness. This contrasted with the lack of responsiveness of the civilian authorities, exemplified by President Zardari's absence in Europe as the floods took their grip.

Judicial Activism

Judicial activism was a crucial legacy of the Musharraf era. Some commentators saw an increasing arrogance of the reinvigorated Supreme Court as a potential danger to democracy. They feared that the court would provide the circumstances for military intervention by overthrowing the Zardari government. The tensions between the PPP-led government and the Supreme Court were rooted in the increasingly politicized activities of the Chief Justice Iftikhar Ahmed Chaudhry, who was reinstated on 21 March 2009. This action had been delayed and was undertaken by Zardari under duress arising from the PML(N) agitation around the issue and the promptings of the military. Public interest litigation burnished the Supreme Court's populist credentials. The Supreme Court objected to the changes in the appointment of higher court judges envisaged by the 18th Amendment, and referred it back to parliament for review. The National Assembly passed a 19th Amendment to address this issue, but it did not end the clash of institutions which reflected both the Supreme Court's guarding of its autonomy and jurisdiction, and its increased confidence post-Musharraf.

The main bone of contention, however, was the instability arising from the Supreme Court's actions involving the National Reconciliation Order (NRO). This gave indemnity to around 8,000 people (including President Zardari) who had corruption and other cases standing against them from the period 1 January 1986 and 12 October 1999. As we saw in Chapter 7, Musharraf's issuing of the NRO in October 2007 had allowed Benazir Bhutto to return to Pakistan. In July 2009, the Supreme Court set 28 November as a deadline for parliamentary approval of the NRO and 36 other ordinances issued by Musharraf. When parliamentary opposition, including that from the PPP's coalition partner the MQM, meant that the law could not be endorsed by parliament, the Supreme Court annulled the NRO on 16 December 2009 and asked the government to revive the corruption cases against the President in the Swiss courts. The government's response of publicly committing itself to implement the Supreme Court's decisions in this and other instances, but seeking to circumvent them through delay, continued the tension between the institutions. It also increased the poor governance performance which came to be seen as a hallmark of the post-2008 period.[49] The judiciary also lost out however in the ensuing stalemate, as the moral halo it had worn since Musharraf's November 2007 emergency began to slip in the welter of controversy.[50]

Centre and Provinces

Tensions between the centre and provinces have undermined political development throughout Pakistan's history. A number of analysts' prescriptions, including the creation of more provinces, increasing the administrative powers of the provinces and fiscal decentralization, were implemented under the Zardari presidency. The creation of Gilgit-Baltistan as a fifth province, the renaming of NWFP as Khyber-

Pakhtunkhwa, the removal of the Concurrent List by the 18th Constitutional Amendment, and agreement of the 7th National Financial Commission (NFC) Award would in different circumstances have been regarded as epochal events. Ironically the weakening capacity of provincial administrations not only raises issues as to whether they will be able to discharge new responsibilities, but also whether long-desired reform will close the alarming gap that has opened between the state and its citizens as a result of its inability to deliver basic services. A rebalancing of centre-province relations may thus not address long-standing political legitimization problems, but may increase trends towards incoherence and fragmentation within the Pakistan polity.

These question marks notwithstanding, the unanimous approval of the Seventh National Financial Commission Award in December 2009 was a major achievement for President Zardari. The 1979, 1984 and 2000 Financial Commissions had all ended in deadlock. The 2009 award thus highlighted improved relations between the provinces. It also marked two other important developments which represented a break with the past. Firstly, the provinces' share of the divisible pool of taxation revenues accruing from income taxes, general sales tax, wealth taxes, capital gains taxes and customs duties was increased from 47.5 per cent under Musharraf to 56 per cent in the first year of the award (2010–11), rising to 57.5 per cent in the remainder of the five-year interval. This set in motion financial transfers of around an additional 70 billion rupees to the provinces. Secondly, the demands of such provinces as Balochistan and Sindh were met in that poverty, revenue generation and urban-rural density were added to the previously sole criterion of population when distributing the provincial allocation. Under the new multiple weightage indicators, the significance of population fell to 82 per cent of the total. The award thus signalled steps forward with respect to fiscal decentralization and the concerns of the smaller provinces regarding Punjabization of Pakistan.

The 18th Amendment to the Constitution followed shortly after the NFC award. While most attention was devoted to the removal of presidential powers regarding the dissolution of parliament and suspension of the constitution and the removal of the two-term limit on Prime Ministers,[51] the Amendment also marked an important decentralization of power through its abolition of the Concurrent List that had been established at the time of the 1973 Constitution. This had enshrined 47 subjects on which both federal and provincial governments could legislate. With its abolition, subjects within the Concurrent Legislative List, such as education, health, population, labour, social welfare and tourism, were transferred to the domain of the provinces. This increase in their responsibilities was accompanied by concerns as to whether there would be sufficient expertise to administer institutions such as the Higher Education Commission, which had previously been a federal responsibility. Most importantly, given Pakistan's 'demographic time bomb', it raised the question as to whether the provinces could effectively finance and administer the programmes of the Federal Population Welfare Ministry.

Provincial powers were also increased as a result of equalizing the representation of the provinces and federal government on the Council of Common Interest (CCI) and transferring some items such as census and estate duty from the sole domain of the federal government to the purview of the CCI. Another important change involved sharing the federal government's prior sole ownership of raw materials such as oil, gas and minerals within the provinces and their adjacent territorial waters. This could potentially address some of the Baloch nationalists' long-standing grievances against the federal government.

The PPP Government and External Relations

India's offer of a $5 million donation for flood victims masked the fact that democratization had not improved relations. Similarly the US financial support which by mid-August was promised at $150 million was indicative of concerns in Washington regarding Pakistan's stability, rather than evidence of growing trust between the two allies in the conflict against Islamic militancy. It was precisely the awareness that Pakistan was too important to fail because of its geo-strategic significance, not to mention its 100 or so nuclear warheads, that prevented a cessation of US military and economic aid in the wake of the Osama Bin Laden episode, despite public anger on Capitol Hill.

Pakistan's democratic travails have been historically linked not only with its elitist political culture and uneven socio-economic structure but also with its external relations. It is well established that the state's geopolitical significance has encouraged long-term ties with the US which have bolstered the military and their allies. The US has historically maintained close relations with all three of Pakistan's military rulers, Ayub, Zia and Musharraf, although they found it increasingly difficult to escape demands to display democratic credentials and legitimacy.

Benazir Bhutto in particular used her Washington contacts to strengthen the growing belief in the West that democracy alone could stabilize Pakistan. It was well known that both London and Washington worked hard behind the scenes to enable her return to Pakistan.[52] Her assassination removed the hope that she might work in tandem with Musharraf to ensure stability in the front-line state in the 'War on Terror'. Her widower had neither the standing nor contacts that she possessed. The West, however, bolstered President Zardari and encouraged him to pose resolute opposition to extremist pressures. Simultaneously, channels to the Pakistan army via the Pentagon remained open, and it is known that Kayani was in discussions with Admiral Mike Mullen, US Chairman of the Joint Chiefs of Staff, at the time of the March 2009 Punjab crisis.

The PPP government was useful to Washington in that relations between Zardari and Karzai were noticeably better than they had ever been at the time of the Musharraf presidency. This was important to the new Af-Pak strategy of the Obama administration, which needed Pakistan's leverage in the reintegration of Taliban insurgents in Afghanistan. This was a central plank of the Afghanistan Peace and Reintegration Programme, which had been approved at the January 2010 London Conference. Financial incentives, jobs and immunity from prosecution were to be offered as part of a reintegration programme for insurgents, provided that they dissociated themselves from Al-Qaeda and renounced violence. Without a successful policy of reconciliation, the transfer of security responsibility from US and NATO troops to the Afghan National Army would be impossible by the end of 2014. Osama bin Laden's death, the Arab Spring of 2011 and the shifting of Al-Qaeda's operational centre to southern Yemen all reduced Afghanistan's strategic importance for the US. Washington was nonetheless keen to avoid the mistakes of its earlier withdrawal from the region in the 1990s. It was acutely aware that another civil war in Afghanistan would have wide-ranging regional implications.

The interaction of the civilian leaderships of Afghanistan and Pakistan, including the visit of a delegation of the Afghan High Peace Council under the leadership of the former President Burhanuddin Rabbani to Islamabad in January 2011, was accompanied by military and intelligence meetings which would have been impossible in the tense relations of the Musharraf era. Pakistan's importance for the settlement of Afghanistan moderated Washington's ire at the military in the wake of the Osama bin Laden affair. Nonetheless, Pakistan had its own interests in Afghanistan which complicated its value to the West as a regional peace-broker. These involved an enhanced role for the Pakhtun in any post-settlement Afghanistan and the desire to limit Indian involvement in the country. India's growing economic aid commitment was accompanied by a 'partnership council' to enhance cooperation on security and law enforcement issues. A further sign of the growing Indian presence was provided by Manmohan Singh's visit to Kabul in May 2011 during which he addressed a joint session of the Afghan parliament. Some commentators have noted that New Delhi's growing influence in Afghanistan since 2001 could become as important a source of tension with Pakistan as the long-running Kashmir flashpoint.[53]

There was not a post-2008 blossoming in Indo-Pakistan relations, despite the fact that some in Pakistan saw President Zardari as taking a soft tone towards India and the prevalent view that New Delhi would engage more with civilian than military leaders. Dialogue remained hostage to terrorist activity. On 7 July there was a bomb attack on the Indian Embassy in Kabul. Indian claims that this bore the hallmarks of the ISI do not appear far from the mark as leaked US cables contain an alleged admission by Mahmood Durrani, the National Security Adviser, that the Pakistan government, while not directly involved, did 'have some contacts with bad guys and perhaps one of them did it'.[54] The much more serious terrorist outrage in Mumbai on 26 November 2008, in which LeT was implicated, dealt an even more grievous blow to the faltering composite dialogue process.

The issue of terrorism dominated relations between the countries before talks resumed at Foreign Secretary level in June 2010. These were conducted in an atmosphere of low expectations. Indeed it was clear that US pressures arising from the shifting strategic tide in Afghanistan, rather than any change of outlook in New Delhi, were the main factors in their resumption. The issues of terrorism and the future of Afghanistan as much as the long-running Kashmir dispute will determine Indo-Pakistan relations in the period up to 2014. If Pakistan is sure-footed, it may well be able to regain some of the ground it has lost in Afghanistan as the US winds down its operation in the country. At the same time, if there is any redirection of *jihadist* activities from Afghanistan to Kashmir, tensions between the distant South Asian neighbours will escalate to dangerous levels. The diplomatic and strategic fall-out from the Abbottabad episode at the beginning of May 2011 undoubtedly further soured relations between Islamabad and New Delhi. It is certain however that the military's overweening influence in Pakistan can only be scaled down if there is a normalization of relations with India.

Civil-Military Relations

The dramatic events of 2 May 2011 in Abbottabad have provoked intense debate concerning the civil-military relationship in Pakistan. Has the best opportunity for reducing military influence since 1971 already been forfeited? Will there be a gradual erosion of military power, rather than a dramatic civilian push-back? Is the army's long-term internal unity imperilled? Will its lower-ranking officers become more radicalized?

While some Western commentators[55] portrayed the army as beleaguered, its ability to recover from the much greater humiliation of the 16 December 1971 surrender at Dhaka gives cause for pause. Any report into the 'Abbottabad incident' is likely to be as tightly constrained by the military as was the 1971 report by Justice Hamidoor Rehman. Survey polls continue to reveal public support for the military establishment's claims that it is indispensable for maintaining Pakistan's sovereignty, despite mounting evidence to the contrary. Air Chief Marshal Rao Qamar Suleman revealed during the security briefing to parliament on the bin Laden affair that the Shamsi air base in Balochistan was under the control of the United Arab Emirates, not the Pakistan air force. Leaked US cables not only reveal Washington's agreement to compensation for civilians killed in drone attacks, but that the Pakistan military, despite public protests, have not only acquiesced in drone attacks, some of which are launched from within Pakistan, but have called for their increase. Referring to the Waziristan situation in February 2008, according to a leaked US State Department cable, the Chief of Army Staff General Kayani asked Admiral William Fallon (Commander US Central Command) if he could assist in providing continuous predator coverage of the conflict area. Fallon is reported to have responded that he did not have the assets to support this request.[56]

The PPP-led government studiously avoided criticism of the military in the wake of a humiliation if not debacle at Abbottabad. The circumstances surrounding Osama bin Laden's death on 2 May 2011 could not have been more humiliating for Pakistan's military establishment, with its revelation that Al-Qaeda's iconic leader had been living for five years in a compound with high walls topped with barbed wire within walking distance of the country's elite military academy at Kakul. They confirmed international observers' long-held suspicions about the security establishment's ability to 'look two ways'. While there were some attempts to mend fences between Washington and Islamabad at the time of Senator John Kerry's and Secretary of State Hillary Clinton's visit to Pakistan, the anger on Capitol Hill was palpable. Prime Minister Gilani however absolved the Security Service of either complicity or incompetence.[57] The government acted slowly in establishing a commission of enquiry. It was left to the opposition PML(N) to voice criticism. Nawaz Sharif even went so far in a press conference on 17 May as to demand that defence and security expenditures be presented in parliament for discussion and approval. The PPP's approach may have been motivated solely by a survival instinct. Certainly, when President Zardari had attempted to increase civilian oversight of ISI in July 2008, this was quickly squashed. Similarly, Prime Minister's Gilani's promise to despatch the Director-General of ISI, Lieutenant-General Ahmed Shuja Pasha, to India to investigate claims of Pakistan involvement in the Mumbai bombings in November 2008 was blocked. Tensions between the government and the army bubbled to the surface over the Kerry-Lugar Bill in September-October 2009. Its proposal to authorize $1.5 billion of civilian aid to Pakistan for five years predated the Obama administration, but fitted into his new strategy for Afghanistan and Pakistan. The conditions for this material assistance were clearly designed to increase civilian oversight of the military.[58] Zardari called the passage of the bill through Congress the greatest foreign policy success of his year in office. The sniping of parliamentary opponents that it infringed Pakistan's 'sovereignty' was of little concern to him. The government was however put firmly on the back foot when the army publicly aired its objections following a meeting of the powerful Corps Commanders on 7 October.

The lack of PPP initiative and the continued high public approval ratings of General Kayani do not mean however that nothing may have changed as a result of Abbottabad. The trend towards linking Western military aid with improved governance and democratic consolidation will have been strengthened. Within Pakistan, the PML(N)'s criticism of the military has been unprecedented and could form the prelude to a future Nawaz Sharif-led government increasing civilian oversight of military expenditure. None of this signals an immediate civilian assertion of control, but the army's resistance to such attempts will have been weakened by public criticism and by the fact that the head of ISI, Lieutenant-General Ahmad Shuja Pasha, and top military officials admitted failure and accepted accountability in a five-hour in camera briefing to parliament on 13 May. Democratic consolidation in the long term requires the army's exposure to the same levels of accountability as elected politicians. It would not only involve full parliamentary scrutiny of military expenditure, but review of security policies.

The Pakistan army's unified command structure has prevented the colonels' coups seen elsewhere in Asia, Africa and Latin America. The changing social composition of its middle ranks has raised concerns of a divide opening up between a more radical junior officer corps and conservative generals. Military losses as a result of actions in the Tribal Areas and civilian collateral damage since around 2007 onwards have been cited as further factors in stretching the army's loyalties. Certainly, General Kayani's 'town hall meetings' with junior officers in the wake of the 2 May episode were as unprecedented as public criticism. Unconfirmed reports of the garrison meetings suggest that the Chief of Army Staff faced robust criticism for his pro-US policies. This may explain the subsequent withdrawal of visas for US military trainers. This does not presage Kayani's removal, far less a junior-officer-led coup. All the time that Kayani retains the support of the Corps Commanders, his position is secure. The middle ranks of the army still have sufficient perks and pensions to see their best interests served by bolstering rather than undermining the hierarchy. Finally, despite the tensions with Washington, which are likely to continue as troops are drawn down in Afghanistan, the Pakistan military has a range of regional concerns which can only be secured by longer-term cooperation with the West.

Conclusion

Even before the national calamity of the July-August 2010 floods, Pakistan's third democratic transition was beset by crises. Some of these were of the government's making, others were external and revealed the fragility of the state's economy and institutions. Inevitably the euphoria generated by the 2008 polls could not be sustained. A single parliament is manifestly insufficient to introduce the structural economic and institutional reforms conducive to democratic consolidation. With respect to traditionally 'backward' areas such as FATA, where literacy rates, access to health care and safe drinking water are well below the Pakistani average, a generation of developmental activity is required.[59] In the short term, the best that can be achieved alongside improved security is the establishment of job-creation schemes in neighbouring settled areas which would increase the economic prospects of FATA residents.[60] Militancy in south Punjab is rooted not only in poverty and political marginalization of the lower classes by feudalism, but in deeply entrenched sectarianism. These issues cannot be tackled overnight but require long-term institution building, and a step change in political culture.

The parties' internal lack of democracy is another hindrance to national democratic consolidation. Party politics remained personalized. This discourages both the emergence of a new generation of leaders and 'out of the box' thinking. Competency levels among the political class remain low, thereby perpetuating the dangerous perception that the army is the only efficiently functioning institution. The army's public stance on the Kerry-Lugar Bill graphically illustrated that it would not easily submit to greater civilian oversight through such mechanisms as an empowered Defence Committee of the Cabinet. Its security wing (ISI) remained only nominally under prime ministerial control. Moreover, the revelation of Osama bin Laden's long-term residence in Abbottabad raised the spectre of ISI groups being able to act independently of established command structures. His killing not only put Pakistan under the international spotlight, but resulted in unprecedented domestic criticism of the military and General Kayani. The evolving relationship between the army and the civilian authorities will be of profound significance for Pakistan's future. Its effects will be felt throughout the region and the international community.

EPILOGUE

FUTURE LONG-TERM CHALLENGES, PROSPECTS AND POSSIBILITIES

Most recent scenario-building studies of Pakistan have focused on the immediate future of 3–7 years.[1] This is understandable given the country's volatility and the prevalence of such 'black swan' events as the 1979 Soviet occupation of Afghanistan, 9/11 and the killing of Osama bin Laden in Abbottabad. The consequences for Pakistan of the Western drawing down of troops in contemporary Afghanistan, which may be hastened following his death, remain unpredictable. Could a Taliban-dominated Afghanistan be a source of cross-border terrorism designed to destabilize an 'apostate' government in Islamabad? Will India and Pakistan discover common interests in a post-conflict Afghanistan, or will a further layer of mistrust be added to their 'enduring rivalry'? A further unpredictable 'game changing' event could be the 'blowback' of a major terrorist attack in the US which was linked to Pakistan. All of this provides cause for pause when attempting to assess the country's longer-term future. Nonetheless, a more expansive view is necessary, both to escape the confines of a contemporary security-driven analysis and to ascertain whether some of the longer-term trends discerned in this text will ultimately derail Pakistan's celebrated ability to 'muddle through'.

The few authors who have stepped back from the contemporary rush of events have stressed the need for radical institutional, economic and cultural transformation if the Pakistan state is to survive future population pressures, with their attendant shortages of food, water and power.[2]

In a worst-case scenario, Pakistan could within the next couple of decades have a population of around 220 million people, with a water shortage equivalent to over two-thirds of the present flow of the Indus, 6 million of its youth unemployed and close on 30 million of its citizens out of school.[3] Both an under-employed youth bulge and provincial conflicts over diminishing water resources could present even greater threats to Pakistan's survival than that posed in recent times by the surge in Islamic militancy. In order to surmount these longer-term challenges, in the words of a former leading civil servant, Tasneem Ahmad Siddique, 'Pakistan has no option but to change for the better'.[4]

As we have seen throughout this text, however, Pakistan's history is littered with missed opportunities for building political institutions, addressing socio-economic imbalances and inequalities and moving beyond ad-hocism to establish a vision for the country. Moreover, the power of landed and social elites which has blocked Islamist political advance could ironically impede effective response to longer-term demographic and environmental challenges.

Will Pakistan muddle through its contemporary security problems only to be undone by the environmental and population challenges facing it in the next two or three decades? Could the state implode under the pressures of power and water shortages and periodic flooding and droughts? There is a view in Pakistan that the international community has too much at stake in terms of regional security and the dangers of nuclear proliferation to allow the state to fail. This attitude has been encouraged by the repeating pattern of IMF 'bail-outs', despite half-hearted and failed attempts to implement prescribed economic and governance reforms. Reliance on international aid has however not only increased dependency, but fuelled domestic consumer-led booms followed by cyclical downturns, rather than encouraging more sustainable development based on increasing rates of investment and export-led growth. What has been termed 'borrowed growth' by Maleeha Lodhi[5] has also reduced incentives for tax reform and helped perpetuate what Tasneem Ahmad Siddiqui calls an 'anachronistic' political system 'where the super-structure…is fast becoming alienated from the realities on the ground'.[6]

The Demographic Time Bomb and the Youth Bulge

The phrase 'demographic time bomb' has been used to dramatize Pakistan's burgeoning population problem. As we saw in the Introduction, the present population is predicted to rise to 335 million by 2050, making Pakistan the fourth largest country in the world. If fertility rates are not decreased, the number could be as high as 460 million. Such a population level would place an immense strain on resources. Even at the current levels, 1 child in 4 is malnourished, almost 36 million people live below the poverty line and half the population is illiterate. Traditionally the export of labour has been one means by which Pakistan has addressed population growth. This is unlikely to be a future option. Internal migration will ease pressure in the countryside, but unless urban development is planned and employment opportunities are increased, projected trends will bring significant environmental, political and social challenges. Historically high rates of economic growth will need to be sustained over a prolonged period if the potential for greater polarization is to be avoided.

A fatalistic view is that the combination of poverty and conservative Islamic values place insurmountable problems in the way of reducing birth rates. Certainly Pakistan has experienced a very chequered history with respect to family planning successes since the Ayub era in the 1950s. Evidence from Bangladesh, however, points to the fact that policies of economic empowerment of women can reduce birth rates even in the context of poverty. Birth rates in Iran have come down in the years since the 1979 revolution, while they also remain significantly lower in Indonesia, with which Pakistan could be compared as a populous Muslim country.[7] Indeed in both Indonesia and Iran fertility rates are half those of Pakistan. In Pakistan's urban areas, at least, it seems that rather than cultural resistance, it is the absence of effective reproductive health services which is the point at issue. The gap between the demand for contraceptive services and their supply (25 per cent) is in fact one of the largest in the world. There may well be scope for ever further provision of contraceptives from the private sector, building on the pioneering efforts of Greenstar Social Marketing, which has seen the private sector account for around 40 per cent of family planning services by 2011.[8]

Pakistan's population problems are symptomatic of many of its future challenges in that the country is at a crossroads. Action is possible to avert a crisis and the challenge could in certain circumstances be turned to an opportunity. The seriousness of the situation however should not be underestimated. The response needs to be holistic in this as in other areas of national challenges. Family planning services alone will be insufficient. They must be accompanied by education and poverty alleviation measures to have an effect. It is now well established that increased female economic participation lowers birth rates and that poverty is both a result of large families and is a contributing factor to them. Education is also of course vital in terms of ensuring that Pakistan's present and future predominantly youthful population is a productive asset, rather than a threat to social cohesion.

The failure of education has contributed to and mirrored the failure of the Pakistan state to achieve its potential since 1947. The failure has resulted both from a 'commitment' gap and an 'implementation' gap. Pakistan has over a sustained period allocated only 2 per cent of its GDP to education; administrative incapacity, which has allowed corruption to thrive, has meant that even these limited resources have been poorly utilized and allocated. The outcomes are apparent in high rates of adult illiteracy, gender and regional disparities, and unconnected public, private and religious systems of education. Within the South Asia region, only Afghanistan has lower educational outcomes. Pakistan is thus ill-prepared to meet the challenges of one of the largest youth bulges in the world which is set to increase until the mid 2020s.[9]

Much has been written about public educational decline since the 1970s and the rise of mosque schools in terms of the current challenges from militancy. Another stereotype of Pakistan is that it is a society which attaches little interest or worth to learning and knowledge. The demand for education is however testified by the burgeoning private sector. Yet this alone cannot ensure the broad access to education which will be crucial for Pakistan's future prospects. Past failures will need to be addressed both in the resource allocation and governance areas. Pakistan can draw on international experience from developing countries with respect to such policies as conditional cash transfer programmes to raise enrolment and retention rates. Nonetheless, hard political choices will have to be made to achieve the degree of progress required. If disaster is to be averted, Pakistan will need to match at least the average of the developing countries' expenditure on education.

How education is delivered and what values it encourages are also crucial for equipping Pakistan to face the challenges of the twenty-first century. Curriculum reform of the *madaris* has long been mooted, but not effectively implemented. The need for reform of the state textbooks which inculcate stereotypes that hinder social cohesion and regional relations has also been long referred to.[10] Behind all of this, there is the necessity firstly for a more mature approach to Pakistan's origins and history, and secondly for the encouragement of education which stimulates rather than suppresses critical thinking.

Improvements in the provision and quality of education will enable Pakistan to benefit from the youth bulge, rather than suffer from its consequences. An increasingly educated population will not only provide opportunities for individual self-fulfilment, and a decent livelihood, but will boost economic growth. Some experts have attributed as much as one third of the growth in China in the 1990s to its 'demographic dividend'. Youthful energies can be directed into positive rather than negative and destructive channels. Pakistan can as a whole benefit from expanding social mobility and entrepreneurial activities. There would of course be the need to ensure that increased educational expenditure was effectively managed and directed in a way that existing regional, rural-urban and gender imbalances were addressed. More emphasis would be required on technical education and on non-university provision than in the past. This will help raise the very low attendance rate of just 50 per cent and 25 per cent respectively at primary and secondary levels of education. The importance of female educational expansion cannot be overstated. Pakistan currently languishes 127th out of 130 countries in the Global Gender Index, with over a third of adult women illiterate and only one fifth participating in the labour force. This represents not only a huge injustice, but a massive waste of potential talent. Moreover it perpetuates the cycle of poor and large families. Across numerous historical periods and cultural contexts there is evident a clear link between increased female literacy and declining birth rates. Educational transformation would broaden Pakistan's already vibrant civil society, which is sometimes overlooked by scholars fixated on security issues and the state in crisis theory.[11] It would also result in a drastic improvement in the country's lowly position in the ranking of the economic competitiveness of its labour force (101 out of 133 countries in the latest Global Competitiveness Index). S. J. Burki has pointed to Pakistan's opportunities for producing services for export not just in IT, but the health, entertainment, education and publishing sectors, provided that there is a sufficiently educated labour force.[12] Its existence could also force the pace of political change and social transformation by unleashing a revolution of rising expectations, especially in less developed rural areas of the country. This could however be a two-edged sword if inequalities are unaddressed, creating the conditions for massive social upheaval with a range of possible political outcomes.[13]

Even with the current levels of awareness of social injustice, there appears to be increasing youth alienation. In 2009 the British Council surveyed a representative sample of 1,500 young people across the country.[14] This was one of a number of national surveys of youth opinion.[15] The findings in the British Council report entitled *Pakistan: The Next Generation* revealed deep disillusionment with Pakistan and its institutions.[16] Only 15 per cent of the respondents believed that the country was heading in the right direction; just 10 per cent thought that Pakistan was doing well; only 10 per cent had confidence in the national government.[17] This reflected not only the well-established problems of corruption and poor governance, but the total exclusion of youthful participation in policy development. This issue needs to be addressed if widespread cynicism is not to store up future problems for the country. Indeed such a mindset provides support for future military intervention, which we have shown to have disastrous political, economic and foreign policy impacts. Pakistan's next generation requires not only better schooling and job creation, but opportunities to become active citizens. Pakistan stands at the crossroads in this as in so many other areas of national life. The British Council sagely warns that only by building a cross-party consensus can the needs of the next generation be truly met and policy continuity be assured.[18]

Water and Energy Security

Alongside a demographic time bomb, Pakistan is facing possible future shortfalls in energy and water supply. These are obviously linked with growing demands because of population increase, but are also impacted by climate change and failures of governance and management. The constant load-shedding is the visible outcome of a current domestic energy shortfall estimated at 4–6 gigawatts. The need for water supply by tankers in urban areas is the equivalent with respect to water supply. Its availability has dropped since the 1950s from around 5,000 cubic metres per capita to about 1,500. The figure projected for 2020 is an alarming 850 with Pakistan running 'dry'. A worst-case scenario points to future 'water wars' between provinces and between India and Pakistan. Certainly the creation of an upstream dam at Baglihar on the Chenab to help address India's electrical supply problems has since 2008 added another element to Indo-Pakistan tensions.

Water could however be a source of potential collaboration as well as conflict in South Asia. Historically the only really effective long-term Indo-Pakistan agreement has been the 1960 Indus Water Treaty. This is coming under increasing pressure now because of India building dams upstream on tributaries to the Indus. Nonetheless the longevity of the agreement provides optimism not only for future effective water management agreements, but for the possibility that progress in these areas could generate increased trust with respect to other divisive issues. India of course has its own water security worries because of China's plans to develop its south-north water diversion project further by building dams on the Brahmaputra in Tibet. India is a lower-riparian country in this respect and may not only empathize with Pakistan and for that matter Bangladesh's fears regarding its own upstream activities, but also see the need for the development of regional multilateral water cooperation mechanisms.

If the situation is not so bleak for Pakistan with respect to regional water security as it appears at first sight, so there are also prospects for increasing domestic water availability. This can be achieved not through financially costly and environmentally damaging new large-scale projects, but by upgrading existing technology. This would enable water to be stored more effectively and prevent the huge losses (perhaps up to 30 per cent of supply) through the country's unlined canals. There could also be advances in water saving technology. Demand could also be decreased if production of rice for example was switched in favour of less water-intensive crops.[19]

Pakistan's current energy crisis also does not mean that its long-term prospects are necessarily as bleak as they may initially appear. The country possesses vast potential energy supplies with respect to coal. The Thar field in Sindh, which extends over 9,000 square miles and contains 175 billion tonnes, represents one of the largest untapped coalfields in the world. It contains as much future energy supply as is available from Saudi Arabia's existing oil reserves. There is great potential also for extending hydroelectricity supply which has seen its production share decline from around 70 per cent in the 1970s to 30 per cent today. China is currently investing in increased coal, hydroelectric and nuclear power production in Pakistan. Increased production will need to be balanced with environmental concerns; these can be partly addressed by community-based small-scale hydroelectric projects and the construction of micro-wind turbines in parts of Khyber Pakhtunkhwa.

As with water supply, electricity shortages arise because of inefficient management due to poor infrastructure and theft. The loss of up to 30 per cent of generated power in transit is a direct result of these problems. Successive governments have fought shy of tackling the issue because of the political influence of landlords, who are the main culprits of power theft. Government installations, including army ones, have further exacerbated the power crisis by non-payment of bills.

Again, as with water, energy security in the region could either exacerbate current political tensions between neighbours or encourage future cooperation. The Turkmenistan-Afghanistan-Pakistan-India natural gas pipeline treaty may be seen in the future as the first tentative step in this direction. It promises not only to meet India's and Pakistan's growing reliance on imported gas, but could provide shared security interests. Pakistan's geo-political strategic situation, which has cost it dear especially over the past three decades, may be transformed into a geo-economic asset.

Pakistan's future challenges could thus create opportunities. They will only be grasped, however, if a series of difficult policy choices are made. It is extremely unlikely that Pakistan will be able to muddle through to a position of stability. For the latter to be achieved a number of previous assumptions will need to be turned on their head and fundamental improvements made to governance. It is to these two areas that we will now turn.

The Need for National Consensus

A recent study has argued that Pakistan's different regime path from India has resulted in part from not just weak political institutionalization inherited from the freedom movement, but a lack of ideational strength. Aside from a vague commitment to Islam, the Pakistan movement was marked by 'negative nationalism' with no vision for the future.[20] Certainly, Pakistan requires a sense of national purpose in the coming years if it is to achieve the uphill task of educating, feeding, employing and providing social justice for a rapidly growing population. This requires coordination and cooperation on a vast scale in a country which has historically been marked by confrontation and short-term thinking. There has been no consistency of policy except resistance to Indian military domination. Can a new generation of Pakistani leaders escape the burdens of over six decades of history?

Pressure of events themselves may nudge Pakistan's leaders and its people in the direction of a national consensus, as was seen in the widespread commitment to tackle militancy in 2009 following the TTP's excesses in Swat. The media explosion of recent years can perhaps play a role here, but this is not guaranteed.

For transformation to be effective, previously politically inexpedient connections between social justice and the sustainability of growth, on the one hand, and between regional security and democratisation, on the other, need to be honestly addressed. A national consensus aimed at turning Pakistan around could emerge from this debate, which would have at its heart a more inclusive economic growth policy than hitherto and an expanded security policy. Economic policy would recognize that past rapid growth, although giving Pakistan temporary advantage over its neighbours, had failed to raise it to middle-income status because it had neglected human development. Pakistan lacked in the long term the human capital to take advantage of globalization. Requirements of international competitiveness as much as of justice and social cohesion should place the tackling of inequality at the heart of future growth models. Security policy would realize that attempts to counterbalance India through arms races, the use of Islamic proxies and the induction of great power rivalries into South Asia have historically come at a high cost of sectarian conflict, economic dependency and democratic fragility. National security policies should in future be defined not solely in terms of conventional and nuclear forces, but encompass food, water and energy security, security from crime, all provided by the state in the context of environmental sustainability and political strength.[21]

Pakistan's security threat from India in one respect will intensify during the next two to three decades as India continues to ascend as a regional and global economic power. This will underpin its military might and dramatically increase the costs of Pakistan's attempt to balance its rival through a combination of conventional and nuclear weapons systems. As with the population bulge, this state of affairs could prove either inherently destabilizing, or provide unforeseen opportunities. In the worst-case scenario Pakistan could destroy itself before seeing through structural reforms, by becoming involved in a nuclear arms race with India which its fragile economy could not ultimately sustain. There are even some hawks in New Delhi who may seek to lure Pakistan into this trap in the hope of doing a 'Reagan' on the country.

Alternatively Pakistan may seek to deepen economic, diplomatic and military ties with Beijing. Such a policy would be strengthened if the lingering Chinese fears of militant support for Uighur separatists were removed. This course of action would however, just as much as an arms race, imperil any transformative reform process. Pakistan's interests would be held hostage to the fate of Sino-Indian relations. If these either dramatically improved or worsened, as a result for example of water disputes, its national interests could be imperilled. Pakistan might have less room for manoeuvre in resolving its own water issues with India. It would also have an increased security risk in resource-rich Balochistan. Finally, hopes of both a 'peace dividend' and of rolling back the domestic influence of the military-security establishment would be dashed.

The Requirement for Improved Governance

Numerous writers have provided their checklists of governance reforms, including improvements in the delivery of services, tax-raising capabilities, along with reform to key institutions including the bureaucracy, the military, the police, state-run corporations, political parties and electoral processes.[22] To these might be added greater transparency in economic life, especially with respect to the privatization of loss-making state enterprises. The direction of the changes would be to empower citizens at the expense of rent-seeking political elites, and increase the resources available for education and health provision.

Successes in one area of reform are in fact likely to improve reform prospects in another. For example if the state is seen as more responsive to its citizens and proactive in delivering basic services, resistance to demands for widening the tax net could be diminished. Increased political legitimacy would also diminish the possibilities of military intervention. In this way a virtuous circle could be established. Just as a 'solution' to the Kashmir dispute may be a generation away, so the normalization of civil-military relations will be a long-term task. Throughout this text we have seen that military intervention has undermined political development, national cohesion and sustainable economic growth. Democratic consolidation will only become irreversible with civilian control over the army and with its expenditures becoming transparent and open for political debate. The reining in of the military influence can only occur within the context of the kind of national reappraisal of Pakistan's future security environment we have referred to above.

Conclusion

Pakistan faces massive future problems arising from population and environmental pressures. They present potentially greater challenges to the state than the current security crisis. It seems unlikely that Pakistan will be able to muddle through in the future, as it has done throughout much of its troubled history. During the next two decades a major turnaround of national policy direction is required in order to avoid future catastrophe. The responsibility for this will lie with Pakistan's leaders and people, although external well-wishers can assist the process through financial and technical expertise. A future stable and sustainable Pakistan state will bring immense benefits to its population. It will enable the South Asia region to fulfil its economic potential. Failure of a nuclear weapons state would have global as well as regional repercussions. Until Pakistan has moved towards economic sustainability and democratic consolidation it will continue to be the focus of heightened international concern.

NOTES

INTRODUCTION

1. Ralph Peters, 'Blood Borders: How a Better Middle East Would Look', *Armed Forces Journal*, June 2006, http://www.armedforcesjournal.com/2006/06/1833899.
2. Stephen P. Cohen, *The Idea of Pakistan* (Washington, DC: The Brookings Institution, 2004).
3. Institute for Defence Studies and Analyses, *Whither Pakistan* http://www.idsa.in/book/WhitherPakistan.
4. Bruce Riedel, 'Armageddon in Islamabad; 23 June 2009', *The National Interest Online* http://www.nationalinterest.org/printerfriendly.aspx?id=21644; John R. Schmidt, 'The Unravelling of Pakistan', June-July 2009, *Survival: Global Politics and Strategy* http://www.iiss.org/publications/survival/survival-2009/year-2009-issue-3/the-unravelling-of-pakistan.
5. Stephen P. Cohen, *The Future of Pakistan* (Washington, DC: The Brookings Institution, January 2011); Stephen P. Cohen. *Pakistan's Future: The Bellagio Papers* http://www.brookings.edu/~/media/Files/rl/papers/2010/09_bellagio_conference_papers/09_bellagio_papers.pdf.
6. Pivotal states were defined as those at a tipping point of success or failure and whose fate would impact on regional and global stability. See Robert Chase, Emily Hill and Paul Kennedy (eds), *The Pivotal States: A New Framework for U.S. Policy in the Developing World* (New York: W.W.W. Norton, 1999).
7. See the following PSRU briefs: Kashif Saeed Khan and Mumar Ahmed Syed, *Conflict, Transformation and Development in Pakistan's North Western Territories*, Brief no. 33 (24 May 2008); Ian Talbot, *The Future Prospects for FATA*, Brief no. 41 (22 September 2008); James Revill, *Pakistan's Tribal Areas: An Agency by Agency Assessment*, Brief no. 42 (29 September 2008); Shaun Gregory, *Towards a Containment Strategy in the FATA*, Brief no. 43 (20 October 2008).
8. See, for example, Civil Secretariat Federally Administered Tribal Areas (FARA),

2007, 'FATA Sustainable Development Plan 2007–2015; Government of Pakistan, Peshawar', http://www.worldsecuritynetwork.com/documents/Booklet on FATA SDP 2006–15.pdf.

9. For a typical security-driven new interest in Pakistan see Jessica Stern, 'Pakistan's Jihad Culture', *Foreign Affairs* 79, 6 (November-December 2000), pp. 115–26.
10. See, for example, C. Fair, 'Militant Recruitment in Pakistan: Implications for Al Qaeda and Other Organizations', *Studies in Conflict and Terrorism* 27, 2 (November/December 2004).
11. R. Looney, 'Failed Economic Take-Offs and Terrorism: Conceptualising a Proper Role for US Assistance to Pakistan', *Asian Survey* 44, 6 (November-December 2004) pp. 771–93.
12. Ibid., p. 786.
13. T. Niazi, 'Modernization, Modernity and Fundamentalism: The Pakistani Experience', *International Journal of Contemporary Sociology* 43, 1 (2006) pp. 125–50.
14. M. Yusuf, 'The Prospects of a Talibanized Pakistan' (The Brookings Institution, 2007) http://www.brookings.edu/opinions/2007/0831pakistan _yusuf.aspx.
15. C. Fair, 'Militant Recruitment in Pakistan: A New Look at the Militancy-Madrassah Connection', *Asia Policy* 4 (July 2007), pp. 107–34.
16. This follows to an extent the earlier assessment of Marc Sageman, *Understanding Terror Networks* (Philadelphia: University of Pennsylvania Press, 2004), pp. 61–98.
17. Tariq Rahman, 'Pluralism and Intolerance in Pakistani Society: Attitudes of Pakistani Students towards the Religious "Other"', 29: http://www.aku.edu/news/majorevents/ismcconf-tr.pdf.
18. Fair, 'Militant Recruitment in Pakistan', pp. 124 ff.
19. The Andrabi report used published household data, and a census of schooling choice maintained that less than 1 per cent of all the educational enrolment in the country was into the *madrasa* system. Tahir Andrabi, Jishnu Das, Asim Khawaja and Tristan Zajonic, 'Religious School Enrolment in Pakistan: A Look at the Data', John F. Kennedy School of Government Working Paper, no. RWP05–024 (March 2005).
20. For this kind of approach see International Crisis Group, 'Pakistan: Karachi's Madrasas and Violent Extremism', ICG Islamabad/Brussels 2007 http://www.crisisgroup.org/library/documents/asia/south_asia/130_pakistan_karachi s madrasas and violent extremism.pdf.
21. Fair, 'Militant Recruitment in Pakistan', pp. 120 ff.
22. Hilary Synnott, *Transforming Pakistan: Ways Out of Instability* (Abingdon: IISS/Routledge, 2009).
23. Ibid., p. 180.
24. Ibid., p. 181.
25. Zahid Hussain, *Frontline Pakistan: The Struggle with Militant Islam* (New York: Columbia University Press, 2007). This was followed up by another

work, *Frontline Pakistan: The Path to Catastrophe and the Killing of Benazir Bhutto* (London: I. B. Tauris, 2008).

26. Hassan Abbas, *Pakistan's Drift into Extremism: Allah, the Army and America's War on Terror* (Armonk, NY: M. E. Sharpe, 2005).
27. Husain Haqqani, *Pakistan: Between Mosque and Military* (Washington, DC: Carnegie Endowment for Peace, 2005).
28. Katja Riikonen, 'Punjabi "Taliban" and the Sectarian Groups in Pakistan', PSRU Brief 55 (12 February 2010); Hassan Abbas, 'Defining the Punjabi Taliban Network', *CTC Sentinel* 2, 4 (April 2009), pp. 1–4; P. K. Upadhyay, 'From FATA to South Punjab: The Looming Leap of Islamic Radicalism in Pakistan', *Institute for Defence Studies and Analyses*, 30 November 2009.
29. Notably the Sipah-e-Sabha Pakistan, the Lashkar-e-Jhangvi and Jaish-e-Muhammad.
30. For an examination of the incidence and intensity of poverty in South Punjab see Ali Cheema, Lyyla Khalid and Manasam Patnam, 'The Geography of Poverty: Evidence from Punjab', *Lahore Journal of Economics*, special edition (September 2008), pp. 163–81.
31. See Safiya Aftab, 'Poverty and Militancy', PIPS *Journal of Conflict and Peace Studies* (October-December 2008) 1, 1, pp. 66–86.
32. Maleeha Lodhi (ed.), *Pakistan: Beyond the 'Crisis State'* (London: Hurst, 2011).
33. Farzana Shaikh, *Making Sense of Pakistan* (London: Hurst 2009), p. 212.
34. Jonathan Paris, *Prospects for Pakistan* (London: Legatum Institute, 2010).
35. Mill's Orientalist work, *The History of British India*, was published in 3 volumes in 1818. Mill never visited India, although as a result of this work he became a London-based examiner of the correspondence of the East India Company.
36. For a typical security-driven new interest in Pakistan, see Jessica Stern, 'Pakistan's Jihad Culture', *Foreign Affairs* 79, 6 (November-December 2000), pp. 115–26.
37. See I. Talbot, *Pakistan: A Modern History*, 2nd edn (London: Hurst, 2009).
38. See Praveen Swami, *India, Pakistan and the Secret Jihad: The Covert War in Kashmir, 1947–2004* (London: Routledge, 2006).
39. Ian Talbot and Gurharpal Singh, *The Partition of India* (Cambridge: Cambridge University Press, 2009), p. 38.
40. Tariq Ali, *Pakistan: Military Rule or People's Power* (New York: William Morrow & Co., 1970).
41. Tariq Ali, *Can Pakistan Survive? The Death of a State* (Harmondsworth: Penguin, 1983).
42. *Dawn*, Internet edition, 22 June 2011.
43. American Embassy Karachi to Department of State, 16 and 21 November 1962, 790.D.00/10–2762 and 790.D.00/11–2762, National Archives at College Park.
44. See, Talbot and Singh, *The Partition of India*, ch. 6.
45. For the view that international concerns are misplaced with respect to the security of Pakistan's nuclear assets, see Rabia Akhtar and Nazir Hussain, 'Safety

and Security of Pakistan's Nuclear Assets' in Usama Butt and N. Elahi (eds), *Pakistan's Quagmire: Security, Strategy and the Future of the Islamic-Nuclear nation* (New York: Continuum, 2010), pp. 175–97.

46. See, for example, Timothy D. Hoyt, 'Pakistani Nuclear Doctrine and the Dangers of Strategic Myopia', *Asian Survey* 41, 6 (November-December 2001), pp. 968–74.
47. The Indian Defence Minister, A. K. Antony, expressed serious concerns about the growing Sino-Pakistan defence ties in the wake of Gilani's visit to Beijing and maintained that India would have to increase its defence capability. See *Dawn*, Internet edition, 21 May 2011.
48. See Yunas Samad, 'Pakistan or Punjabistan: Crisis of National identity' in Gurharpal Singh and Ian Talbot (eds), *Punjabi Identity: Continuity and Change* (New Delhi: Manohar, 1996), pp. 61–87.
49. Frederic Grare, 'Pakistan: The Resurgence of Baluch Nationalism', Carnegie paper no. 65 (January 2006), p. 6.
50. See Willem van Schendel, *A History of Bangladesh* (Cambridge: Cambridge University Press, 2009) pp. 161 ff.
51. On ethnic and linguistic allegiances see Alyssa Ayres, *Speaking Like a State: Language and Nationalism in Pakistan* (Cambridge: Cambridge University Press, 2009).
52. See Ian Talbot, *Pakistan: A Modern History*, 2nd edn, (London: Hurst, 2009), ch. 2 and3.

1. PAKISTAN: LAND, PEOPLE, SOCIETY

1. See K. L. Kamal, *Pakistan: The Garrison State* (New Delhi: Intellectual Publishing House, 1982). A. Waites, 'The State and Civil Society in Pakistan', *Contemporary South Asia* 4, 3 (1995), pp. 229 ff. Altaf Gauhar, *Ayub Khan: Pakistan's First Military Ruler* (Karachi: Oxford University Press, 1996).
2. I. Talbot and G. Singh, *The Partition of India* (Cambridge: Cambridge University Press, 2009), p. 162.
3. Cited in I. H. Malik, *State and Civil Society in Pakistan: Politics of Authority, Ideology and Ethnicity* (Basingstoke: Macmillan, 1987), p. 63.
4. JI activists were grouped in the Al-Badr and Al-Shams groups and received training for military actions by members of the Pakistan army.
5. For an authoritative examination of these legacies see Sana Haroon, *Frontier of Faith: Islam in the Indo-Afghan Borderland* (London: Hurst, 2007).
6. *Dawn*, Internet edition, 24 October 2010.
7. The present Gas Sales Agreement is to provide via the 800 km-long pipeline over 1 billion cubic feet of gas per day, which could be used to generate 4,500 MW of electricity.
8. Pakistan is currently facing a shortfall in its main fuel, compressed natural gas, of around 203 million cubic feet per day. The electricity shortfall with its accompanying 'load-shedding' is in the range of 4–6,000 MW. Pakistan's largely unutilized coal reserves are however amongst the largest in the world. The Thar field, which spreads over an area of 9,100 square miles in Sindh, contains 175

billion tons of coal. Its exploitation to meet Pakistan's energy shortfall would have immense environmental repercussions.

9. See M. K. Bhadrakumar, 'Pipeline Project a new Silk Road', *Asia Times*, 16 December 2010.
10. Ishtiaq Ahmad, 'Beyond the Geopolitics of Resolving Conflict in Afghanistan', unpublished paper, BASAS Conference, University of Southampton, 12 April 2011.
11. *Dawn*, Internet edition, 1 November 2010.
12. John Briscoe and Usman Qamar, *Pakistan's Water Economy: Running Dry* (Washington, DC: Oxford University Press and the World Bank, 2006), p. xiv.
13. For details see *Dawn*, Internet edition, 20 October 2010.
14. See *Dawn*, Internet edition, 5 June 2010.
15. *Dawn*, Internet edition, 5 October 2010.
16. This is the estimate of the CIA *World Factbook* accessed at https://www.cia.gov/library/publications/the-world-factbook/geos/pk.html
17. The Pakistan Institute of Peace Studies, Pakistan Security annual report for 2009 recorded a figure of 12,000 deaths as a result of political, ethnic and sectarian violence, terrorist attacks and government counter-insurgency operations.
18. For an extended discussion of these issues see Michael Kugelman and Robert M. Hathaway (eds), *Reaping the Dividend: Overcoming Pakistan's Demographic Challenges* (Washington, DC: Woodrow Wilson International Centre for Scholars, 2011). See also the Epilogue of this volume.
19. 2005 World Bank data put defence spending at 3.4 per cent of GDP, compared with 1.6 per cent on education and 0.5 per cent on health.
20. Statistics Division, Population Census Organization, Government of Pakistan *1998 Census* Demographic Indicators, accessible at http://www.statpak.gov.pk/depts/pco/statistics/demographic_indicators.html
21. Finance Division, Government of Pakistan, 'Population, Labour Force and Employment', *Pakistan Economic Survey 2008–9*, p. 183.
22. UNDP, (2007–8) Gender Related Index (2000–8) http://hdr.undp.org/en/media/HDR_20072008_GDI.pdf; UNDP (2007–8), Gender Empowerment Measure (2007–8) http://hdr.undp.org/en/media/HDR_20072008_GEM.pdf
23. Zahid Hussain, 'Paradise Lost', *Newsline* (February 2009), online edition.
24. Population Reference Bureau and National Committee for Maternal and Neonatal Health (Pakistan), 'Pakistan on the Move: Family Planning, Reproductive Health and Development in Pakistan', in Michael Kugelman and Robert M. Hathaway (eds), *Reaping the Dividend: Overcoming Pakistan's Demographic Challenges* (Washington, DC: Woodrow Wilson International Centre for Scholars, 2011), p. 48.
25. Ibid., p. 50.
26. Zeba A. Sethar, 'Demographic Doom or Demographic Dreams: Pakistan at the Crossroads', in Kugelman and Hathaway (eds), *Reaping the Dividend*, pp. 33–4.

27. Estimate of the UN Population Division reported in *Dawn*, Internet edition, 28 July 2009.
28. British Council, *Pakistan: The Next Generation* http://www.britishcouncil.pk/pakistan-Next-Generation-Report.pdf
29. Yaqoob Khan Bangash, 'The Integration of the Princely States of Pakistan 1947–55', unpublished Oxford DPhil 2011.
30. Ibid., p. 283.
31. For details see ibid., ch.6.
32. Ibid., p. 283.
33. For further details see Talbot and Singh, *The Partition of India*, ch.4.
34. Population Division of the Department of Economic and Social Affairs of the United Nations Secretariat, *World Population Prospects: The 2007 Revision and World Urbanization Prospects* http://esa.un.org/unup
35. On the Pashtoonization of Islamic ideology in Pakistan see Mohammad Abdul Qadeer, *Pakistan: Social and Cultural Transformation* (New York: Routledge, 2007), p. 70.
36. See Mohsin Ali, 'Violence Drives Settlers Out of Province', *Gulf News*, 28 July 2010, gulfnews.com
37. See Roger Ballard, 'The Context and Consequences of Migration: Jullundur and Mirpur Compared', *New Community* 11,1/2 (Autumn/Winter 1983), pp. 117–36.
38. See Akbar S. Ahmed, '*Dubai chalo*: Problems in the Ethnic Encounter between Middle Eastern and South Asian Muslim Societies', *Asian Affairs* 15, pp. 262–76.
39. *Dawn*, Internet edition, 11 February 2011.
40. See for example Arshi Saleem Hashmi, 'The Arabist Shift from Indo-Persian Civilization and Genesis of Radicalization in Pakistan', *Pak Institute for Peace Studies*, 2009.
41. Judith M. Brown, *Global South Asians: Introducing the Modern Diaspora* (Cambridge: Cambridge University Press, 2006), p. 41.
42. For the best assessment of the US diaspora's demographic size and economic connections with Pakisan see Adil Najam, *A Giving Community: Philanthropy by the Pakistan-American Diaspora* (Harvard: Harvard University Press, 2006).
43. See Safiya Aftab, 'Poverty and Militancy', *PIPS Journal of Conflict and Peace Studies* 1, 1 (October-December 2008), pp. 66–86.
44. This helped prompt the government of Pakistan's drawing up of a Sustainable Development Plan for FATA, 2007–15.
45. Aftab, 'Poverty and Militancy', pp. 79–81.
46. See Shaid Javed Burki, 'The Middle-Class Millions', *Dawn*, Internet edition, 2 November 2010.
47. Sadaf Ahmad, 'Identity Matters, Culture Wars: An Account of Al-Huda (re) Defining Identity and Reconfiguring Culture in Pakistan', *Culture and Religion* 9, 1 (2008), pp. 63–80.
48. On the pervasiveness of 'radical' outlooks amongst the educated middle classes,

see David Hensen, 'Radical Rhetoric-Moderate Behaviour: Perceptions of Islam, *Shari'a* and the Radical Dimensions among Inhabitants of Islamabad and Rawalpindi in the post 9/11 Pakistani Reality', unpublished PhD Thesis, University of Oslo, 2010.

49. Pervez Hoodbhoy, 'Pakistan after Osama June 2011', *Himal* http://www.himalmag.com/component/content/article/4466.html accessed 2 June 2011.
50. *Dawn* Internet edition, 30 May 2011.
51. For a typical assessment see I. H. Malik, *State and Civil Society in Pakistan: Politics of Authority, Ideology and Ethnicity* (Basingstoke: Macmillan, 1997), ch.4.
52. Talbot, *Pakistan: A Modern History*, p. 215.
53. D. Gilmartin, *Empire and Islam: Punjab and the Making of Pakistan* (Berkeley, CA: University of California Press, 1988); S. Ansari, *Sufi Saints and State Power: The Pirs of Sind, 1843–1947* (Cambridge: Cambridge University Press, 1992).
54. Hansen, 'Radical Rhetoric-Moderate Behaviour', p. 361.
55. Waseem conflated 'feudals' with what he terms the political classes as opposed to the middle classes. See Mohammad Waseem, 'A Tale of Two Classes', *Dawn* (Karachi), 15 December 2009.
56. For a wider view of the impact of the rise of the middle class on democratization in Muslim societies see Vali Nasr, *Forces of Fortune: The Rise of the New Muslim Middle Class and What It Will Mean for our World* (New York: Free Press, 2009).
57. Matthew J. Nelson, *In the Shadow of Shari'ah: Islam, Islamic Law and Democracy in Pakistan* (London: Hurst, 2011).
58. It is interesting for example to read Nelson's understanding of the workings of the district and appellate courts, especially with respect to landed property disputes, alongside the comments of Anatol Lieven in ch.3 of *Pakistan: A Hard Country* (London: Allen Lane, 2011).
59. Tariq Rahman, *Language, Ideology and Power: Language-learning Among the Muslims of Pakistan and North India* (Karachi: Oxford University Press, 2002), p. 217.
60. See, Farina Mir, *The Social Space of Language: Vernacular Culture in British Colonial Punjab* (Berkeley, CA: University of California Press, 2010).
61. For details of the Sindhi language movement see Tariq Rahman, *Language and Politics in Pakistan* (Karachi: Oxford University Press, 1998), ch.7.
62. See G. M. Syed, *A Case For Sindhu Desh* (London: Sindh International Council, 2000).
63. Rahman, *Language and Politics*, p. 134.
64. See for example Christophe Jaffrelot, 'India and Pakistan: Interpreting the Divergence of Two Political Trajectories', *Cambridge Review of International Affairs* 15, 2, pp. 251–67.
65. Qadeer, 'Pakistan: Social and Cultural Transformation in a Muslim Nation'.
66. Hansen, 'Radical Rhetoric-Moderate Behaviour'. Farzana Shaikh has termed

this process 'shariatization'. See F. Shaikh, *Making Sense of Pakistan* (London: Hurst, 2009), pp. 107–9.

67. See for example Praveen Swami, *India, Pakistan and the Secret Jihad* (London: Routledge, 2007); Rizwan Hussain, *Pakistan and the Emergence of Islamic Militancy in Afghanistan* (Burlington: Ashgate, 2005).
68. See Zahid Hussain, *Frontline Pakistan: The Struggle with Militant Islam* (New York: Columbia University Press, 2007), especially pp. 89–101.
69. See William Millam, 'Factors Shaping the Future', in S. Cohen (ed.), *Pakistan's Future: The Bellagio Papers* http://www.brookings.edu/~media/Files/rc/papers/2010/09_bellagio_conference_papers/09_bellagio_papers.pdf.
70. At one end of the spectrum, intolerance manifests itself in violent attacks on minorities, or individuals who question narrow sectarian interpretations of Islam; at the other end there is the refusal of sections of the population to condemn such actions, or to engage in self-denying conspiracy theories to 'explain' their existence.
71. For a revisionist understanding see C. Fair, 'Militant Recruitment in Pakistan. A New Look at the Militancy-Madrasah Connection', *Asia Policy* 4 (July 2007), pp. 107–34.
72. Tariq Rahman, 'Education in Pakistan: A Survey', in Craig Baxter (ed.), *Pakistan on the Brink: Politics. Economics and Society* (Karachi: Oxford University Press, 2004), pp. 171–90.
73. Hansen, 'Radical Rhetoric-Moderate Behaviour'.
74. Ibid., pp. 143 ff. Even Deobandis may visit shrines if only to offer prayers *(fateha)* for those who are buried.
75. Delawar Jan, 'Why Did Swat Militants Exhume Pir Samiullah's Body?' *The News* (Karachi), 19 December 2008.
76. Hansen, 'Radical Rhetoric-Moderate Behaviour', p. 59.
77. For an overview see I. Talbot, *India and Pakistan* (London: Arnold, 2000), especially ch.2.
78. Francis Robinson, 'Islam and the Impact of Print in South Asia', in Nigel Crook (ed.), *The Transmission of Knowledge in South Asia* (Delhi: Oxford University Press, 1996), pp. 62–97.
79. See Barbara D. Metcalf, *Islamic Revival in British India: Deoband 1860–1900* (Delhi: Oxford University Press, 1982).
80. See M. Anwarul Haq, *The Faith Movement of Mawlana Muhammad Ilyas* (London: George Allen & Unwin, 1972).
81. On the emerging role of Aligarh and Muslim separatism, see David Lelyveld, *Aligarh's First Generation* (Princeton: Princeton University Press, 1978).

2. UNDERSTANDING THE FAILURE OF PAKISTAN'S FIRST EXPERIMENT WITH DEMOCRACY 1947–58

1. I. A. Rehman has argued that Mirza's attitudes were forged during his years as a political agent in the tribal areas of the NWFP during the Raj. I. A. Rehman, 'Damned by History', *Newsline* (May 1996), p. 129.

2. Allen McGrath, *The Destruction of Pakistan's Democracy* (Karachi: Oxford University Press, 1996), see especially ch. 8.
3. M. M. Syed, 'Pakistan: Struggle for Power 1947–58', *Pakistan Journal of History and Culture* 15, 2 (July-December 1994), pp. 85 ff.
4. Safdar Mahmood, 'Decline of the Pakistan Muslim League and Its Implications (1947–54)', *Pakistan Journal of History and Culture* 15, 2 (July-December 1994), pp. 63–84.
5. Ayesha Jalal, *The State of Martial Rule: The Origins of Pakistan's Political Economy of Defence* (Cambridge: Cambridge University Press, 1990), pp. 299 ff.
6. For a detailed analysis of the accession and integration of the Pakistan Princely States, see Yaqoob Khan Bangash, 'The Integration of the Princely States of Pakistan 1947–44', unpublished 2011 Oxford D.Phil thesis.
7. Yunas Samad, *A Nation in Turmoil: Nationalism and Ethnicity in Pakistan 1937–58* (New Delhi: Sage, 1995), p. 169.
8. See Clive Dewey, 'The Rural Roots of Pakistani Militarism', in D. A. Low (ed.), *The Political Inheritance of Pakistan* (Basingstoke: Macmillan, 1991), pp. 255–83.
9. See I. Talbot, *Khizr Tiwana, The Punjab Unionist Party and the Partition of India* (Karachi: Oxford University Press, 2002).
10. I. Talbot, *Pakistan: A Modern History*, 2nd edn (London: Hurst, 2009), pp. 54 ff.
11. M. Waseem, *The 1993 Elections in Pakistan* (Lahore, 1994), pp. 30–1.
12. Bangash, 'The Integration of the Princely States of Pakistan 1947–55'.
13. Ibid., p. v.
14. Ibid., pp. 184–8.
15. Ibid., p. 221.
16. For details within the Punjab region see I. Talbot, *Punjab and the Raj 1849–1947* (New Delhi: Manohar, 1988).
17. Ibid. See also D. Gilmartin, *Empire and Islam: Punjab and the Making of Pakistan* (Berkeley: California University Press, 1988).
18. Proceedings of the visit of the Committee of Action to the North West Frontier Province, FMA vol. 343 NWFP ML Part III, 1944.
19. Jinnah to Khuhro, 13 October 1945, SHC Sind V1:10.
20. Dow to Wavell, 20 September 1945, L/P&J/5/261 IOR.
21. During an election tour in November 1945, Jinnah had declared: 'Every vote in favour of the Muslim League candidates means Pakistan. Every vote against the Muslim League candidates means Hindu Raj'. *Dawn* (Delhi), 29 November 1945.
22. Ashok Kapur, *Pakistan in Crisis* (London: Routledge, 1991), p. 2.
23. Harun-or-Rashid, *The Foreshadowing of Bangladesh: Bengal Muslim League and Muslim League Politics, 1936–1947* (Dhaka: Asiatic Society of Bangladesh, 1987), p. 164.
24. *Statesman* (Calcutta), 28 October 1950.
25. Waseem, *The 1993 Elections in Pakistan*, p. 163.

26. Ayesha Jalal, *The State of Martial Rule: the Origins of Pakistan's Political Economy of Defence* (Cambridge: Cambridge University Press, 1990).
27. Cited in Chaudhuri Muhammad Ali, *The Emergence of Pakistan* (New York: Columbia University Press, 1967), p. 376.
28. Yunas Samad, *A Nation in Turmoil: Nationalism and Ethnicity in Pakistan, 1937–1957* (New Delhi: Sage, 1995), p. 128.
29. For new insights into how 'path dependency' eventually institutionalized the military's presence in Pakistan politics, see Mazhar Aziz, 'The Parallel State: Understanding military control in Pakistan', unpublished PhD, University of Nottingham, 2006.
30. Jalal, *The State of Martial Rule*, p. 198.
31. Ibid., p. 1.
32. Niaz, 'The Culture of Power', p. 115.
33. Samad, *A Nation in Turmoil*, p. 143.
34. Jalal, *The State of Martial Rule*, p. 208.
35. Yunus Samad, 'Pakistan or Punjabistan: Crisis of national identity', in Gurharpal Singh and Ian Talbot (eds), *Punjabi Identity: Continuity and Change* (New Delhi: Manohar, 1996), pp. 61–87.
36. For the impact on locals' attitudes to refugees in the Punjab in circumstances where refugees were economic assets rather than competitors see I. Talbot, *Divided Cities: Partition and its Aftermath in Lahore and Amritsar 1947–1957* (Karachi: Oxford University Press, 2006), ch.6.
37. Waseem, 'Partition migration assimilation', p. 216.
38. See Tariq Rahman, *Language and Politics in Pakistan* (Karachi: Oxford University Press, 1996), ch.11.
39. Samad, *A Nation in Turmoil*, p. 147.
40. S. Ansari, *Life After Partition: Migration, Community and Strife in Sindh 1947–1962* (Karachi: Oxford University Press, 2005), p. 57.
41. Ibid., p. 62.
42. Ibid., p. 98.
43. This included the Sindh Awami Mahaz, the Sindh Hari Committee and members of the Sindh Muslim League.
44. Deputy High Commissioner's Report for East Bengal, period ending 11 July 1948, L/P&J/5/322 IOR.
45. Deputy High Commissioner's Report for East Bengal, 12–18 January 1948, L/P&J/5/322 IOR.
46. See M. Habibur Rahman, 'Bhasa Andolan (Language Movement) and the Beginning of the Break-up of Pakistan', *Indo-British Review* XV11, nos. 1 and 2 (September and December 1989), pp. 169–73.
47. T. M. Murshid, *The Sacred and the Secular: Bengal Muslim Discourses 1871–1977* (Oxford: Oxford University Press, 1995), pp. 310–11.
48. See G. F. Papanek, *Pakistan's Development: Social Goals and Private Incentives* (Cambridge Mass: Harvard University Press, 1967), p. 20.
49. Jalal, *The State of Martial Rule*, p. 156.
50. Zaheer, *Separation of East Pakistan*, pp. 30–31.

51. Safdar Mahmood, *Pakistan Divided*, p. 19.
52. Ziring, *Ayub Khan Era*, p. 91.
53. Jalal, *The State of Martial Rule*, p. 189.
54. In these riots, Bengali labourers were pitted against West Pakistani managers.
55. Samad, *A Nation in Turmoil*, p. 185.
56. On the Muslim League's weak political institutionalization and its consequences see Safdar Mahmood, 'Decline of the Pakistan Muslim League and its Implications (1947–54)', *Pakistan Journal of History and Culture* 15, 2 (July-December 1994), pp. 63–84.
57. See Mazhar Aziz, *Military Control: The Parallel State* (London: Routledge, 2008).

3. AYUB'S PAKISTAN: THE END OF THE BEGINNING

1. There has been no major study since Lawrence Ziring's now classic text, L. Ziring, *The Ayub Khan Era: Politics in Pakistan, 1958–1969* (Syracuse, NJ: Syracuse University Press, 1971).
2. He later wrote in his autobiography, 'Yesterday's "traitors" were today's Chief Ministers, indistinguishable as Tweedledum and Tweedledee!' Ayub Khan, *Friends Not Masters: a Political Biography* (London: Oxford University Press, 1967), p. 55.
3. Mohammad Ayub Khan, *Speeches and Statements*, vol. 1 (Karachi: Pakistan Publications, 1961), p. 2.
4. Cited in R. Jahan, *Pakistan: Failure in National Integration* (New York: Columbia University Press, 1972), p. 64.
5. For details see I. Talbot, *Pakistan: A Modern History* 2nd edn (London: Hurst, 2009), pp. 154–6.
6. A. T. Rafiqur Rahman, *Basic Democracies at the Grass Roots* (Comilla: Pakistan Academy for Village Development, 1962), p. 253.
7. Hasan-Askari Rizvi, *Military, State and Society in Pakistan* (Basingstoke: Macmillan, 2000), p. 89.
8. M. Waseem, *Politics and the State in Pakistan* (Lahore: Progressive, 1989), p. 155.
9. Z. Niazi, 'Towards a Free Press', in V. Schofield (ed.), *Old Roads, New Highways: Fifty Years of Pakistan* (Karachi: Oxford University Press, 1997), p. 182.
10. Iftikhar H. Malik, *State and Civil Society in Pakistan: Politics of Authority, Ideology and Ethnicity* (Basingstoke: Macmillan, 1997), p. 135.
11. The centre could still intervene with respect to railways and industries in the name of coordination and uniformity of policy. Moreover any provincial scheme which cost more than Rs 5 million in foreign exchange required central approval.
12. Tariq Rahman, *Language and Politics in Pakistan* (Karachi: Oxford University Press, 1996), p. 99.
13. S. Ansari, 'Punjabis in Sind-Identity and Power', *International Journal of Punjab Studies* 2, 1 (January-June 1995), pp. 12 ff.

14. See for example the issue for 11 June 1946, Sindh Muslim League, Part IX, 1944–6, vol. 386, Freedom Movement Archives.
15. Harun-or-Rashid, 'The Ayub Regime and the Alienation of East Bengal', *Indo-British Review* 17, nos. 1 and 2 (September 1989 and December 1989), p. 181.
16. Rahman, *Language and Politics in Pakistan*, p. 117.
17. T. Rahman, 'Language and Politics in a Pakistan Province: The Sindhi Language Movement', *Asian Survey* 35, 11 (November 1995), pp. 1010–11.
18. Consul-General Dacca to Department of State, 8 February 1962, 790.D.00/2–162, National Archives at College Park.
19. During the seventeen-day Indo-Pakistan war, the eastern wing was left to fend for itself in defence and economic matters.
20. Just 75 out of 280 members of the commissions of inquiry were from East Pakistan. See Jahan, *Pakistan: Failure in National Integration*, p. 98.
21. American Consul-General Lahore to Department of State, 22 January 1963, 790.D.00/1–1663, National Archives at College Park.
22. For details see G. F. Papanek, *Pakistan's Development: Social Goals and Private Incentives* (Cambridge, MA: Harvard University Press, 1967), p. 20.
23. Ayesha Siddiqa, *Military Inc: Inside Pakistan's Military Economy* (London: Pluto Press, 2007), p. 131.
24. For details see Talbot, *Pakistan: A Modern History*, 2nd edn, pp. 164 ff.
25. This refers to the extension of the legal code contained in the Quran and the Sunnah (Prophet's example) by analytical extrapolation and consideration of the public good.
26. Muhammad Ayub Khan, *Speeches and Statements*, vol. 1, pp. 110–11.
27. Idem, *Friends Not Masters*, p. 14.
28. American Consul Lahore to Department of State, 13 August 1962, 790.D.00/18–1062, National Archives at College Park.
29. Farzana Shaikh, *Making Sense of Pakistan* (London: Hurst 2009), pp. 159 ff.
30. Ibid., p. 160.
31. During the period 1960–65 Pakistan received $2,365 million in total foreign assistance, nearly 80 per cent of which took the form of loans. Anita Weiss, *Culture, Class and Development in Pakistan: The Emergence of an Industrial Bourgeoisie in Punjab* (Colorado: Westview Press, 1991), p. 35.
32. Shaikh, *Making Sense of Pakistan*, p. 128.
33. Siddiqa, *Military Inc.*, p. 131.
34. Ibid., p. 209.
35. Ibid., p. 135.
36. Ibid., p. 183.
37. Talbot, *Pakistan: a Modern History* 2nd edn (London: Hurst, 2009), p. 364.
38. S. J. Burki, 'Twenty Years of the Civil Service of Pakistan; A Re-evaluation', *Asian Survey* 9, 4 (April 1969), p. 248.
39. For details see H. Feldman, *From Crisis to Crisis: Pakistan 1962–1969* (London: Oxford University Press, 1972), pp. 305–9, 325–7.
40. Siddiqa, *Military Inc.*, p. 17.
41. Sir Morrice James, *Pakistan Chronicle* (London: Hurst, 1992), p. 157.
42. Ayub Khan, *Friends Not Masters*, p. 136.

43. Gary Power's U-2 spy plane had begun its ill-fated flight of 5 May 1960 from a base near Peshawar. Khruschchev warned the world that not only would future flights be shot down, but the foreign bases from which they had taken off would 'receive shattering blows'. This strengthened anti-Western sentiment in Pakistan. Ayub was moreover troubled by the fact that he had been kept in the dark about Power's mission.
44. For details see Brian Cloughley, *A History of the Pakistan Army: Wars and Insurrections* (Karachi: Oxford University Press, 1999), pp. 61 ff.
45. American Embassy Karachi to Department of State, 16 November 1962, 790.D.00/10–2762, National Archives at College Park.
46. American Embassy Karachi to Secretary of State, 21 November 1962, 790.D.00/11–2062, National Archives at College Park.
47. Embassy Karachi to Department of State, 8 January 1963, 790.D.00/1–363, National Archives at College Park.
48. The Chinese Foreign Minister, Chen Yi, had issued a number of statements in support of Pakistan's 'just action'. On 16 September, China accused India of constructing military works on the Sikkim frontier and called for their dismantling.
49. See General K. M. Arif, *Khaki Shadows: Pakistan 1947–1997* (Karachi: Oxford University Press, 2001), pp. 46 ff.
50. For discussions of the Pakistan army's irredentist motivations see Stephen M. Saideman, 'At the Heart of the Conflict: Irredentism and Kashmir', in T. V. Paul (ed.), *The India Pakistan Conflict: An Enduring Rivalry* (Cambridge: Cambridge University Press, 2005), pp. 218 ff.
51. On the Hazratbal episode and the strategic misreading of its legacy, see Victoria Schofield, *Kashmir in Conflict: India, Pakistan and the Unfinished War* (London: I. B. Tauris, 2000), pp. 103–4;,108–9.
52. See Praveen Swami, *India, Pakistan and the Secret Jihad: The Covert War in Kashmir 1947–2004* (London: Routledge, 2007), pp. 60 ff.; Shaikh, *Making Sense of Pakistan*, pp. 160 ff.
53. Swami, *India, Pakistan and the Secret Jihad*, p. 61.
54. On the 1951 Rawalpindi Conspiracy see Hasan Zaheer, *The Times and Trial of the Rawalpindi Conspiracy, 1951: The First Coup Attempt in Pakistan* (Karachi: Oxford University Press, 1998).

4. BHUTTO'S PAKISTAN: A MISSED OPPORTUNITY

1. A. H. Syed, 'The Pakistan People's Party: phases One and Two' in L. Ziring, R. Braibanti and W. Howard Wriggins, *Pakistan: The Long View* (Durham, NC: Duke University Press, 1977), p. 75.
2. Hasan-Askari Rizvi, *Military, State and Society in Pakistan* (Basingstoke: Macmillan, 2000), pp. 142–3.
3. Yahya had expected a better show from the Qayyum Muslim League and the Islamic parties favoured by his regime. Instead the PPP had triumphed in the

West, and the Awami League had swept to a landslide victory in the East, capturing 160/162 seats allocated for East Pakistan in the National Assembly.

4. For further details on all these issues see R. Sisson and Leo E. Rose, *War and Secession: Pakistan, India and the Creation of Bangladesh* (Berkeley, CA: University of California Press, 1990).
5. *Daily Javadan* (Lahore), 19 December 1971. The previous issue had boldly declared '*Pakistan ki Shikast ka zimmadar Yahya Khan hain*' (Yahya Khan is responsible for Pakistan's defeat). Cited in Hasan-Askari Rizvi, *The Military and Politics in Pakistan, 1947–86* (Delhi: Konark, 1988), p. 195.
6. T. Ali, *Can Pakistan Survive? The Death of a State* (Harmondsworth: Penguin, 1983), p. 95.
7. Lt-Gen. A. A. K. Niazi, *The Betrayal of East Pakistan* (Karachi: Oxford University Press, 1998), p. 194.
8. S. Wolpert, *Zulfi Bhutto of Pakistan* (Oxford: Oxford University Press, 1993), p. 234.
9. Zulfiqar Ali Bhutto, *Speeches* (Islamabad: Government of Pakistan, 1973), p. 13.
10. J. Piscatori, 'Asian Islam: International Linkages and their Impact on International Relations', in J. L. Esposito (ed.), *Islam in Asia* (New York: Oxford University Press, 1987), p. 247.
11. For further details see, Ian Talbot, *Pakistan: A Modern History* 2nd edn (London: Hurst, 2009), p. 221.
12. Z. A. Bhutto, *If I Am Assassinated* (New Delhi: Vikas, 1979), p. 19.
13. This dispute was not solely about Bhutto's intolerance of political rivals, as Sardar Muhammad Daoud, who had come to power after the overthrow of the Afghan King Zahir Shah in July 1973, had reopened the Pakhtunistan issue which had lain dormant for many years.
14. See, Talbot, *Pakistan: A Modern History*, p. 226.
15. For conflicting interpretations of the significance of the Iranian involvement see S. Harrison, 'Baluch Nationalism and Superpower Rivalry', *International Security* 5, 3 (1980/81), p. 154; R. G. Wirsing, *Pakistan's Security under Zia: The Policy Imperatives of a Peripheral Asian State* (Basingstoke: Macmillan, 1991), pp. 105–6.
16. See Frederic Grare, 'Pakistan: The Resurgence of Baluch Nationalism', Carnegie Paper 65 (January 2006), p. 6.
17. Maleeha Lodhi, 'The Pakistan People's Party', unpublished 1979 thesis, London School of Economics, p. 124.
18. Philip E. Jones, *The Pakistan People's Party Rise to Power* (Karachi: Oxford University Press, 2003), p. 439.
19. Ibid.
20. Ibid., p. 441.
21. Ibid., p. 429.
22. A. H. Syed, 'The Pakistan People's Party', p. 111.
23. He was the father of Raza Khan Qasuri, a founder member of the PPP who had become a major critic of Bhutto and had been expelled from the party in October 1972. Qasuri's car had been fired on in November 1974 while returning

from a wedding in Lahore. The investigation into the murder of the Nawab, who was widely regarded as not the main target of the attack, was reopened by Zia and its initiative allegedly traced to Bhutto.

24. On Bhutto's abolition of the CSP and his induction of party loyalists (so called Bhuttocrats) into the bureaucracy see C. Kennedy, *Bureaucracy in Pakistan* (Karachi: Oxford University Press, 1987).
25. William B. Milam, *Bangladesh and Pakistan: Flirting with Failure in South Asia* (London: Hurst, 2009), p. 48.
26. Farzana Shaikh, *Making Sense of Pakistan* (London: Hurst, 2009), pp. 62–3.
27. Jhangvi was to form the *Sipah-i-Sahaba Pakistan* (SSP) and to have its paramilitary splinter organization *Lashkar-e-Jhangvi* (LeJ) named after him. See the next chapter for details.
28. Rizvi, *The Military and Politics in Pakistan*, p. 197.
29. Ibid., p. 146.
30. Ibid., p. 150.
31. Bhutto secured the 'cover' of the 1974 Islamic summit to recognize Bangladesh. India had been linking the release of the POWs with this step, but had eventually agreed in separate negotiations to their repatriation.
32. Arif, *The Betrayal of East Pakistan*, p. 240.
33. Rizvi, *Military, State and Society in Pakistan*, p. 145.
34. S. J. Burki, *Pakistan Under Bhutto 1971–1977* (London: Macmillan, 1980), Table 2, p. 105.
35. For discussion of this issue see Shaikh, *Making Sense of Pakistan*, pp. 163–4; Praveen Swami, *India, Pakistan and the Secret Jihad: The Covert War in Kashmir 1947-2001* (Milton Park, Abingdon: Routledge, 2007), pp. 127–8.
36. Swami, *India, Pakistan and the Secret Jihad*, p. 128.
37. General Khalid Mahmud Arif, *Working with Zia: Pakistan's Power politics, 1977–1988* (Karachi: Oxford University Press, 1995), p. 80.
38. Ibid., p. 73.
39. Ibid., p. 88.
40. See, S. Taheer, *Bhutto: a Political Biography* (London: Ithaca Press, 1979); S. Wolpert, *Zulfi Bhutto of Pakistan* (Oxford: Oxford University Press, 1993).
41. For details see W. E. Gustafson, 'Economic Reforms Under Bhutto', *Journal of Asian and African Studies* 8, 3–4 (July-October 1973), pp. 241–58.
42. Nita Weiss, *Culture, Class and Development in Pakistan: The Emergence of an Industrial Bourgeoisie in Punjab* (Colorado: Westview Press, 1991), p. 134.
43. Z. A. Bhutto, 'Address to the Nation Announcing Nationalisation of Ten Categories of Industries', 12 January 1972, *Speeches and Statements (20 December 1971–31 March 1972)* (Karachi, 1972), p. 33.
44. Burki, *Pakistan under Bhutto*, p. 126.
45. Iftikhar H. Malik, *State and Civil Society in Pakistan: Politics of Authority, Ideology and Ethnicity* (Basingstoke: Macmillan, 1997), p. 120.
46. Mohammad Waseem, *Politics and the State in Pakistan* (Islamabad: National Institute of Historical and Cultural Research, 1994), pp. 115–19.

47. Jones, *The Pakistan People's Party*, p. 459.
48. Ibid.

5. ZIA AND THE QUEST FOR PAKISTAN'S STABILITY

1. Cited in Iftikhar H. Malik, *State and Civil Society in Pakistan: Politics of Authority, Ideology and Ethnicity* (Basingstoke: Macmillan, 1997), p. 92.
2. Nighat Said Khan, 'The New Global Order: Politics and the Women's Movement in Pakistan', in Soofia Mumtaz, Jean-Luc Racine, Imran Anwar Ali (eds), *Pakistan: The Contours of State and Society* (Karachi: Oxford University Press, 2002).
3. See Matthew J. Nelson, *In the Shadow of Shari'ah: Islam, Islamic Law and Democracy in Pakistan* (London: Hurst, 2011), p. 168.
4. Iqbal Akhund, *Memoirs of a Bystander: a Life in Diplomacy* (Karachi: Oxford University Press, 1998), p. 353.
5. O. Noman, 'The Impact of Migration on Pakistan's Economy and Society', in Hastings Donnan and Pnina Werbner (eds), *Economy and Culture in Pakistan: Migrants and Cities in a Muslim Society* (London: Palgrave Macmillan, 1991), p. 85.
6. J. S. Addleton, *Undermining the Centre* (Karachi: Oxford University Press, 1992), p. 79.
7. Cited in I. Talbot, *Pakistan: a Modern History* (Hurst: London, 2009), p. 254.
8. J. Piscatori, 'Asian Islam: International Linkages and their Impact on International Relations', in J. L. Esposito (ed.), *Islam in Asia: Religion, Politics and Society* (New York: Oxford University Press, 1987), p. 248.
9. They financed 50 per cent of the trade gap and 50 per cent of total investment through the period 1978–88. Asad Sayeed, 'State-Society Conjunctures and Disjunctures: Pakistan's Manufacturing Performance', in S. M. Naseem and Khalid Nadvi (eds), *The Post-Colonial State and Social Transformation in India and Pakistan* (Karachi: Oxford University Press, 2002), p. 227.
10. Shahid Javed Burki, 'Politics of Power and its Economic Imperatives: Pakistan, 1947–99', in Anita M. Weiss and S. Zulfiqar Gilani (eds), *Power and Civil Society in Pakistan* (Karachi: Oxford University Press, 2001), p. 148.
11. See Aijaz Ahmad, 'The Rebellion of 1983: A Balance Sheet', *South Asia Bulletin* 4, 1 (Spring 1984), p. 33; O. Noman, 'The Impact of Migration on Pakistan's Economy and Society', in Donnan and Werbner (eds), *Economy and Culture in Pakistan*, p. 90.
12. S. Cohen, *The Idea of Pakistan* (New Delhi: Oxford University Press, 2004), p. 112.
13. James Raymond Vreeland, 'Between the Lines: Pakistan's Debt of Gratitude', *Foreign Policy* 129 (March-April 2002), p. 72.
14. See R. G. Wirsing, *Pakistan's Security Under Zia, 1977–1988: The Policy Imperatives of a Peripheral Asian State* (Basingstoke: Macmillan,1991), pp. 110 ff.; Adrian Levy and Catherine Scott-Clark, *Deception: Pakistan, the*

United States and the Secret Trade in Nuclear Weapons (New York: Walker and Company, 2007).

15. Praveen Swami, *India, Pakistan and the Secret Jihad: The Covert War in Kashmir, 1947–2004* (London: Routledge, 2007), p. 145.
16. Akhund, *Memoirs of a Bystander*, p. 392.
17. Ibid., p. 366.
18. *Al-Mushir* 26, 1 (1983), p. 172.
19. See such works as Afzal Tauseef, *Testimony*; Badar Abro, *Furnance Days*; Siraj, *The Eighth Man*.
20. K. K. Aziz, *The Pakistani Historian: Pride and Prejudice in the Writing of History* (Lahore: Vanguard, 1993).
21. M. Gazdar, *Pakistani Cinema 1947–1997* (Karachi: Oxford University Press, 1997), p. 187.
22. Ibid., p. 191.
23. Akhund, *Memoirs of a Bystander*, p. 393; Lt-Gen. Faiz Ali Chishti, *Betrayals of Another Kind: Islam, Democracy and the Army in Pakistan* (London: Asia Publishing House,1989), pp. 81, 101.
24. For details see Talbot, *Pakistan: A Modern History*, p. 261.
25. Akhund, *Memoirs of a Bystander*, p. 388.
26. For a detailed study see Mohammad Waseem, 'Election Politics 1985', *The Muslim* 9, nos. 10, 11 and 22 (April 1985).
27. See Benazir Bhutto, *Daughter of the East: An Autobiography* (London: Hamilton, 1988).
28. Farzana Shaikh, *Making Sense of Pakistan* (London: Hurst, 2009), p. 98.
29. Hasan-Askari Rizvi, *The Military and Politics in Pakistan* (London: Palgrave Macmillan, 2003), p. 242.
30. Shaikh, *Making Sense of Pakistan*, pp. 107–10.
31. Cited in S. V. R. Nasr, 'Islam, the State and the Rise of Islamic Militancy', in C. Jaffrelot (ed.), *Pakistan: Nationalism Without a Nation* (New Delhi: Manohar, 2002), p. 91.
32. Ibid., p. 109.
33. This measure, which was enacted by Presidential Ordinance in October 1984, laid down that the evidence of two women was only equal to that of one man. The Hudood Ordinances, which were designed to introduce Islamic punishments laid down in the Quran and Sunnah, were controversially based on the Law of Evidence for sexual crimes. This was either self-confession or the witness of four *salah* (upright) males. For men in rape cases self-confession was verbal; for women however it could be pregnancy or medical examination. Women who had been raped could thus be punished by flogging for adultery (*zina*) while their assailants went unconvicted.
34. Equally divisive was the fixing of *diyat* (blood money for a murder victim) for a female victim as half that of a man.
35. Talbot, *Pakistan: A Modern History*, p. 279.
36. Cohen, *The Idea of Pakistan*, p. 181.
37. See Saeed Shafqat, 'From Official Islam to Islamism: The Rise of Dawat-ul-

Irshad and Lashkar-e-Toiba', in C. Jaffrelot (ed.), *Pakistan: Nationalism Without a Nation?* (New Delhi: Manohar, 2002), pp. 141 ff.

38. The Zikris are followers of Syed Muhammad whom they consider to be the Mahdi. They possess no mosques or prescribed prayers, although they regard themselves as Muslims. Their greatest affront to the orthodox Muslims is the practice of pilgrimage to the Koh-e-Murad in the city of Turbat in Makran rather than to Mecca.
39. Wirsing, *Pakistan's Security Under Zia*, p. 52.
40. Shaikh, *Making Sense of Pakistan*, p. 205.
41. For a translation of his influential poem 'Love for Homeland' see Talbot, *Pakistan: A Modern History*, p. 253.
42. For an examination of the background to the MQM's emergence see I. Malik, 'Ethno-Nationalism in Pakistan: A Commentary on Muhajir Qaumi Mahaz (MQM) in Sindh', *South Asia* 18, 2 (1995), pp. 60–1. Ayesha Siddiqa is of the view that MQM like IJI was a tool of the army to counter Bhutto's continuing popularity in his home province of Sindh. A. Siddiqa, *Military Inc. Inside Pakistan's Military Economy* (London: Pluto Press, 2007), pp. 86–7.
43. *Newsline* (Karachi), 28 March 1994, p. 27.
44. R. LaPorte, 'Administrative Restructuring During the Zia period', in S. J. Burki and C. Baxter (eds), *Pakistan Under the Military: Eleven Years of Zia ul-Haq* (Boulder, CO: Westview Press, 1991), p. 129.
45. See Siddiqa, *Military Inc.*, pp. 125 ff.
46. Ibid., p. 147.
47. Ibid.
48. The National Logistics Cell had been ostensibly created in 1978 in the context of a cargo-handling crisis at Karachi.
49. For the CIA's training and sharing of expertise with ISI see J. L. Cooley, *Unholy Wars, Afghanistan, America and International Terrorism* (London: Pluto Press, 1999).
50. Saira Yamin, *Peace Building in Afghanistan: Revisiting the Global War on Terrorism* (Colombo: Regional Centre for Strategic Studies, 2008), p. 16.
51. For the political consequences of the explosion see Talbot, *Pakistan: A Modern History*, p. 284. For the possibility that this was an ISI cover-up see Y. Samad, 'In and Out of Power but Not Down and Out: Mohajir Identity Politics', in C. Jaffrelot (ed.), *Pakistan: Nationalism Without a Nation?* (New Delhi: Manohar, 2002), p. 71.
52. Ibid.
53. Siddiqa, *Military Inc.*, p. 142.

6. PAKISTAN'S DEMOCRATIC INTERLUDE 1988–99

1. Cited in Ayesha Siddiqa, *Military Inc. Inside Pakistan's Military Economy* (London: Pluto Press, 2007), p. 93.
2. Ibid., p. 92.

3. Zahid Hussain, 'Benazir Bhutto Fall From Grace', *Newsline* (November 1996), pp. 24–31.
4. *Dawn*, Internet edition, 15 January 1997.
5. Iqbal Akhund, *Trial and Error: The Advent and Eclipse of Benazir Bhutto* (Karachi: Oxford University Press, 2000), p. 43.
6. See I. Talbot, *Pakistan: A Modern History* (London: Hurst, 2009), p. 330.
7. Cited in Siddiqa, *Military Inc.*, p. 92.
8. Akhund, *Trial and Error*, p. 65.
9. Ibid., pp. 77 ff.
10. Ibid., p. 45.
11. Ibid., pp. 69 ff.
12. Ibid., p. 140.
13. Siddiqa, *Military Inc.*, p. 91.
14. Akhund, *Trial and Error*, p. 139.
15. Ibid., p. 120.
16. Saeed Shafqat, 'Pakistan Under Benazir Bhutto', *Asian Survey* 36, 7 (July 1996), p. 663.
17. *Dawn* (Karachi), 18 January 1991.
18. See Tahir Amin, 'Pakistan in 1993: Some Dramatic Changes', *Asian Survey* 34, 2 (February 1994), pp. 197–8.
19. For further details see Talbot, *Pakistan: A Modern History*, pp. 320 ff.
20. Nawaz had identified 100 state-owned undertakings for privatization, including the Muslim Commercial Bank. See Stephen Cohen, *The Idea of Pakistan* (New Delhi: Oxford University Press, 2004), p. 251.
21. For a comprehensive study of the elections see M. Waseem, *The 1993 Elections in Pakistan* (Lahore: 1994).
22. For details see Zahid Hussain, 'Who Killed Mirtaza Bhutto?', *Newsline* (Karachi), October 1996, pp. 23–30.
23. Siddiqa, *Military Inc.*, p. 95.
24. Ibid., p. 163.
25. Shafik H. Hashmi, 'Privatization Policy', in C. H. Kennedy and R. B. Rais (eds), *Pakistan in 1995* (Boulder, CO: Westview Press, 1995), pp. 42–3.
26. Siddiqa, *Military Inc.*, p. 151.
27. Ibid., p. 152.
28. Ibid., pp. 154, 160.
29. *Dawn* (Karachi), 29 September 1989.
30. L. Ziring, 'Pakistan in 1989: The Politics of Stalemate', *Asian Survey* 30, 2 (February 1990), p. 131.
31. See Iftikhar H. Malik, *State and Civil Society in Pakistan: Politics of Authority, Ideology and Ethnicity* (Basingstoke: Macmillan, 1997), ch.10; Talbot, *Pakistan: A Modern History*, pp. 303 ff; Yunas Samad, 'In and Out of Power but not Down and Out: Mohajir Identity Politics', in C. Jaffrelot (ed.), *Pakistan: Nationalism Without a Nation?* (New Delhi: Manohar, 2002), pp. 63–85.
32. *Dawn* (Karachi), 9 February 1990.

33. Hasan-Askari Rizvi, *Military, State and Society in Pakistan* (London: Palgrave Macmillan, 2003), p. 207.
34. Akhund, *Trial and Error*, p. 144.
35. *Herald* (Karachi), 20, 10 (October 1989), p. 78.
36. *Dawn* (Karachi), 1 December 1989.
37. *Herald* (Karachi), 20, 10 (October 1989), p. 89.
38. The notion of a common Saraiki language itself was founded on bringing together local tongues such as Multani and Derajati.
39. S. A. Kochanek, 'Ethnic Conflict and the Politicization of Business', in C. H. Kennedy and R. B. Rais (eds), *Pakistan in 1995* (Boulder, CO: Westview Press, 1995), p. 149.
40. See Mariam Abou Zahab, 'The Regional Dimension of Sectarian Conflicts in Pakistan', in C. Jaffrelot (ed.), *Pakistan: Nationalism Without a Nation?* p. 121.
41. S. V. R. Nasr, 'Islam, the State and the Rise of Sectarian Militancy', in C. Jaffrelot (ed.), *Pakistan*, p. 94.
42. His most controversial public statement in 1995 was to become an SSP slogan: '*Agar pakistan main musulman bun kar rehna hey, to Shia ko kaafir kehna hey*'. ('If Islam is to be established in Pakistan, then Shia must be declared infidels'.)
43. Amir Ziqa, 'Tribes and Tribulations', *Newsline* (Karachi), October 1996, pp. 71–5.
44. *Newsline* (Karachi), March 1995, p. 24.
45. See Nasr, 'Islam, the State and the Rise of Sectarian Militancy', in C. Jaffrelot (ed.), *Pakistan*, p. 97
46. Ibid., p. 104.
47. See Praveen Swami, *India, Pakistan and the Secret Jihad: The Covert War in Kashmir, 1947–2004* (London: Routledge, 2007), pp. 152 ff.
48. Ibid., p. 184.
49. Ibid., p. 173.
50. Ibid., p. 181.

7. THE JANUS STATE: PAKISTAN UNDER MUSHARRAF

1. Owen Bennet Jones, *Pakistan: Eye of the Storm* (New Haven: Yale, 2002).
2. Hassan Abbas, *Pakistan's Drift into Extremism: Allah, the Army and America's War on Terror* (Armonk, NY: M. E. Sharpe, 2008).
3. A. Z. Hilali, *US-Pakistan Relationship: Soviet Invasion of Afghanistan* (Aldershot: Ashgate, 2005), pp. 256 ff.
4. Abbas, for example, focuses on the fact that Musharraf's 'unhappy mix of the conventional and the revolutionary' made him a 'master of half measures', the 'poor man's Attaturk'. Abbas, *Pakistan's Drift into Extremism*, pp. 235–6.
5. See Shahid Javed Burki, *Changing Perceptions, Altered Realities: Pakistan's Economy Under Musharraf 1999–2006* (Oxford: Oxford University Press, 2007).

6. Musharraf's autobiography provides a particularly colourful account. P. Musharraf, *In the Line of Fire: A Memoir* (London: Simon &Schuster, 2006).
7. For the AQ network's threat to attempts to limit nuclear proliferation see Adrian Levy and Catherine Scott-Clarke, *Deception:Pakistan, the United States and the Global Nuclear Weapons Conspiracy* (London: Atlantic Books, 2007); Shuja Nawaz, *Crossed Swords: Pakistan, Its Army and Wars Within* (Oxford: Oxford University Press, 2008).
8. See Robert Looney, 'Failed Economic Take-Offs and Terrorism in Pakistan: Conceptualizing a Proper Role for US Assistance', *Asian Survey* 44, 6 (November-December 2004), p. 780.
9. Overseas Pakistanis feared that their assets might be impounded by Western governments in the wake of 9/11. By 2002, remittances had reached US$ 3.5 billion.
10. Looney, 'Failed Economic Take-Offs', p. 782.
11. Mahbub ul Haq, *Human Development in South Asia 2007: A Ten Year Review* (Karachi: Oxford University Press, 2008), p. 90.
12. See Jawaid Bokhari, 'Consumer Focused Growth: "Frozen Mind-Sets"', *Dawn*, Internet edition, 25 August 2003.
13. For criticism of Musharraf's economic orientation see Masooda Bano, 'What Reforms', *News International*, 15 November 2002.
14. For an assessment see Shaun Gregory, *Towards a Containment Strategy in the FATA* PSRU Brief no. 43.
15. Zahid Hussain, *Frontline Pakistan: The Path to Catastrophe and the Killing of Benazir Bhutto* (London: I. B. Tauris, 2008), p. 190.
16. Abbas, *Pakistan's Drift into Extremism*, p. 225.
17. See Selig S. Harrison, 'Global Terrorism: US Policy after 9/11 and its Impact on the Domestic Politics and Foreign Relations of Pakistan', in Rajshree Jetley (ed.), *Pakistan in Regional and Global Politics* (New Delhi: Routledge, 2009), pp. 20–45.
18. See Husain Haqqani, *Pakistan: Between Mosque and Military* (Lahore: Vanguard, 2005), p. 306.
19. See Imtiaz Ali, 'The Haqqani Network and Cross-Border Terrorism in Afghanistan', *Terrorism Monitor* 6, 6 (24 March 2008), pp. 1–3.
20. The reform commission established by Nawaz Sharif to investigate economic and political irregularities was generally recognized as an instrument of political coercion. S. P. Cohen, *The Idea of Pakistan* (New Delhi: Oxford University Press, 2005), p. 154.
21. Ayesha Siddiqa, *Military Inc. Inside Pakistan's Military Economy* (London: Pluto Press, 2007), p. 100.
22. Cohen, *The Idea of Pakistan*, p. 154.
23. Transparency International, *Global Corruption Barometer 2007* (6 December 2007) http:www.transparency.org/content
24. Alan B. Krueger and Jita Maleckova, *Education, Poverty, Political Violence and Terrorism: Is There a Causal Connection?* (Cambridge, MA: National Bureau of Economic Research, 2002).

25. This term has been coined by Shahid Javed Burki; see his work, *Changing Perceptions, Altered Realities: Pakistan's Economy Under Musharraf, 1999 - 2006* (Oxford: Oxford University Press, 2007), p. 39.
26. Reported in *Dawn*, Internet edition, 2 May 2002.
27. *Dawn*, Internet edition, 28 August 2004.
28. Siddiqa, *Military Inc.*, p. 100.
29. Critics such as Ayesha Siddiqa have nevertheless maintained that, even before 2007, Musharraf's regime selectively targeted journalists who stepped too far out of line resulting in harassment and even more sinisterly in 'disappearances'. Siddiqa, *Military Inc.*, p. 98.
30. Mohammad Waseem, *Democratization in Pakistan: A Study of the 2002 Elections* (Karachi: Oxford University Press, 2006), p. 71.
31. See F. Grare, 'The Resurgence of Baloch Nationalism', *South Asia Project* Pakistan paper 65 (January 2006).
32. *Dawn*, Internet edition, 7 May 2004.
33. Muhammad Amir Rana, *Baloch Insurgency—A Backgrounder*, SouthAsiaNet-Pakistan, Pakistan Institute for Peace Studies, 19.04.2006 http://san-pips.com/PIPS-SAN-Files/SAN-Pakistan/SAN-PAK-Article47/San-Pak-Main-A47-D.asp
34. The Marri family have been identified as providing leadership (Nawab Khair Bakhsh and the late Balach Marri) and fund-raising (Hyrbyair Marri) for the BLA. It remains committed to the goal of an independent Greater Balochistan which would include Baloch population areas of Iran, Pakistan and Afghanistan.
35. South Asia Terrorism Portal, Pakistan Assessment 2008 http://www.satp.org/satporgt/countries/pakistan/index.htm
36. These were military commando style attacks used against security establishment targets within Pakistan and with immense international effect in New Delhi and Mumbai in India.
37. See http://www.satp.org/satporgrp/countries/pakistan/
38. See International Media Support, *Media in Pakistan* (July 2009) http:www.m-s-s.dk/files/publication
39. *Dawn*, Internet edition, 16 May 2004.
40. See Salman Masood, 'Pakistan Moves Toward Altering Rape Law', *New York Times*, 16 November 2006.
41. For an articulation of this understanding see for example the following International Crisis Group Reports: International Crisis Group, 2004 'Pakistan: Reforming the Education Sector', http://www.crisisgroup.org/library/documents/asia/south_asia/084_ppakistan_reforming the education sector.pdf. International Crisis Group, 2007 'Pakistan: Karachi's Madrasas and Violent Extremism' http://www.crisisgroup.org/library/documents/asia/south_asia/130_pakistan_karachis madrasas_and violent extremism.pdf
42. See Robert Nichols, 'Challenging the State: 1990s Religious Movements in the Northwest Frontier Province', in Craig Baxter and Charles Kennedy (eds), *Pakistan, 1997* (Boulder, CO: Westview Press, 1998), pp. 123–42.
43. David Hansen, 'Radical Rhetoric-Moderate Behaviour: Perceptions of Islam,

Shari'a and the Radical Dimensions among Inhabitants of Islamabad and Rawalpindi in the post-9/11 Pakistani Reality', Unpublished PhD Thesis, University of Oslo, June 2010, p. 219.

44. Ibid., pp. 231–2.
45. Ibid., pp. 217–18.
46. For details see I. Talbot, *Pakistan: A Modern History* (London: Hurst, 2009), pp. 422 ff.
47. Some analysts maintain however that the Marriott bombing was in response to the army's launching of Operation Sher Dil in Bajaur.
48. Sartaj Aziz, 'The Economic Cost of Extremism', in Usama Butt and N. Elahi (eds), *Pakistan's Quagmire: Security, Strategy, and the Future of the Islamic-Nuclear Nation* (New York: Continuum, 2010), p. 78.
49. The MMA finally agreed to the NSC when Musharraf promised to give up his position as Army Chief by December 2004. He went back on this, citing the terrorist threat arising from Pakistan's front-line state status in the 'War on Terror'. Musharraf's reneging on his promise, along with what was seen as an excessively pro-American policy, soured his relations with the MMA.
50. Siddiqa, *Military Inc.*, p. 171.
51. Ibid., p. 110.
52. For more details see ibid., pp. 194–8.
53. UN, *Report of the United Nations Commission of Inquiry Into the Facts and Circumstances of the Assassination of Former Prime Minister Mohtarma Benazir Bhutto* http://www.un.org/News/dh/infocus/Pakistan/UN_Bhutto_Report_15April2010.pdf
54. For a detailed analysis of the results see Talbot, *Pakistan: A Modern History*, pp. 432 ff.
55. Zardari jointly chaired the party with Benazir's son, Bilawal, who was a student at Oxford University.

8. SURVIVING THE STORM: ZARDARI'S PAKISTAN

1. Asif Zardari, who had married Benazir in December 1987, claimed that charges against him were politically motivated. While he may have favoured friends and family, his portrayal as 'Mr 10 per cent' was exaggerated. In all he spent 11 years in jail facing various corruption and criminal charges. He left Pakistan to go overseas for medical treatment after being granted bail in mid 2004.
2. Sartaj Aziz, 'The Economic Cost of Extremism', in Usama Butt and N. Elahi (eds), *Pakistan's Quagmire: Security, Strategy and the Future of the Islamic-Nuclear Nation* (New York: Continuum, 2010), p. 80.
3. Hilary Synnott, *Transforming Pakistan: Ways out of Instability* (Abingdon: Routledge, 2009), p. 56.
4. Pakistan's GDP reached the peak of 8.6 per cent in 2004–5. Ibid.
5. For the rapid decline in Pakistan's current account see *Dawn* (Karachi), 23 October 2008; Robert Looney, *Failed Take-Off: An Assessment of Pakistan's*

October 2008 Economic Crisis, Pakistan Security Research Unit Brief no. 46, October 2008

6. In July 2007 they had stood at $13.3 billion. Synnott, *Transforming Pakistan*, p. 83.
7. William B. Milam, *Bangladesh and Pakistan: Flirting with Failure in South Asia* (London: Hurst, 2009), pp. 137 ff.
8. *Dawn*, Internet edition, 19 July 2010.
9. This figure was quoted by the World Bank President, Robert Zoellick, on 13 August. *Dawn*, Internet edition (14 August 2010).
10. See *Dawn*, Internet edition, 13 and 16 August 2010.
11. *Dawn*, Internet edition, 16 August 2010.
12. See the article by Saeed Shah in guardian.co.uk, 15 August 2010.
13. *Dawn*, Internet edition, 13 August 2010.
14. *Dawn*, Internet edition, 18 August 2010.
15. Synnott, *Transforming Pakistan*, p. 81.
16. See the Epilogue for further reflection on Pakistan's demographic 'time bomb'.
17. Asad Hashim, 'Public Support for Militancy', *Dawn*, Internet edition, 22 June 2010.
18. Robert Nicholls, 'Class, State and Power in the Swat Conflict', unpublished paper, Association of Asian Studies Conference, Honolulu, 2 April 2011.
19. Ibid.
20. See N. Ilahi, 'The Existential Threat: Tehreek-e-Taliban Pakistan (TTP) and al-Qaeda in Pakistan?' in Usama Butt and N. Elahi (eds), *Pakistan's Quagmire: Security, Strategy and the Future of the Islamic-Nuclear Nation* (New York: Continuum, 2010), p. 144.
21. Synott, *Transforming Pakistan*, p. 94. The figure for militant deaths may well be exaggerated, with the numbers standing instead at around 1,000.
22. For details see Brian Cloughley, 'Insurrection, Terrorism and the Pakistan Army', in U. Butt and N. Elahi, *Pakistan's Quagmire*, pp. 93–123.
23. See *Dawn*, Internet edition, 18 October 2009.
24. Cited in *Dawn*, Internet edition, 7 June 2010.
25. Cited in *Dawn*, Internet edition, 22 June 2010.
26. Cited in *Dawn*, Internet edition, 13 June 2010.
27. For a discussion of the utility of this term see Katja Riikonen, '"Punjabi Taliban" and the Sectarian Groups in Pakistan', PSRU Brief no. 55, 12 February 2010.
28. See *Dawn*, Internet edition, 11 October 2009.
29. See Hassan Abbas, 'Defining the Punjabi Taliban Network', *CTC Sentinel* 2, 4 (April 2009), pp. 1–4.
30. See P. K. Upadhyay, 'From FATA to South Punjab: The Looming leap of Islamic Radicalism in Pakistan', *Institute for Defence Studies and Analyses*, 30 November 2009.
31. There are a number of differing classifications of the Punjab's regions, depending on such factors as administrative and geographical boundaries, agronomic and cultural zones. The smallest area defined as South Punjab includes the four

districts of Bahawalnagar, Bahawalpur, Dera Ghazi Khan and Rahim Yar Khan. The most comprehensive includes, along with these, the Bhakker, Jhang, Khanewal, Layyah, Lodhran, Multan, Rajanpur and Vehari districts.

32. See 'Southern Punjab leaks' in *Dawn*, Internet edition, 24 May 2011.
33. Aftab, 'Poverty and Militancy', p. 82.
34. See Ayesha Siddiqa, 'Terror's Training Ground', *Newsline* (September 2009) http://www.newsline.com.pk/NewsSep2009/bookmarksep.htm
35. Siddiqa, 'Terror's Training Ground'.
36. Tahir Kamran, 'Contextualising Sectarian Militancy in Pakistan: A Case Study of Jhang', *Journal of Islamic Studies* 20, 1 (2009), pp. 55–85.
37. He had originally been active in SSP, before going on to involvement with the Kashmir *jihad* organizations, *Harkat-ul-Mujahadin* (HUM) and *Harkat-ul-Ansar* (HUA).
38. *Dawn*, Internet edition, 21 August 2010.
39. *Dawn*, Internet edition, 15 August 2010.
40. Ibid.
41. See Pervez Hoodbhoy, 'Pakistan after Osama June 2011', *Himal* http://www.himalmag.com/component/content/aericle/4466.html accessed 2 June 2011.
42. *Dawn*, Internet edition, 3 October 2009.
43. Baloch nationalism is rooted in a sense of economic exploitation and political marginalization. For the encouragement to *shariatization* arising from poverty, corruption and lack of social justice see Farzana Shaikh, *Making Sense of Pakistan* (London: Hurst, 2009).
44. Cited in *Dawn*, Internet edition, 13 June 2010.
45. *Dawn*, Internet edition, 5 June 2010.
46. *Dawn*, Internet edition, 19 June 2011.
47. According to the 2009–10 Economic Survey, energy shortages caused a loss of 2 per cent of GDP during the current fiscal year. *Dawn*, Internet edition, 5 June 2010.
48. Zardari's approval rating was just 20 per cent; Kayani's was 61 per cent. Over 70 per cent of PML(N) supporters had a positive opinion of the army chief, while even those who identify with the ruling PPP had a 59 per cent approval rating. *Dawn*, Internet edition, 2 August 2010.
49. Mohammad Waseem, 'Judging Democracy in Pakistan: Conflict between the Executive and the Judiciary', unpublished paper, 25th. Annual BASAS Conference, University of Southampton, 13 April 2011, p. 15·
50. Ibid., p. 18.
51. Musharraf's block on a return of Nawaz Sharif to power was thus removed.
52. Synnott, *Transforming Pakistan*, pp. 71–2.
53. India since 2001 has contributed $750 million for reconstruction in Afghanistan, has 4,000 civilian and security personnel working in the country and has provided vital assistance in road-building and training of Afghan police and civil servants. Pakistan has claimed that the Indian presence is directed against its interests not only in the country, but in the sensitive Balochistan province. See Synnott, *Transforming Pakistan*, pp. 137 ff.

54. See http://abcnews.go.com/Blotter/wikileaks-cable-pakistan-asked-fewer-drones/story?id=13647893 accessed 3 June 2011.
55. See for example Declan Walsh, 'In the Shadow of Bin Laden: Pakistan Still Reeling from the Raid that Killed al-Qaida Chief', *Guardian* (London), 2 June 2011.
56. http://abcnews.go.com/Blotter/wikileaks-cable-pakistan-asked-fewer-drones/story?id=13647893 accessed 3 June 2011.
57. Hoodbhoy, 'Pakistan after Osama', *Himal* http://www.himalmag.com/component/content/article/4466.html accessed 2 June 2011.
58. They included greater civilian control over promotions and appointments and parliamentary oversight of military budgets, along with certification that the security forces were not subverting the political and judicial processes.
59. The literacy rate in FATA is for example 17.5 per cent compared with the Pakistani average of 44 per cent. For an assessment of the future prospects of FATA see Ian Talbot, *Future Prospects for FATA*, Pakistan Security Research Unit Brief no. 41, 22 September 2008.
60. Synnott, *Transforming Pakistan*, p. 170.

EPILOGUE

1. See Introduction to this volume.
2. Ahmad Faruqi, *Rethinking the National Security of Pakistan: The Price of Strategic Myopia* (Aldershot: Ashgate, 2003); Tasneem Ahmad Siddiqui, *Towards Good Governance* (Karachi: Oxford University Press, 2001); Maleeha Lodhi (ed.), *Pakistan: Beyond the Crisis State* (London: Hurst, 2011).
3. These figures are cited in Shanza Khan and Moeed Yusuf, 'Education as a Strategic Imperative', in Maleeha Lodhi (ed.), *Pakistan: Beyond the Crisis State* (London: Hurst 2011), pp. 261–2.
4. Siddiqui, *Towards Good Governance*, p. 210.
5. Maleeha Lodhi, 'Beyond the Crisis State', in Maleeha Lodhi (ed.), *Pakistan: Beyond the Crisis State* (London: Hurst, 2011), p. 57.
6. Ibid.
7. For a comparison between Pakistan's performance with respect to family planning and that of Bangladesh and Iran see Mehtab S. Karim, 'Pakistan's Demographic Scenario, Past and Present: Population Growth and Policies, with Lessons from Bangladesh and Iran', in Michael Kugelman and Robert M. Hathaway (eds), *Reaping the Dividend: Overcoming Pakistan's Demographic Challenges* (Washington: Woodrow Wilson International Centre for Scholars, 2011), pp. 121–44.
8. See Sohail Agha, 'The Role of the Private Sector on Reproductive Health Service Delivery in Pakistan', in Kugelman and Hathaway (eds), *Reaping the Dividend*, pp. 160–75.
9. Khan and Yusuf, 'Education as a Strategic Imperative', in Lodhi (ed.), *Pakistan: Beyond the Crisis State*, p. 261.

10. See Moeed Yusuf, 'A Society on the Precipice? Examining the Prospects of Youth Radicalization in Pakistan', in Kugelman and Hathaway (eds), *Reaping the Dividend*, pp. 76–105.
11. For a typical approach see Christine Fair et al., *Can the US Secure an Insecure State?* (Santa Monica, CA: Rand, 2010).
12. This would of course be following the Indian example. Burki has maintained that the IT sector alone could supply annual export earnings of $20 billion by 2013–15. See Shahid Javed Burki, 'Historical Trends in Pakistan's Demographics and Population Policy', in Kugelman and Hathaway (eds), *Reaping the Dividend*, pp. 56–75.
13. Analysts have pointed to military dictatorship, regional separatism, Islamist revolution, as possible outcomes.
14. See http://www.britishcouncil.pk/pakistan-Next-Generation-Report.pdf
15. See also *Herald* 'Youth Speak', 41, 1 (January 2010), pp. 52–105.
16. http://www.britishcouncil.pk/pakistan-Next-Generation-Report.pdf, p. 6.
17. Ibid., p. 18.
18. Ibid., p. 26.
19. For a fuller discussion of Pakistan's water challenges and responses see Anatol Lieven, *Pakistan: A Hard Country* (London: Allen Lane, 2011), pp. 29–33.
20. Maya Tudor, 'Twin Births, Divergent Democracies: The Social and Institutional Origins of Regime Outcomes in India and Pakistan', unpublished Princeton University PhD Thesis, 2010.
21. For a further reflection on this see Faruqi, *Rethinking the National Security of Pakistan*.
22. See the various contributors to the Maleeha Lodhi volume.

SELECT BIBLIOGRAPHY

Private Papers

Caroe Papers, India Office Records, Mss.Eur F203.
Cunningham Papers, India Office Records, Mss.Eur 670.
Linlithgow Papers, India Office Records, Mss.Eur F125.
Mian Fazl-i-Husain Papers, India Office Records, Mss.Eur F325.
Mountbatten Papers, University of Southampton, MB1.
Mudie Papers, India Office Records, Mss.Eur F164.
Quaid-e-Azam Papers, National Archives of Pakistan, Islamabad.

Government Records

India Office Records

Records of the Military Department 1940–2.
Records of the Political and Secret Department 1928–47.
Records of the Public and Judicial Department 1929–47.

National Archives of India

Records of the Home Political Department 1927–45.

National Archives (US) at College Park

State Department Central Files 1960–3, 1964–6.

National Security Archives, George Washington University

LBJ Presidential Files Country Files (Pakistan).
India-Pakistan (4 boxes).

Freedom Movement Archives

All-India Muslim League Records.

Committee of Action 1944–7.
Working Committee 1932–7.
Provincial Muslim League Records.

Newspapers and Journals

Dawn (Karachi).
The Nation (Lahore).
Herald (Karachi).
Newsline (Karachi).
Nawa-i-Waqt (Lahore).

Printed Secondary Works

Adeney, Katharine, *Federalism and Ethnic Conflict Resolution in India and Pakistan* (New York: Palgrave, 2007).

Ahmad, Syed Nur, *From Martial Law to Martial Law: Politics in the Punjab 1919–1958* (Boulder, CO: Westview Press, 1985).

Ahmed, Akbar S., *Jinnah, Pakistan and Islamic Identity: The Search for Saladdin* (London: Routledge, 1997).

Alavi, Hamaza, 'Pakistan and Islam: Ethnicity and Ideology' in Fred Halliday and Hamza Alavi (eds), *State and Ideology in the Middle East and Pakistan* (New York: Macmillan, 1988), pp. 64–111.

Ali, Chaudhri Muhammad, *The Emergence of Pakistan* (New York: Columbia University Press, 1967).

Ali, Imran, *The Punjab under Imperialism, 1885–1947* (Princeton: Princeton University Press, 1988).

Ali, S. Mahmud, *The Fearful State: Power, People and Internal Wars in South Asia* (London: Zed Books, 1993).

Ali, Tariq, *Pakistan: Military Rule or People's Power* (New York: William Morrow & Co., 1970).

——— *Can Pakistan Survive? The Death of a State* (Harmondsworth: Penguin, 1983).

Ansari, Sarah, *Sufi Saints and State Power: The Pirs of Sind, 1843–1947* (Cambridge: Cambridge University Press, 1992).

——— *Life after Partition: Migration, Community and Strife in Sindh 1947–1962* (Karachi: Oxford University Press, 2005).

Ayres, Alyssa, *Speaking Like a State: Language and Nationalism in Pakistan* (Cambridge: Cambridge University Press, 2009).

Aziz, Mazhar, *Military Control: The Parallel State* (London: Routledge, 2008).

Banerjee, Mukulika, *The Pathan Unarmed: Opposition and Memory in the North West Frontier Province* (Oxford: Oxford University Press, 2000).

Baxter, Craig and Kennedy, Charles, *Pakistan 1997* (Boulder, CO: Westview Press, 1998).

Bhutto, Benazir, *Daughter of the East: An Autobiography*, revised edition (London: Simon & Schuster, 2007).

Burke, S. M., and Salim Al-Din Qureshi, *Quaid-i-Azam Mohammad Ali Jinnah: His Personality and Politics* (Karachi: Oxford University Press, 1997).

Burki, Shahid Javeed, *Pakistan under Bhutto, 1971–77* (Basingstoke: Macmillan, 1980).

——— *Pakistan: Fifty Tears of Nationhood* (Boulder, CO: Westview Press, 1999).

Butt, Usama and Ilahi, N. (eds), *Pakistan's Quagmire: Security, Strategy and the Future of the Islamic-Nuclear Nation* (New York: Continuum, 2010).

——— *Changing Perceptions, Altered Reality: Pakistan's Economy Under Musharraf, 1999–2006* (Oxford, Oxford University Press, 2007).

Cheema, Pervaiz Iqbal, *The Armed Forces of Pakistan* (New York: New York University Press, 2003).

Chester, Lucy P., *On the Edge: Borders, Territory and Conflict in South Asia* (Manchester: Manchester University Press, 2008).

Cohen, S. P. 'State Building in Pakistan' in A. Banuazizi and M. Weiner (eds), *The State, Religion and Ethnic Politics: Afghanistan, Iran and Pakistan* (New York: Syracuse University Press, 1986).

——— *The Idea of Pakistan* (Washington, DC: The Brookings Institution, 2004).

——— *The Pakistan Army* (Karachi: Oxford University Press, 1998).

——— *The Future of Pakistan* (Washington, DC: The Brookings Institution, 2011).

——— (ed.) *Pakistan's Future: The Bellagio Papers* (Washington, DC: The Brookings Institution, 2010).

Correra, Gordon, *Shopping for Bombs: Nuclear Proliferation, Global Insecurity and the Rise and Fall of the A.Q. Khan Network* (Melbourne: Scribe, 2006).

Daechsel, Markus, *The Politics of Self-Expression: The Urdu Middle Class Milieu In Mid-Twentieth Century India and Pakistan* (London: Routledge, 2006).

——— 'Military Islamisation in Pakistan and the Spectre of Colonial Perceptions', *Contemporary South Asia* 6, 2 (1997), pp. 141–60.

Devji, Faisal, *Landscapes of the Jihad: Militancy, Morality, Modernity* (New York: Cornell University Press, 2005).

Dewey, Clive, 'The Rural Roots of Pakistani Militarism' in D. A. Low (ed.), *The Political Inheritance of Pakistan* (Basingstoke: Macmillan, 1991), pp. 255–84.

Donnan, Hastings and Werbner, Pnina (eds) *Economy and Culture in Pakistan: Migrants and Cities in a Muslim Society* (London: Palgrave Macmillan, 1991).

Fair, Christine, *The Madrassah Challenge: Militancy and Religious Education in Pakistan* (Washington: United States Institute of Peace Press, 2008).

——— et al., *Can the US Secure an Insecure State?* (Santa Monica, CA: Rand, 2010).

Faruqi, Ahmad, *Rethinking the National Security of Pakistan: The Price of Strategic Myopia* (Aldershot: Ashgate, 2003).

Feldman, Herbert, *The End and the Beginning: Pakistan, 1969–1971* (Karachi: Oxford University Press, 1976).

Ganguly, Sumit, *Conflict Unending: India-Pakistan Tensions Since 1947* (New York: Columbia University Press, 2001).

——— *The Crisis in Kashmir: Portents of War, Hopes of Peace* (Cambridge: Cambridge University Press, 1997).

Gilmartin, David, *Empire and Islam: Punjab and the Making of Pakistan* (Berkeley, CA: University of California Press, 1998).

Grare, Frederic, *Rethinking Western Strategies Towards Pakistan: An Action Agenda for the United States and Europe* (Washington, DC: Carnegie Endowment for International Peace, 2007).

Haq, Farhat 'Rise of MQM in Pakistan. Politics of Ethnic Mobilization', *Asian Survey* 35, 11 (November 1995), pp. 900–1004.

Haqqani, Husain, *Pakistan: Between Mosque and Military* (Washington, DC: Carnegie Endowment for International Peace, 2005).

Hardy, Peter, *The Muslims of British India* (Cambridge: Cambridge University Press, 1972).

Hasan, Mushirul, 'India and Pakistan: Why the Difference?' in Mushirul Hasan and Nariaki Nakazato (eds), *The Unfinished Agenda: Nation-Building in South Asia* (New Delhi: Manohar, 2001), pp. 328–37.

——— (ed.), *India's Partition: Process, Strategy and Mobilization* (New Delhi: Oxford University Press, 1993).

Hassan, Abbas, *Pakistan's Drift into Extremism: Allah, the Army and America's War on Terror* (Armonk, NY: M. E. Sharpe, 2005).

Hayat, Sikander, *The Charismatic Leader: Quaid-i-Azam Mohammad Ali Jinnah and the Creation of Pakistan* (Karachi: Oxford University Press, 2008).

Hussain, Zahid, *Frontline Pakistan: The Struggle with Militant Islam* (New York: Columbia University Press, 2007).

International Crisis Group, 'After Bhutto's Murder: A Way Forward for Pakistan' (Islamabad/Brussels Asia Briefing 2 January 2008).

Jaffrelot, Christophe (ed.), *A History of Pakistan and Its Origins* (London: Anthem Press, 2002).

——— (ed.), *Pakistan: Nationalism Without A Nation?* (London: Zed Books, 2002).

Jalal, Ayesha, *The Sole Spokesman: Jinnah, The Muslim League and the Demand for Pakistan* (Cambridge: Cambridge University Press, 1985).

——— *The State of Martial Rule: The Origin of Pakistan's Political Economy of Defence* (Cambridge: Cambridge University Press, 1990).

——— *Self and Sovereignty: Individual and Community in South Asian Islam Since 1850* (London: Routledge, 2000).

Jahan, Rounaq, *Pakistan: Failure in National Integration* (New York: Columbia University Press, 1972).

James, Sir Morrice, *Pakistan Chronicle* (London: Hurst, 1993).

Jansson, Erland, *India, Pakistan or Pakhtunistan? The Nationalist Movements in the North-West Frontier Province, 1937–47* (Uppsala: Acta Universitatis Upsaliensis, 1981).

Johnson, Rob, *A Region in Turmoil: South Asian Conflicts Since 1947* (London: Reaktion Books, 2008).

Jones, Owen Bennett, *Pakistan: Eye of the Storm* (New Haven, CT: Yale Nota Bene, 2002).

Jones, Philip E. *The Pakistan People's Party: Rise to Power* (Karachi: Oxford University Press, 2003).

Kamran, Tahir, 'Contextualising Sectarian Militancy in Pakistan: The Case of Jhang', *Journal of Islamic Studies* 20, 1 (January 2009), pp. 55–85.

Kennedy, C. H. *Bureaucracy in Pakistan* (Karachi: Oxford University Press 1987).

——— (ed.) *Pakistan in 1992* (Boulder, CO: Westview Press,1992).

——— and R. B. Rais (eds), *Pakistan in 1995* (Boulder, CO: Westview Press 1995).

Kepel, Gilles, *Jihad: The Trail of Political Islam* (London and New York: I. B. Tauris, 2002).

Khan, Adeel, *Politics of Identity: Ethnic Nationalism and the State in Pakistan* (London: Sage Publications, 2005).

Khan, M. Asghar, *We've Learnt Nothing from History: Pakistan—Politics and Military Power* (Karachi: Oxford University Press, 2005).

Khan, Yasmin, *The Great Partition: The Making of India and Pakistan* (New Haven, CT: Yale University Press, 2007).

Kugelman, Michael and Robert M. Hathaway (eds), *Reaping the Dividend: Overcoming Pakistan's Demographic Challenges* (Washington, DC: Woodrow Wilson International Centre for Scholars, 2011).

Kukreja, Veena, *Contemporary Pakistan: Political Processes, Conflicts and Crises* (New Delhi and London: Sage Publications, 2003).

Kurin, Richard, 'Islamization in Pakistan: A View from the Countryside', *Asian Survey*, 25, 8 (August 1985), pp. 589–612.

Kux, Dennis, *The United States and Pakistan, 1947–2000: Disenchanted Allies* (Washington and Baltimore: Woodrow Wilson Centre and Johns Hopkins University Press, 2001).

Laporte, Robert, 'Pakistan in 1995: The Continuing Crises', *Asian Survey* 36, 2 (February, 1996), pp. 179–89.

Lelyveld, David, *Aligarh's First Generation: Muslim Solidarity in British India* (Princeton: Princeton University Press, 1978).

Lieven, Anatol, *Pakistan: A Hard Country* (London: Allen Lane, 2011).

Lodhi, Maleeha (ed.), *Pakistan: Beyond the 'Crisis State'* (London: Hurst, 2011).

Low, D. A. (ed.), *The Political Inheritance of Pakistan* (Basingstoke: Macmillan, 1991).

Malik, Iftikhar Haider, *State and Civil Society in Pakistan: Politics of Authority, Ideology and Ethnicity* (Basingstoke: Macmillan, 1997).

——— *Jihad, Hindutva and the Taliban: South Asia at the Crossroads* (Karachi: Oxford University Press, 2005).

——— *Culture and Customs of Pakistan* (Westport, CT: Greenwood Press, 2005).

Mascarenhas, Anthony, *The Rape of Bangladesh* (Delhi: Vikas, 1971).

Matinuddin, Kamil, *The Nuclearization of South Asia* (Karachi: Oxford University Press, 2002).

McGrath, Allen, *The Destruction of Pakistan's Democracy* (Karachi: Oxford University Press, 1996).

Metcalf, Barbara D., *Islamic Revival in British India: Deoband, 1860–1900* (Princeton: Princeton University Press, 1982).

Mumtaz, Khawar and Farida Shaeheed (eds), *Women of Pakistan: One Step Forward Two Steps Back* (London: Zed Books, 1987).

Murshid, T. M., *The Sacred and the Secular: Bengal Muslim Discourses 1871, 1977* (Calcutta: Oxford University Press, 1995).

Musharraf, Pervez, *In the Line of Fire: A Memoir* (London: Simon & Schuster, 2006).

Nasr, Seyyed Vali Reza, *The Vanguard of the Islamic Revolution: The Jamaat-i-Islami of Pakistan* (Berkeley: University of California Press, 1994).

——— *Maududi and the Making of Islamic Revivalism* (Oxford: Oxford University Press, 1996).

——— *Islamic Leviathan: Islam and the Making of State Power* (New York: Oxford University Press, 2001).

Nawaz, Shuja, *Crossed Swords: Pakistan, Its Army and the Wars Within* (Karachi: Oxford University Press, 2008).

Nelson, Matthew, *In the Shadow of Shari'ah: Islam, Islamic Law and Democracy in Pakistan* (London: Hurst, 2010).

——— 'Muslims, Markets and the Meaning of a "Good" Education in Pakistan', *Asian Survey* 46, 5 (2006) pp. 690–720.

——— Dealing with Difference: Religious Education and the Challenge of Democracy in Pakistan', *Modern Asian Studies* 43, 2 (March 2008), pp. 361–90.

——— 'Religious Education in Non-Religious Schools: A Comparative Study of Bangladesh and Pakistan', *Journal of Comparative and Commonwealth Politics* 46, 3 (July 2008), pp. 337–67.

Noman, Omar, *The Political Economy of Pakistan, 1947–85* (New York: Keegan Paul, 1988).

Noon, Feroz Khan, *From Memory* (Lahore: Ferozesons, 1966).

Pande, Sivita, *Politics of Ethnic and Religious Minorities in Pakistan* (New Delhi: Shipra, 2005).

Pandey, Gyanendra and Samad, Yunas, *Fault Lines of Nationhood* (Delhi: Lotus Collection, Roli Books, 2007).

——— *Remembering Partition: Violence, Nationalism and History* (Cambridge: Cambridge University Press, 2002).

Paul, T. V., *The India-Pakistan Conflict: An Enduring Rivalry* (Cambridge: Cambridge University Press, 2005).
Rahman, Tariq, *Language and Politics in Pakistan* (Karachi: Oxford University Press, 1996).
Rais, Rasul Bakhsh (ed.), *State, Society and Democratic Change in Pakistan* (Karachi: Oxford University Press, 1997).
Rana, Muhammad Amir, trans. Saba Ansari, *A to Z of Jehadi Organizations in Pakistan* (Lahore: Mashal Books, 2004).
Rashid, Ahmed, *Descent into Chaos: How the War Against Islamic Extremists is Being Lost in Pakistan, Afghanistan and Central Asia* (London: Penguin, 2008).
Rashid, Harun-or, *The Foreshadowing of Bangladesh: Bengal Muslim League and Muslim League Politics, 1936–1947* (Dhaka: Asiatic Society of Bangladesh, 1987).
Rittenberg, S. A., *Ethnicity, Nationalism and Pakhtuns: The Independence Movement in India's North-West Frontier Province, 1901–1947* (Durham, NC: Duke University Press, 1988).
Rizvi, Hasan Askari, *Military, State and Society in Pakistan* (London: Palgrave Macmillan, 2003).
Robinson, Francis, *Separatism among Indian Muslims: The Politics of the United Provinces' Muslims 1860–1923* (Cambridge: Cambridge University Press, 1974).
Samad, Yunas, 'The Military and Democracy in Pakistan', *Contemporary South Asia* 3, 3 (1994), pp. 189–203.
——— *A Nation in Turmoil: Nationalism and Ethnicity in Pakistan 1937–1958* (New Delhi: Sage, 1995).
——— 'Pakistan or Punjabistan: Crisis of National Identity', in Gurharpal Singh and Ian Talbot (eds), *Punjabi Identity: Continuity and Change* (New Delhi: Manohar, 1996), pp. 61–87.
——— 'Pakistan from Minority Rights to Majoritarianism' in Gyanendra Pandey and Yunas Samad, *Fault Lines of Nationhood: Cross-Border Talks* (New Delhi: Lotus Collection, Roli Books, 2007) pp. 67–138.
Sayeed, Khalid bin, *Pakistan: The Formative Phase 1857–1948* (Oxford: Oxford University Press, 1968).
Schofield, Victoria, *Kashmir in the Crossfire* (London: I. B. Tauris, 1996).
——— *Kashmir in Conflict: India, Pakistan and the Unending War* (London: I. B. Tauris, 2003).
Shah, Syed Waqar Ali, *Muslim League in NWFP* (Karachi: Royal Book Company, 1992).
Shaikh, Farzana, *Community and Consensus in Islam: Muslim Representation in Colonial India, 1860–1947* (Cambridge: Cambridge University Press, 1989).
——— *Making Sense of Pakistan* (London: Hurst, 2009).
Siddiqa, Ayesha, *Military Inc. Inside Pakistan's Military Economy* (London/ Anne Arbor: Pluto Press, 2007).

Siddiqui, Tasneem Ahmed, *Towards Good Governance* (Karachi: Oxford University Press, 2001).

Sikand, Yoginder, *The Origins and Development of the Tablighi Jama'at* (New Delhi: Sangam Books, 2002).

Singh, Gurharpal, 'On the Nuclear Precipice: India, Pakistan and the Kashmir Crisis', *OpenDemocracy* (6 August 2002), www.opendemocracy.net/conflict-india_pakistan/article_194.jsp.

Swami, Praveen, *India, Pakistan and the Secret Jihad: The Covert War in Kashmir 1947–2001* (Milton Park, Abingdon: Routledge, 2007).

Syed, Anwar H., *Pakistan: Islam, Politics and National Solidarity* (New York: Greenwood Press, 1982).

Talbot, Ian, *Divided Cities: Partition and its Aftermath in Lahore and Amritsar 1947–1957* (Karachi: Oxford University Press, 2006).

——— *India and Pakistan* (London: Arnold, 2000).

——— *Khizr Tiwana, the Punjab Unionist Party and the Partition of India* (Karachi: Oxford University Press, 2002).

——— *Pakistan: A Modern History*, 2nd edn (London: Hurst, 2009).

——— *Punjab and the Raj, 1949–1947* (Delhi: Manohar, 1988).

——— (ed.) *The Deadly Embrace: Religion, Politics and Violence in India and Pakistan, 1947–2002* (Karachi: Oxford University Press, 2007).

Talbot, Ian and Gurharpal Singh (eds), *The Partition of India* (Cambridge: Cambridge University Press, 2009).

Waseem, Mohammad, *Politics and the State in Pakistan* (Islamabad: National Institute of Cultural and Historical Research, 1994).

Weiss, Anita and S. Zulfiqat Gilani (eds), *Power and Civil Society in Pakistan* (Karachi: Oxford University Press, 2001).

——— (ed.), *Islamic Reassertion in Pakistan: The Application of Islamic Laws in a Modern State* (New York: Syracuse University Press, 1986).

Weiss, Anita, *Culture, Class and Development in Pakistan: The Emergence of and Industrial Bourgeouisie in Punjab* (Colorado: Westview Press, 1991).

Whaites, Alan, 'The State and Civil Society in Pakistan', *Contemporary South Asia* 4, 3 (1995), pp. 229–54.

Widmalm, Sten, *Kashmir in Comparative Perspective: Democracy and Violent Separatism in India* (Karachi: Oxford University Press, 2006).

Wilcox, Wayne, *Pakistan: The Consolidation of a Nation* (New York: Columbia University Press, 1963).

Wirsing, Robert, *Pakistan's Security Under Zia, 1977–88: The Policy Imperatives of a Peripheral Asian State* (Basingstoke: Macmillan, 1991).

——— 'Pakistan's Transformation: Why it Will Not (and need not) Happen', *Asia-Pacific Centre for Security Studies* 4, 2 (2005), pp. 1–6.

Wolpert, Stanley, *Jinnah of Pakistan* (New York: Oxford University Press, 1984).

Zaheer, Hassan, *The Separation of East Pakistan: The Rise and Realization of Bengali Muslim Nationalism* (Karachi: Oxford University Press, 1994).

Zaman, Muhammad Qasim, *The Ulama in Contemporary Islam: Custodians of Change* (Princeton: Princeton University Press, 2002).

Zamindar, Vazira-Fazila Yacoobali, *The Long Partition and the Making of Modern South Asia: Refugees, Boundaries, Histories* (New York: Columbia University Press, 2007).

Ziring, Lawrence, *Pakistan: The Enigma of Political Development* (Boulder, CO: Westview Press, 1980).

——— *Pakistan in the Twentieth Century: A Political History* (Karachi: Oxford University Press, 1997).

——— *Pakistan: At the Cross-Current of History* (Oxford: Oxford University Press, 2003).

Unpublished Theses

Aziz, Mazhar, 'The Parallel State: Understanding Military Control in Pakistan', PhD Thesis, University of Nottingham, 2006.

Bangash, Yaqoob Khan, 'The Integration of the Princely States of Pakistan 1947–55', DPhil Thesis, University of Oxford, 2011.

Hansen, David, 'Radical Rhetoric-Moderate Behaviour: Perceptions of Islam, *Shari'a* and the Radical Dimensions among Inhabitants of Islamabad and Rawalpindi in the post-9/11 Pakistani Reality', PhD Thesis, University of Oslo, 2010.

Tudor, Maya, 'Twin Births, Divergent Democracies: The Social and Institutional Origins of Regime Outcomes in India and Pakistan', PhD Thesis, Princeton University, 2010.

INDEX